Buddhadhamma

SUNY series in Buddhist Studies
Matthew Kapstein, editor

BUDDHADHAMMA

Natural Laws and Values for Life

Phra Prayudh Payutto

Translated by Grant A. Olson

State University of New York Press

Published by
State University of New York Press, Albany

Printed in the United States of America

For information, address State University of New York Press,
State University Plaza, Albany, NY 12246

Production by Cynthia Tenace Lassonde
Marketing by Nancy Farrell

Library of Congress Cataloging-in-Publication Data

Phra Thēpwēthī (Prayut)
[Phutthatham. English]
Buddhadhamma : natural laws and values for life / Phra Prayudh Payutto ; translated by Grant A. Olson.
p. cm. — (SUNY series in Buddhist studies)
Translation of: Phutthatham.
Summary: On Buddhist doctrine (dhamma) according to principles of Theravada Buddhism.
Includes bibliographical references and index.
ISBN 0-7914-2631-9 (hc : alk. paper). — ISBN 0-7914-2632-7 (pb : alk. paper)
1. Buddhism—Doctrines. I. Olson, Grant A. II. title.
III. Series.
BQ4150.P46813 1995
294.3'42—dc20 95-15504
CIP

10 9 8 7 6 5 4 3 2 1

There are. . . many schools in Buddhism that still handle Buddhism as a concept. But real Buddhism is to focus on the process itself. The process is you.

—Dainin Katagiri, *Returning to Silence*

To all the priceless teachers and teachings
and the various forms they may take.

Contents

A Concise Note on the Name and Ecclesiastical Titles of Phra Prayudh Payutto

Without getting too involved in the intricacies of the system of ecclesiastical ranks in Thailand's monastic system, allow me to list in one place the various ranks and titles of the author of *Buddhadhamma*. For the most part, this information is also written into the biography that follows.

The author was born Prayudh Aryangura. Upon Prayudh's ordination as a novice, he was known as Samanen Prayudh (or Novice Prayudh). Pali is the sacred language of the Theravada Buddhist texts, and when men receive higher ordination as monks, they have a Pali "ordination name" bestowed upon them that generally replaces their family name. Upon his ordination as a full-fledged monk, the Pali name Payutto was added; and because he had passed the state Pali examinations, he was then known as Phra Maha Prayudh Payutto (with the term *phra* indicating his status as a monk and *maha* indicating his Pali language accomplishments).

After further recognition, he was given the titles of Phra Srivisuddhimoli (1969); Phra Rajavaramuni (1973); Phra Debvedi (1987); and Phra Dhammapitaka (1993). Despite these presitigious changes in title, many people still refer to him, according to his earlier rank, as Phra Maha Prayudh or, reflecting his royal titles, Chaokhun Prayudh.

Since monk's titles are in flux and can lead to confusion, some recent English language books by the author have come out under the name Bhikkhu P. A. Payutto, employing *bhikkhu*, a more generic Pali term for monk, and the author's initials followed by the name bestowed upon him at the time of his ordination as a monk. Not wishing to add to this confusion, I have elected to use the name Phra Prayudh Payutto, employing *phra*, a more common term for Thai monks. This simplification, however, is not intended as a way of leaving this monk's titles unrecognized. Another justification for the use of Prayudh Payutto is that in official listing of monks' names, a monk's given name and ordained name usually follow his title;

for example, an official listing of Phra Prayudh's current rank would be Phra Dhammapitaka (Prayudh Payutto). In other words, even if this monk's rank were to change again, the parenthetical use of Prayudh Payutto would remain constant. Needless to say, because of changing titles and ranks and the various systems of romanization that exist for Thai, students of Buddhism who now attempt to engage in on-line searching of bibliographic records have their work cut out for them.

Acknowledgments

Much of the text of *Buddhadhamma* discusses the importance of realizing how interrelated and interdependent factors cause various things to come into existence or allow people to attain certain goals. I wish to acknowledge some of the factors related to the task of this translation.

First and foremost, I would like to thank Phra Prayudh Payutto for being so generous with his time and skills; I have learned a great deal through his direct and indirect guidance. Phra Prayudh's assistant, Phra Khrupalat Insorn Duangkid, was always on hand to help. Khunying Krachangsri Raktakanit offered a great deal of assistance to me in the field. If I remember correctly, originally it was Sulak Sivaraksa, Wisit Wangwinyoo, and Athorn Techatada, who agreed that the translation of *Buddhadhamma* should be a "one-man show," and I am grateful that they thought that I was the one to do it. But special thanks must go to Sulak who provided unflagging encouragement and read an earlier draft during his travels through Chicago in the summer and fall of 1992 while in exile following the charge of lèse majesté made against him in late 1991. I would like to thank Maha Nakorn Khemapali, Maha Narong Cittasobhano, and Maha Prayoon Mererk (Phra Medhidhammaporn) at Mahachulalongkorn Buddhist University, who have lent their ears, offered encouragement, and given crucial advice over the years (and I apologize if I have not listed the most recent ecclesiastical ranks of these venerable monks). I thank "Dhamma-vijaya" (Wat Pa Nanachat) for his earlier translation of a section of *Buddhadhamma* entitled, *Sammāsati: An Exposition of Right Mindfulness* (Bangkok: Buddhadhamma Foundation, 1988) and allowing me to cross-check my version with his preexisting work. Chalermsee Olson often stopped what she was doing to help me with an odd turn of phrase. The following people often offered encouragement and showed an ongoing interest in this translation: William Klausner, Suwanna Satha-Anand, Samana Bodhirak, Edwin Zehner, and Duncan McCargo. I thank Chuen Jantaro and family for giving me a place to stay in Bangkok, and Nongnoot and Praphrut for allowing to use their truck and a desk on their porch in Rayong. Various professors at different parts of my graduate career steered me in the right direction and offered suggestions about portions of this translation work: Robert Bobilin at the University of Hawaii, and A. Thomas Kirsch and Milton Barnett at Cornell University.

During the final stages of this translation work, the following people gave me good advice and assistance: Achan Sunthorn, Phra Banyat, Maha Somsong, Phra Nyanasobhano, and the board members of Wat Buddhadharma, Hinsdale, Illinois; Steven Collins, University of Chicago, jogged my memory about several things and reminded me of certain standards that I probably have not met; and Charles Hallisey, Harvard University, saved me a great deal of time by sending me crucial e-mail messages while I was putting the finishing touches on this work. A. Thomas Kirsch, John Hartmann, Ted Mayer, and David Mullikin commented on various versions of the introductions.

Initial funding for this translation work was received from the John F. Kennedy Foundation, Bangkok. Later, two trips were made to Thailand to complete this research, one with funding from the Henry Luce Foundation/SEAC Committee of the Association for Asian Studies and another with the assistance of a Fulbright Senior Scholar Research Award under the Southeast Asian Regional Research Program, which is funded through the United States Information Agency. During my Fulbright trip, I was based in Bangkok at the Thai Khadi Research Institute, Thammasat University. Doris Wibunsin, formerly of the Thai-U.S. Educational Foundation, Bangkok, never failed to cheer me on. The Center for Southeast Asian Studies, Northern Illinois University, and the Centre for South-East Asian Studies, University of Hull, graciously allowed me the leeway to complete this project.

This work is dedicated to the memory of Buddhadasa Bhikkhu, who passed away in July of 1993; the legacy of his life and thought is a never-ending source of inspiration. I also want to thank Donald Swearer and Frank and Mani Reynolds for their inspiration and good examples. And, as always, I could not have done this work without the help of my whole family, especially Chalermsee and Teal Metta.

Pali Text Abbreviations Used in the Notes

A	*Aṅguttaranikāya* (5 volumes)
Abhid-s	*Abhidhammatthasaṅgaha*
D	*Dīghanikāya* (3 volumes)
Dh	*Dhammapada*
DhA	*Dhammapada Aṭṭhakathā*
Dhs	*Dhammasaṅganī* (*Abhidhamma*)
DhsA	*Dhammasaṅganī Aṭṭhakathā* (*Aṭṭhasālinī*)
It	*Itivuttaka* (*Khuddakanikāya*)
J	*Jātaka*
M	*Majjhimanikāya* (3 volumes)
MA	*Majjhimanikāya Aṭṭhakathā* (*Papañcasūdanī*)
Nd[1]	*Mahānidesa* (*Khuddakanikāya*)
Ps	*Paṭisambhidāmagga* (*Khuddakanikāya*)
PsA	*Paṭisambhidāmagga Aṭṭhakathā* (*Saddhadhammapakāsinī*)
S	*Saṁyuttanikāya* (5 volumes)
SA	*Saṁyuttanikāya Aṭṭhakathā* (*Sāratthapakāsinī*)
Sn	*Suttanipāta* (*Khuddakanikāya*)
SnA	*Suttanipāta Aṭṭhakathā* (*Paramatthajotikā*)
Thīg	*Therīgāthā*
Ud	*Udāna* (*Khuddakanikāya*)
UdA	*Udāna Aṭṭhakathā* (*Paramatthadīpanī*)
Vbh	*Vibhaṅga* (*Abhidhamma*)
VbhA	*Vibhaṅga Aṭṭhakathā* (*Sammohavinodanī*)
Vin	*Vinaya Piṭaka* (5 volumes)
Vism	Visuddhimagga

Translator's Introduction

> Translation is never perfect, but it is possible, and the effort to achieve it rewards us not by giving us an exact copy (which would be of little real interest, after all), but by expanding our boundaries.
> —Elizabeth Kamarck Minnich, *Transforming Knowledge**

There are too few translators who go into any detail about the task of translating. There is a whole literature on the subject but very little of it is published in conjunction with translations. If any discussion of the task of translation is attempted, it is usually incorporated into an all-too-brief preface or acknowledgments section. Ben Anderson's *In the Mirror* offers one paragraph; after reading Donald Swearer's translations of Buddhadasa Bhikkhu's works, I was left with many questions; and it was not until I actually met Theodora Bofman and heard her give a talk about her translation of the *Ramakian* that I discovered, despite the different nature of our texts, that we had encountered similar obstacles.[1] More elaboration on the actual task of translation would have been helpful to future translators. I remember talking with Professor Frank Reynolds about the translation of the *Three Worlds According to King Ruang* that he did with his wife, Mani—"it came very close to ending our marriage," he said frankly.[2] This type of information, however, usually ends up on the cutting room floor and never makes it into the final drafts of introductions. So, let us at least start to say something for and about translating.

Compared to other academic activities, translation seems such a tentative task. While I have worked on this version until I was willing to let it out of my grasp, I am still trying to master parts of it. But perhaps at least part of this is due to the fact that it is a Buddhist text. This translation work, and the text itself, have meant different things to me at different points in time. Initially, having realized the value of the text, I looked forward to the challenge of working on *Buddhadhamma*, of testing my language skills, and trying to convey the text in the most readable form possible. Then, as the translation progressed and I was doing more work on the

* From Elizabeth Kamarck Minnich, *Transforming Knowledge* (Philadelphia: Temple University Press, 1990), 164.

thought of the author, I began learning through the translation: it gave me additional clues about how the author conceived the principles of Buddhism and how he was attempting to order them and keep them relevant for modern society. At one point, I envisioned a portion of *Buddhadhamma* as a part of my dissertation on the life of Phra Prayudh, but then my dissertation and the translation outgrew one another.

The Metamorphosis Of

Translation requires a great deal of forbearance and just plain stubbornness. It is a task that tries and eventually changes the translator. As translation work progresses, both it and the translator evolve—"The more I translated, the more questions I asked myself."[3] No translator's language skills are the same at the beginning of a project as they were at the end; no translator's conception of a manuscript remains unchanged throughout the act of translation. Nor will any major translation remain unchanged by the life changes experienced by the translator in the course of completing the work. This also means that once a translation is "finished," it is still not done. It must be reconsidered from the beginning all over again. This is a process that grows less rewarding as time goes on, and, naturally, succumbing to the extremes of this tendency can lead to never finishing a translation.

This translation work has been a long, ongoing process that has been "running in the background" while I have been passing through many phases of my education and academic work. Beginning in 1985, I dabbled with this translation in my spare time while attending graduate school at Cornell University. At that time, even though I had tried my hand at a few other Thai translations, I was still taking classes in the formal study of Thai. The translation of *Buddhadhamma* began when my language was at one level and then actually became a tool, a part of my education, as a means to improve both my language skills and my understanding of doctrinal Buddhism.

At times in my career I wished that I could have stopped everything to finish this work, but in the real world this is usually not possible. And other, unanticipated things happened in the field to delay the completion of this project: for example, in 1991, when I took time off to go to Thailand on a Fulbright grant to work toward the completion of this translation, Phra Prayudh contracted an eye infection that almost caused him to permanently lose sight in one of his eyes.

Furthermore, anyone who has seen the merits of a particular work when read in its original language and then begins to translate it into another, will come to realize the nature of these merits must change. While reading a work in the original language can yield one impression, reading a translation may offer still another. Many Western-educated Thais actually told me that they would prefer to read an English version of *Buddhadhamma* because they felt that potentially it would be clearer than the Thai version—perhaps they were more used to seeing scholarly works of this nature in English not Thai, or perhaps they found the level of the Thai language in the text to be still quite daunting and still too "monkish," even though this book has been widely praised for its modern prose. Most often, however, even after undergoing a metamorphosis in the process of translation, a meritorious work will tend to maintain its essential merits.

The Faith Of

There is a book entitled *Quality in Translation* that offers an international smorgasbord of opinions on translating. While many of the people in this book give conflicting, dramatic, and even sarcastic presentations concerning the task of translating, most of them agree on the importance of being faithful to the following: the spirit of the original text, the letter of the original text, and the gracefulness of the language used in the translation. If these precepts are observed, the effort can be called a "faithful translation."[4] Such a noble ideal involves a precarious balance; perhaps it constitutes the middle path of the translator.

On the other hand, Buddhist texts are unique in certain ways. In July of 1993, while attending the 5th International Conference on Thai Studies at the University of London, I took the opportunity to confer with another translator of Thai, Professor David Smyth. I asked him about a couple of troublesome terms that seemed to have unique Buddhist meanings and he replied, "Well, you know, most Buddhist texts sound pretty strange anyway." Somehow this comment from a master came as a bit of a relief.

In any language certain Buddhist texts and statements sound strange, and this is part of their intended effect. In the same *Quality in Translation* volume, Simon Pietro Zilahy states that "a translation is good when it arouses in us the same effect as did the original."[5] But according to whom? My interviews on the effects of *Buddhadhamma* in Thailand led to varied conclusions; there was little agreement on its effect. But let us assume that we know what Professor Zihaly is talking about. Buddhadasa Bhikkhu coined the term "dhammic language" (as opposed to everyday, "people language") for part of the intended effect of certain Buddhist teachings.[6] In other words, many Buddhist teachings intend to shake us out of our ordinary frame of mind and confound us with the Truth—and many times such teachings just sound strange. Still, this translation attempts to balance the intentions of the original author and the various traditions of Buddhist scholarship and present them in a readable form. I thank Charles Hallisey and other friends for reminding me that, like everything else, Buddhism deserves to be a dynamic thing.

The Rewards (Or Lack) Of

Even though translation is such a demanding task, academic rewards for this endeavor have tended to be minimal. However, in order for a translation to work, the translator must know at least two languages, and two cultures as well. In this way, translation tests the complete skills of the translator's understanding of a language, the writer of the original work, and the culture in which it arose. In translating *Buddhadhamma*, a fundamental knowledge of Thai is required, along with a familiarity with Buddhist Pali terminology. In order to appreciate the hermeneutics of Phra Prayudh's presentation, a sense of how certain Pali terms have changed over time into common Thai terms is also necessary. Furthermore, to gain an appreciation for the reasoning behind the creation of *Buddhadhamma* itself, a historical context must be provided; and so, this volume and the introduction that follows are an attempt to put yet another wedge into the trunk of Thai history, to split its wood and gain access to its rings.

Even after employing all of these skills, translation is usually not viewed as "original" work; most academic departments give little credit to those engaged in this activity. As I have mentioned elsewhere, one of my past teachers stopped doing translations, citing the reason that if a translation is good, the original author gets all the credit, and if a translation is bad, the translator catches all the flak. Translation is done in spite of this.

In the realm of the humanities (especially literature and religion), a translation seems to have more value in itself; whereas, in the social sciences, the act of translation has required much more justification and lengthy apologetics. But perhaps if a more holistic view of translations can be achieved, then we might come to see the task of translation as being in line with the goals of ethnography, and these efforts would then require less justification to social scientists.[7] Often, however, this is not the case, and it is the hope of this translator that the fruits of our task will come to be appreciated as original presentations and interpretations of cultural texts and "artifacts."

The Intended Audience Of

As I have mentioned, the translation of *Buddhadhamma* has been a valuable exercise in a variety of ways. On one level, it has been an academic activity in itself. Its form became part of an interpretive framework, and its principles have been of practical value in my own life. Accordingly, I hope that this work will make a contribution to Thai studies as well as to academic and practical dimensions of Buddhist studies and the understanding of the evolution of the Theravada tradition.

Since Phra Prayudh assumes some familiarity with Buddhism on the part of his readers, there is liberal use of Pali terminology in this text. Most of it is glossed and explained in passing and additional notes have been added by the translator. The reader can look forward to learning some Pali in the reading, and in certain sections Pali and English terms are used interchangeably.

The Tools Of

Like any other job that you want done correctly, first you need the right tools. Since Mary Haas' *Thai-English Student's Dictionary* contains a dearth of Pali-Sanskrit loans words and Buddhist terminology, George McFarland's *Thai-English Dictionary* remains one of the best and most accurate dictionaries for more serious translation work. For literary terminology, occasionally the Thai-Thai dictionary of the Royal Institute comes in handy. But for this particular work, Phra Prayudh's *Dictionary of Buddhism* was the most indispensible tool, since it offered his preferred translations of Thai or Pali terms and usually put them in the contexts of the groups of Buddhist concepts. The *Pali-Thai-English-Sanskrit Dictionary* by Prince Kitiyakara Krommaphra Chandaburinarnath contains many esoteric terms. The London Pali Text Society's *Pali-English Dictionary* is one of the best references for checking romanized Pali terms. And for standardization of the names of people and places that appear in the Pali texts, I used G. P. Malalasekera's *Dictionary of Pali Proper Names*. In the final stages of this work, I used what turned out to be a remarkable research tool: Phra Prayudh's own *saṅgāyanā* version of the Thai Pali Tipiṭaka.

In his personal copy of the canon, Phra Prayudh had carefully pencilled in cross-rerefences to other canons, which were used in the occasional checking and "cleansing" of the Buddhist canon, an activity in which this scholarly monk has often played a key role. This unique resource turned out to be invaluable. There was one drawback, however. At one point, Phra Prayudh had made the decision to rebind these volumes and in the process "economize" by cutting down the size and weight of these books. The unfortunate result was that some of his marginal notes were lost in the process.

Some Nuts And Bolts Of

There are certain common Thai terms that have unique Buddhist senses, and these pose special challenges for the translator. Often this is because these terms are Pali loan words that have evolved into somewhat different concepts in common Thai discourse. For example, especially troublesome was the compound verb *prungtaeng*. *Prung* is quite common in day-to-day Thai, often used in terms of spicing something up, perking up the flavor (as in *prungrot*). *Taeng* is generally used to refer to dressing with clothes (as in *taengkai, taengtua*) or to decorate. But in Thai Buddhist literature, *prungtaeng* is used in a psychological sense, especially in passages dealing with meditation. In such passages, you often see *prungtaeng khwamkhit*, referring to the penchant to build thought upon thought, to "decorate" thought, hang ideas or opinions on other ideas, build up mental notions, habits, and predispositions. It, therefore, carries negative connotations. Most of the time, in the practice of meditation, we are to observe things for what they are and not interfere or "add on." After much consideration (and not complete satisfaction) I arrived at a translation for this term: embellishment. And so, the reader will occasionally find passages talking about the relative merits of the embellishment of thought. This is one example.

There are other terms that are somewhat more straightforward, though heavily contextual and potentially misleading. The Thai terms *sangkhan* (Pali, *saṅkhāra*) and *arom* (Pali, *ārammaṇa*) can take on a whole different sense in a Buddhist context. In typical daily conversation, *sangkhan* would generally refer to the body and *arom* to mood or emotions. But the Pali Buddhist meaning of the former can refer to compounded things (by implication this includes but is not limited to the physical body) or predispositions of thought, and the latter relates to mind-objects or objects of consciousness. Furthermore, in a Buddhist context the Thai word for food (*ahan*) can also refer to a thing that sustains thought or a state of mind. *Ahanchai* can refer to an object of meditation, for example.

Occasionally a difficult Thai idiom appears, such as *pen tua khong tua eng*. There is no easy way to literally render this notion, so we must leap. This idiom refers to a person with confidence, a flair, a way about him that is accomplished and perhaps self-motivated. In Buddhist writings it can also suggest an appropriate harmony with nature and society—being yourself or acting in accordance with your true nature—and, therefore, it has positive connotations. Dare I say, it is less like Frank Sinatra's signature tune "My Way" and more like Billie Holiday's "God Bless the Child (that's got his own)."

Aside from difficulties related to the ambiguity of the meanings of the terms above, there is the more perennial problem of the lack of subjects in Thai sentence constructions. Sometimes this information is implied, and in other cases the reader has to surmise a subject or return to a much earlier point in the text to find one. Also, rendering some Pali passages into Thai can cause problems related to the ambiguity of singular and plural subjects. The troublesome term dhamma, for example, ends up being ambiguous in many cases—is it dhamma or dhammas? The only recourse is to return to the Pali texts when the answer to this question seems crucial.

Because of the ambiguity of subjects, the translator must also make certain decisions about the use of pronouns. To maintain a certain instructional tone of familiarity, I have often employed the second person "you," but in other cases when it seemed appropriate, "people," "we," or "a person" were also used. When using "a person" in a didactic construction—such as, "when a person experiences. . . he then. . ."—I have maintained the more traditional use of "he," and this is generally meant to be generic and all inclusive, except in places in the Buddhist texts where the audience was a group of monks.

Another difficulty relates to the tricky use of the term "self" in works dealing with Buddhism. On a conventional level Buddhism acknowledges a self, but at a higher level any notion of self is denied. Therefore, the translator has to be very careful about the use of terms such as the following: the self vs. a self, oneself vs. one's self, yourself vs. your self, or even the self itself, and so on.

In a lengthy note that appeared in the original text of *Buddhadhamma* at the end of the introduction, the author explains that he has attempted to include parenthetical English translations of many Pali terms in order to clear up misunderstandings in Buddhist scholarship that may have evolved over time and to help Thai scholars expand their knowledge of Buddhist technical terminology in English. In this translation, these terms have been incorporated into the text for ease of reading. If anyone is interested in singling out such terms for study, it will be necessary to refer to the original Thai text and Phra Prayudh's *Dictionary of Buddhism*. Also, aside from the parenthetical glosses of Pali words, other parenthetical information added by the author has generally been preserved as such. Occasionally, additions or clarifications made by the translator appear in brackets. For the romanization of Thai terms, I have simplified the Library of Congress standard. The Three Gems of Buddhism—Buddha, Dhamma, and Sangha—have been capitalized, along with other major "groups"—such as the Four Noble Truths, the Five Aggregates, and the Eight-fold Path—that constitute some of the most significant sections in this text.

Readers who are not used to Thai or Buddhist discourse are certain to feel that some explanations are rather lengthy and repetitive. This tends to be the style of much Thai literature and especially Theravada Buddhist discourse. When translating spoken sermons, some people have made apologies for all of the verbiage, or they have sacrificed the feel of this oral tradition and made significant cuts. *Buddhadhamma*, however, is a written work; and, for scholarly reasons, the text has been left virtually in its entirety. While Phra Prayudh's style has been praised as modern, Western readers may still feel that this work is often quite wordy.

As for the Pali passages, I have attempted to remain more faithful to Phra Prayudh's versions. I believe that this adherence allowed me to make the text as a whole more seamless and to remain truer to the original intentions of the author.

Notes

1. Benedict R. O.'G. Anderson's *In the Mirror: Literature and Politics in Siam in the American Era* (Bangkok: Duang Kamol, 1985); Theodora Bofman, *Poetics of the Ramakian*, Special Report no. 21 (DeKalb: Center for Southeast Asian Studies, Northern Illinois University, 1984); Buddhadasa, *Toward the Truth*, trans. by Donald K. Swearer (Philadelphia: The Westminster Press, 1971) and Donald K, Swearer, *Me and Mine: Selected Essays of Bhikkhu Buddhadasa* (Albany: SUNY Press, 1989). And other recent translations are no different; see, for example, Siburapha, *Behind the Painting and Other Stories*, trans. by David Smyth (Singapore: Oxford University Press, 1990); Katherine A. Bowie, *Voices from*

the Thai Countryside: The Short Stories of Samruam Singh, Monograph 6 (Madison: Center for Southeast Asian Studies, University of Wisconsin, 1991); and Dokmaisot, *A Secret Past*, trans. by Ted Strehlow (Ithaca: Southeast Asia Program, Cornell University, 1992).

2. Frank E. and Mani B. Reynolds, *Three Worlds According to King Ruang: A Thai Cosmology*, Berkeley Buddhist Studies Series 4 (Berkeley: University of California, 1982).

3. Bofman (1984), 10.

4. See esp. A. A. A. Fyzee in *Quality in Translation* (Proceedings of the IIIrd Congress of the International Federation of Translators, 1959), ed. by E. Cary and R. W. Jumpelt, 156 (New York: Macmillan, 1963).

5. *Quality in Translation* (1963), 285.

6. See Buddhadasa Bhikkhu, *Two Kinds of Language* (Bangkok: Siva Phorn, 1974) and Swearer (1989), 126–140.

7. For more on this, see Herbert P. Phillips, *Modern Thai Literature: An Ethnographic Interpretation* (Honolulu: University of Hawaii Press, 1987).

Introduction

A Brief Biography of Phra Prayudh Payutto

On January 12, 1939, a fourth son was born to Chunki and Samran Aryankura, who were merchants in the market village of Ban Krang, Siprachan, in the central province of Suphanburi, Thailand. They named him Prayudh. From the time of his birth Prayudh suffered a number of ailments and was in chronically bad health. His family sought to cure him through traditional and nontraditional methods—trying everything from the advice of local government health workers to herbal doctors. But his poor health persisted. At the age of 7, Prayudh's parents had him ordained as a novice monk, hoping that the merit accrued through this Buddhist ritual might improve his health. But this initial stay in the monkhood was very brief: only one week.

After Prayudh, three daughters were born. Prayudh's early years were spent playing with and helping his sisters. Often he would play the role of teacher and lead them in classroom lessons. He tended to prefer reading and studying to the rougher play in which other boys were involved. He completed the first four years of compulsory education near his hometown, and then, under a scholarship from the government, he moved to Wat Pathumkhongkha School in Bangkok to begin the next level of his studies. Like many young, upcountry boys, he depended on the temple as a dwelling place while he pursued his schooling in the city. Prayudh became a temple boy (*dek wat*) at Wat Phra Phirain, where his father had acquaintances from his home village and his own period of ordination into the Buddhist Order. Samran held education in very high regard, and Prayudh's brothers were also staying at Wat Phra Phirain while they attended various Bangkok schools.

About halfway through his first year at Wat Pathumkhongkha School, Prayudh developed intestinal problems and returned home. His second oldest brother, Pasuka, and his father convinced him that it might be a good idea to enter the novicehood. Once again, they had his health in mind. He would be able to live a peaceful life and stay at a temple closer to home, Wat Ban Krang. This time, Prayudh was 11 years old. He spent his first year at Wat Ban Krang and then, in order to gain access to further schooling, he moved to the provincial capital of Suphanburi and stayed at Wat Prasatthong. Since many upcountry temples had limited classes in Buddhist studies and the Pali language, it was necessary for monks in search of higher education to head to the capital. According to his monk-teachers, Prayudh had shown himself to be a very adept and resourceful student. He distinguished himself by never dozing in class and by keeping his own meticulous notebooks of canonical references that his teachers mentioned in class; and according to his instructors, his memory was unsurpassed. In order to obtain still more schooling, young novice Prayudh went to Bangkok once again to stay at Wat Phra Phirain, while he studied the Buddhist canonical language of Pali at the royal temple of Wat Suthat. Novice Prayudh began working his way through the various levels of Pali study (*parian*), of which there are nine. After having passed level 4, he was eligible to enter the Buddhist university of Mahachulalongkorn. In 1961, he became one of a very small circle of ordinands to have passed the highest level of Pali study, level 9, while still a novice. This made him eligible to have his higher ordination sponsored by King Bhumibol Adulyadej at Wat Phra Kæo, The Temple of the Emerald Buddha. He then became known as Phra Maha Prayudh Payutto.[1] In 1962, he was graduated at the top of his class with a B.A. degree (the highest degree offered at that time) from Mahachulalongkorn Buddhist University.

Following graduation, Phra Maha Prayudh Payutto began teaching at Mahachulalongkorn Buddhist University. He prepared a number of classroom materials, including English-language texts that are still in use. In 1964, he received the position of assistant to the secretary-general of the university and later became deputy secretary-general. He is credited with improving the university's curriculum, its system of grading and credits, and its Buddhist Sunday school for the general public. He also helped to institute some of the programs involving monks in national development projects as a part of their education. It was during his tenure at Mahachulalongkorn that he wrote the bulk of his masterpiece on Buddhist doctrine, *Buddhadhamma* (2514 [1971]). People still describe this monk-scholar as so dedicated that he often sacrificed sleep and worked late into the night, often never returning to his temple and ending up "sleeping where he worked."

In 1969, he was given the royal title of Phra Srivisuddhimoli (Prayudh Payutto), and in 1972 he was made abbot of Wat Phra Phirain.[2] In 1973, promotion to another royal rank soon followed, when he was made Phra Rajavaramuni. In 1974, after disagreeing with certain aspects of the politicization of the monkhood taking place during this more liberal period in Thai history, Phra Rajavaramuni resigned from the Buddhist university, and later he resigned his position as abbot of Wat Phra Phirain.[3] He now wished to devote himself to writing and creating a number of works related to the study and application of Buddhism. At the time of his resignation, Phra Rajavaramuni was working on the first edition of his *Dictionary of Buddhism*.[4] This resource, which includes standardized Thai and English translations of Pali terms, lists of major Dhamma concepts from the Pali canon, and numerous cross-references to the canonical texts, has become an indispensable tool for people doing research on Buddhism. Furthermore, its organization is a marvel of precomputer-era scholarship.

In 1972, Phra Rajavaramuni traveled with a small group of Thai monks to the United States to lecture at the University of Pennsylvania and study aspects of American life. While Phra Rajavaramuni reported that this group of travelers was given the opportunity to visit such places as Hollywood and the Grand Canyon, they chose instead to visit universities with programs in Southeast Asian studies, paying calls on about eight East Coast universities in the course of two weeks. In 1976, at the invitation of Professor Donald Swearer, Phra Rajavaramuni taught at Swarthmore College; and later in 1981, he team taught again with Professor Swearer, this time at Harvard University. One of the fruits of Phra Rajavaramuni's travels to the United States was the publication of his lecture *Mong Amerika ma kae panha Thai* [Looking to America to Solve Thailand's Problems] in which he warns Thai people about shunning their own valuable traditions and heedlessly borrowing too many trends of social and material development from the West.[5]

In 1987, after not having been promoted for some fourteen years, he was given the rank of Phra Debvedi.[6] Several people felt that because Phra Prayudh had not been involved in some of the more typically recognized "tracks" that often help to raise a monk's title, such as being an abbot of a major temple or being involved in the monastic bureaucracy or administration, he had been overlooked. A major part of the justification for this recognition was apparently the writing of *Buddhadhamma*, which had now evolved from a book of some two hundred pages to a tome of over a thousand pages. In 1993, he received the rank of Phra Dhammapitaka, a fitting title for a monk who has firmly grounded his learning in the Buddhist canon or Tipiṭaka.

Since 1982, further recognition from Thai institutions of higher learning has come Phra Prayudh's way. For example, in 1982, he was given an honorary doctorate in Buddhist studies from Mahachulalongkorn Buddhist University; in 1986 an honorary doctorate in philosophy was bestowed upon him by Thammasat University; in 1987 in curriculum and teaching from Silpakorn University; in 1987 in education and teaching from Kasetsart University; in 1988 in linguistics from Chulalongkorn University; and in 1990 another degree in education from Srinakarinwirot University. And the recognition does not stop there. In 1994, Phra Prayudh became the first Thai to receive the UNESCO Prize for Peace Education. As a result of his intellectual accomplishments, he has come to be seen as one of the major figures in the history of Thai Buddhism and stands as one of the foremost examples of a monk-scholar (*phra nakwichakan*).

Phra Prayudh has plans for many ongoing projects, including an encyclopedia of Buddhism and a more comprehensive treatment of Buddhist ethics. At present, his health remains troublesome, but he perseveres, still working late into most nights with the help of his assistant Phra Khrupalat Insorn, saying, with a certain amount of Buddhist detachment, that he thinks his body can take it—"there is so much work that remains to be done, and we are constantly competing with time."

Phra Prayudh and the Middle Path

I first met Phra Prayudh in the summer of 1982 while gathering information for a master's thesis on two new Thai Buddhist reformist movements—the Santi Asoke movement and a meditation center in Southern Thailand called Nawachiwan.[7] I had been to a number of temples, had even spoken with the Supreme Patriarch of the Thai Sangha, but I was not encountering many people who were willing to discuss the practices and views of these reform-minded groups. One of the major reasons why monks refused to comment was that these two groups had both said that they wished to be free of the governing body of the Thai Sangha—the Mahatherasamakhom (or Council of Elders). Many monks, therefore, simply said that Santi Asoke, the most ascetic and strict of the two movements, really had nothing new to offer: they just observe vegetarianism. A month of interviewing people outside of these movements had yielded precious little.

When I went to the field I had a list of potential subjects for interviews. One of those names was Phra Prayudh (at that time holding the ecclesiastical rank of Phra Rajavaramuni). I had made inquiries about this monk, who had worked at Mahachulalongkorn Buddhist University but had resigned to spend most of his time writing at Wat Phirain on Vorachak Road near the edge of Chinatown in Bangkok. Most of the people I spoke with said that he was in bad health and should not be bothered; as a junior scholar, I was discouraged from disturbing him. Nevertheless, I continued to ask questions about him when I spoke with other people. It was not until I went to see Maha Nakorn Khemapali, a prominent administrator in charge of ecclesiastical education at Mahachulalongkorn Buddhist University, that I was told, "You must see him." He said in no uncertain terms that my thesis would not be complete until I had a chance to talk with the monk-scholar Phra Prayudh.

In many respects, I really had no thesis until I spoke with Phra Prayudh. Based on my meetings with him and the generous amount of time that he was willing to spend with me, my hunches began to take shape. I had gone to the field wondering about some of the new practices that these groups advocated. I had wanted to discover the motivation behind their reasons for breaking away from the Council of Elders. I suspected that much of what these groups were advocating was connected with a certain amount of stodginess and unwillingness to address the challenges of the modern world on the part of the Elders in the Order; lax practices and poor guidance of monks was behind many of these reforms. Furthermore, each of these reform groups had grown tired of state-initiated reforms and were seeking a path that would allow them more spiritual creativity. When I spoke with Phra Prayudh, his understanding of these issues was deep. He was eloquent in both English and Thai and could go into the background and development of these problems in the Thai Sangha. I did not know it then, but he had already written several essays on this subject. Also, it was fortuitous that I happened to be in the field when the extensively revised edition of his major summary of Buddhist doctrine *Buddhadhamma* had just been published (2525 [1982]).

As my field research evolved beyond my master's thesis, I continued to follow the work of Phra Prayudh. It became more and more clear that his appearance and position in my thesis constituted a different perspective on the reform of the Thai Sangha—reform from within the traditional structure of the Order. When it came time for me to propose a dissertation topic, I chose to research in depth the life and contribution of Phra Prayudh by gathering extensive interviews with Phra Prayudh and those around him—both monks and laity.

The position of Phra Prayudh's reforms is especially fascinating and is tied to various aspects of his own life story.[8] Having made his way through the rigors of the ecclesiastical education system, which tends to rely heavily on rote learning, he transcended this system's limitations and has come to be one of its major constructive critics. His objective, carefully worded critiques of Thai society and Thai Theravada Buddhism attempt to care for the best of tradition while advocating a spiritually meaningful course for the future development of his country.[9] Many scholars at secular universities—who had turned away from Buddhism as a foundation for their thought because they found the traditional treatises on Buddhism and the predominantly superstitious outlook of the Thai people had little to offer the modern world—embraced Phra Prayudh's work; this learned monk-scholar's updated and competent applications of Buddhist doctrine started a new wave of writings on the social applications of Buddhism.

Phra Prayudh has stayed solidly within the Theravada tradition by using the Buddhist Pali canon as the basis for his writings on Buddhism, thereby avoiding some of the criticism that Buddhadasa Bhikkhu has incurred because of his more liberal theological interpretations and applications of the Dhamma and his relatively free approach to incorporating aspects of other religious traditions, such as Zen and even Christianity, into the Theravada world. Phra Prayudh's designation of the Thai Pali canon as the foundation for his works has, therefore, made his scholarship more generally accepted by those who embrace Theravada Buddhism. In a Sangha (or state for that matter) that is often administered according to regional favoritism, Phra Prayudh, a monk who comes from rural Central Thailand, has been largely viewed as "standing in the middle," remaining neutral. To date, *Buddhadhamma* has been recognized as Phra Prayudh's best scholarly effort to objectively represent the essence of the teachings of Buddhism.

The Publication History of *Buddhadhamma*

What started out as an article for a festschrift volume eventually evolved into a masterpiece of modern Thai Buddhist scholarship. In 1970 [2513], on behalf of a social science textbook project, Sulak Sivaraksa contacted

Phra Prayudh (who then held the rank of Phra Srivisuddhimoli) to ask him to contribute to a festschrift commemorating the eightieth birthday of Prince Wan Waithayakon, a prominent Thai statesman and man of letters.[10] It was the goal of the committee, which had Magsaysay award-winner Dr. Puey Ungphakorn as an advisor, to put together an educational textbook that would show the current state of the art of several branches of knowledge, including politics, philosophy, literature, and the arts.[11] Phra Prayudh was invited to write the section on philosophy. As he continued to write, his outline of Buddhist philosophy soon grew beyond the bounds of the planned festschrift.

In the years just prior to this invitation, Phra Prayudh had emerged as an astute critic of the condition of Buddhism and its relation to the state in modern-day Thai society. His perceptive, well-thought-out, and balanced critiques had started to gain him a new audience of educated monks and lay intellectuals. Some of his foremost supporters recount that they first encountered his works in relationship to a Weberian-type debate taking place in certain circles of Thai society.[12] Some people in the Ministry of Education, perhaps influenced by Western scholarship, were putting forth the notion that Thai people were lazy and unprogressive because of the Buddhist value of "contentedness" (Thai, *sandot*; Pali, *santosa*). In 1971, Phra Prayudh first published an article entitled *"Sandot"* to correct any misuse of the term and to set the record straight.[13] His article provided a very comprehensive and succinct treatment of this term as it is used in the Buddhist canon—suggesting that it deals more with appropriate effort and desire and not lethargy—and this helped the debate to subside.

Critiques of the three pillars of Thai society—the Nation, the Religion, and Royalty—began to emerge in the post-Field Marshal Sarit era.[14] Prior to that time, criticisms of social institutions were rarely made public. This radical criticism would eventually build as a major force in ousting Prime Minister Thanom, coming to a head with the events of the 14th of October 1973 student uprising. Nor was the Sangha left out of the critiques taking place during these turbulent times; indeed, as Mattani Rutin points out,

> In the late 1960s and early seventies some young extremists strongly criticized the loose moral conduct of modern monks, the emphasis on the external ceremonial aspects of Buddhism, and the activities of monks who seek their fortunes in performing black and white magic, soothsaying, or astrology, or who endorse immoral establishments such as bars, night clubs and massage

> parlours. These critical works were written however, with constructive purposes to purify Buddhist institutions rather than to destroy them.[15]

The foundation for the moralist stance of the controversial Santi Asoke Buddhist movement was laid in this climate. Some of this movement's more scathing treatises criticizing the superstitious and capitalistic practices of the Sangha were produced (and later confiscated) during this time. But the Santi Asoke movement still bases its actions and its claims to purity on their reaction to lax practices of other members of the Buddhist Order. In the context of much of the polemics of this era, Phra Prayudh's statements aspire to provide a voice of reason.

For most scholars and students, Phra Prayudh's views first became known after being published in the *Social Science Review*, a "radical," revisionist forum for the discussion of modern and traditional ideas and ideals initiated by editor and social critic Sulak Sivaraksa in 1963.[16] One of Phra Prayudh's first publications in this journal was entitled "*Panha, thana, lae pharakit khong song* [Problems, status, and activities of the Sangha]" (*Sangkhomsat Barithat* [Social Science Review], Special Issue 4, "*Botbat phutthasatsana kap sangkhom Thai* [The role of Buddhism in Thai society]," August 2505 [1962]). Subsequently, Phra Prayudh was invited to lecture at a seminar given by the Siam Society in August of 2512 [1969] on the subject of "Buddhism and Present-day Thai Society." He gave a talk, entitled "*Botbat khong phrasong nai sangkhom Thai patchuban* [The role of Buddhist monks in present-day Thai society]," that was later published in a proceedings volume, *Phutthasatsana kap sangkhom Thai patchuban* [Buddhism and present-day Thai society] (Bangkok: Siam Society, 2513 [1970]). His analysis of the conditions of the Buddhist Order and his challenges to those in charge of the Buddhist religion in Thailand were so honest that, according to Sulak Sivaraksa, he made some Thai women in the audience weep.[17] However, with the demeanor of equanimity expected of Buddhist monks, he stated his position very diplomatically—people listened and took note. In his Siam Society talk, he pointed out the following issues: the dearth of monks in the Order (especially those of long standing); the poor state of the ecclesiastical education system (both in terms of curriculum and funding); that recently many foreigners were coming to Thailand to study about Buddhism and that few people were prepared to instruct them (he also warned against foreigners claiming to be "Buddhists" and who, either intentionally or out of confusion, might defame the national religion); the lack of social applications of Buddhism in the development of the nation; the increase of beliefs in the powers of sacred objects rather than increased interest in the application of Buddhist values related to critical thinking, which could be used to solve the problems facing Thai society; and the penchant for temples to become involved in building expensive, ornate edifices instead of other structures that might better serve social and monastic welfare. All of these themes were to be sustained and developed in his future published works.

The prominence Phra Prayudh gained from his presence and participation at the Siam Society seminar (together with the resulting publication) made several people feel that perhaps he was the best mind available for writing the section on Buddhist philosophy for the festschrift dedicated to Prince Wan Waithayakon. Phra Prayudh answered the committee's request by saying he would be pleased to accept their request for a work on "Buddhadhamma," or Buddhist doctrine.

The first version of *Buddhadhamma*—written while Phra Prayudh was serving as an administrator at Mahachulalongkorn Buddhist University—was just over two hundred pages long (2514 [1971]), and it is this version that has been translated here. This version of *Buddhadhamma* has subsequently been occasionally reprinted as a cremation volume for the funerals of some prominent, high-ranking monks.[18]

With the publication of *Buddhadhamma*, Phra Prayudh's reputation grew even further. The book began to be used by educators as a textbook and quickly became suggested reading for monks studying at Mahachulalongkorn Buddhist University. *Buddhadhamma* had also attracted the attention of Dr. Rawi Bhavilai, head of the unit at Chulalongkorn University dedicated to religious studies called Thamma-sathan. Dr. Rawi thought the published volume of such merit that he encouraged its republication when he discovered that the first edition had gone out of print.

Dr. Rawi had first encountered Phra Prayudh's *Buddhadhamma* in the wake of the events following October of 1973. Being a kind of renaissance man himself, he was caught up in various activities taking place at this time. Dr. Rawi taught astronomy and physics, but maintained a parallel interest in religion and philosophy. As protests were escalating in Thailand towards the end of 1975, has was elected to a position on the Legislative Panel of the National Assembly and became involved in revising the Constitution. He started a group called Radom-tham, or the "Dhamma Mobilization" group. Through some of its activities during this period of Thai history, the Radom-tham group recognized the value of *Buddhadhamma*.

Rawi Bhavilai: At this time, I became more interested in society and politics, and I felt that there was going to be a "crisis." I felt that we must look for a way out of this. . . .There is an old belief held by many Thais that if the leader of the country knows something bad is about to happen, he will be ordained into the monkhood, adhere to the moral precepts, and practice the Dhamma. Those in the government will follow this example. By doing this, they can divert the "crisis." I tried to find a way to speak with those in power at all levels along these lines—at the "grassroots," too. I could not know, but [a crisis] was to happen in October [of 1976]. But I believe there was increased awareness established in Buddhist circles. After this, there was a committee formed around me called Khana Radom-tham that had this symbol. [He holds up the cover of the version of *Buddhadhamma* he sponsored.] We found the book *Buddhadhamma* [version 2514 (1971)] to be very good. We decided that at each lunchtime we would meet and read it together and discuss it. We chose it first and read it in its entirety. A few days after we had finished it, the events surrounding the 6th of October took place.

At that time, we tried to find more copies of this book. Most stores were sold out. So we had to go to the place that printed it and there we were able to obtain just a few copies. Our group agreed that we would reprint it. I, therefore, went to see Chaokhun [Prayudh]. This was the first time I went to see him. I asked him if we could republish this book in the name of Khana Radom-tham. This was my reason for visiting him. This was in 2519 [1976]. But when I went to see him, he said he had already turned over the copyright to the textbook project of the Social Studies Society (*samakhom sangkhomsat*) of Thailand. I knew Saneh Chamarik, who was a part of this project. Professor Saneh worked at Thammasat, and he was happy to give us permission. But then, Chaokhun [Prayudh] asked to revise the book and add some things. We waited for him to make his changes and had to wait a very long time because just when he began to do this, he traveled abroad, occasionally returning to Thailand. But he continued with his alterations of the text. From a small book of some 200 pages, it became a work of some 940 pages. This process took over two years. I learned later that he worked very hard, that he became ill many times.[19]

Although Phra Prayudh's *Buddhadhamma* was being revised and reconsidered during these turbulent times in Thai society, its influence was felt during this period of great searching and questioning. *Buddhadhamma* is widely viewed as a part of the new trends of thought (*khwamkhit naeo mai*) that were emerging at this time.[20] However, it would be going too far to say that the scholarly publication *Buddhadhamma* somehow advocated or contributed directly to activism. Moreover, during Phra Prayudh's tenure as an administrator Mahachulalongkorn Buddhist University, he eschewed and advised against monk-students taking part in any of the political actions.[21] From memos he distributed at that time, it was clear that his feeling was that monks should not disrupt their education (nor the educators in charge of their education) by taking a public political role; they should complete their studies and attain a position of responsibility that would allow them to carry out meaningful change from within the system. These disagreements over the role of monks in Sangha politics became one reason why Phra Prayudh eventually asked to be relieved of his administrative duties at Mahachulalongkorn.[22]

According to Phra Prayudh, when he was asked by Khana Radom-tham to reprint *Buddhadhamma,* he asked for some more time to make futher revisions and additions. For a variety of reasons, the republication of *Buddhadhamma* ended up taking over three years. It was during this time that he had been invited by professor of religion Donald Swearer to teach at Swarthmore, and in 1981 he was asked to return and teach a class on Buddhism with Swearer at Harvard University. His travels, his poor health, the loss of a chapter of the final draft of the book, together with the slow pace of the government printing house in charge of the production led to an eventual publication date of 1982.

In the introduction to this second edition, Rawi Bhavilai wrote,

> Khana Radom-tham is delighted to have the opportunity to publish the revised and expanded edition of *Buddhadhamma* by Phra [Prayudh]. . . . We are certain that it is a diamond of the first water and that it will serve as a foundation and reference for future Buddhist studies. The unintentional coincidence of the republication of this volume and the celebration of the Rattanakosin Bicentennial is especially auspicious and worthy of note.[23]

Some Buddhist scholars expressed their initial uncertainty over the hasty proclamation that the work was a "diamond of the first water"—they said they would wait and see. Today, however, *Buddhadhamma* is widely held to be a masterpiece of modern Buddhist scholarship and Thai literature. Chetana Nagavajara, a scholar of Thai literature, has praised the "elegance" of Phra Prayudh's prose and the "freshness" of his Pali translations.[24] For the year 1982, in conjunction with the celebration of the Rattanakosin Bicentennial commemorating the founding of Bangkok and the beginning of the Chakri dynasty in 1782, *Buddhadhamma* was awarded first prize for literary prose (*roikaeo*) by the Bangkok Bank Foundation (with Professor Rawi Bhavilai making the nomination); and in the same year Phra Prayudh was selected by the Department of Religious Affairs as an outstanding contributor to Buddhism, for which the creation of *Buddhadhamma* was cited as a prominent contribution.[25] Giving a work of Buddhist theology an award for literature is further evidence of both Phra Prayudh's artistry and how the definition of Thai literature has expanded from its more classical roots in poetry.[26] Such expansion and diversity has indeed made the Thai literary heritage rich and complex and bears out the statement that, at least for the modern period since the mid-19th century and the advent of printing, the "Thai always take the term 'literature' to cover a wider meaning than the Western notion of 'imaginary literature'."[27]

The next edition of *Buddhadhamma* was published by Mahachulalongkorn Buddhist University in 2529 [1986]. This time the volume had been expanded to 1145 pages, which included additional revisions and an extensive 100-page index of its contents. As of this writing, Mahachulalongkorn University Press is completing the fourth revised edition. In the minds of most scholars, *Buddhadhamma* has been deemed Phra Prayudh's principal contribution to Thai Buddhist scholarship—and beyond the Thai realm it has been accepted as a work of international standards. *Buddhadhamma* is widely viewed as the most significant Thai contribution to Buddhist scholarship in the last two hundred years.

While later, expanded versions of *Buddhadhamma* have improved and fleshed out certain parts of the original in a number of ways, the earlier version of *Buddhadhamma* offered here still serves as a more concise overview to the author's thought. Without a doubt the later versions of *Buddhadhamma* serve as more complete reference tools containing expanded concepts and additional material from the Buddhist Commentaries; however, in many ways the earlier version remains more accessible and readable as an essay (albeit a long one), and for this reason it continues to be published in Thailand.

In recounting the history of the publication of *Buddhadhamma*, it would perhaps be remiss not to mention a case involving an unsanctioned publication of this work. This case involves the alleged reprinting of *Buddhadhamma* by the government's Department of Religious Affairs without permission. It is an interesting example of the kind of bureaucratic "corruption" that takes place in Thailand, from which, apparently, religious literature is not exempt.[28]

On April 5, 1984, an article appeared in *Matimaharat* explaining some of the details of the publication of *Buddhadhamma* by the Department of Religious Affairs. According to the writer, ex-monk, and Pali scholar Sathienpong Wannapok, the Department of Religious Affairs in 1981 published *Buddhadhamma* and four other texts without asking permission from the writers or publishers. In the introduction to their version of *Buddhadhamma*, it was claimed that the Department had asked Phra Prayudh to write the book, and they had formed a committee to check the language and content before the book went to press. Sathienpong states this to be false, because the book was originally published some ten years earlier. Furthermore, he asserts their saying a committee was necessary to oversee his work was a form of condescension. An official of the Ethics Section—who Sathienpong claims was unethical—forged the signature of Phra Prayudh on reimbursement forms at the rate of 150 baht per page. The book was 206 pages, and so this amounted to the considerable sum of 30,900 baht.[29]

When Phra Prayudh saw this republication, he checked with the Department of Religious Affairs. The same official from the Ethics Section came to apologize to him. Phra Prayudh made two suggestions: one, that they seek the consent of Professor Saneh Chamarik, the head of the foundation for the creation of social science and humanities texts, who originally invited him to write the book; and, second, that they rewrite the introduction according to the truth. The official said these would be done, but no such action was taken to rectify the situation. In October of 1983, the chairman of the foundation wrote a letter to the Minister of Education asking him to correct this situation or they would press charges.[30] The same official from the Ethics Section changed the introduction on only about five hundred copies and then sent them to the foundation; the surplus copies remained as they were.

The case was almost forgotten until a newspaper picked up on the story and mentioned that there was also copyright reimbursement involved and that this amounted to tens of thousands of baht going into the hands of Religious Affairs Department officials. The same official once again went to see Phra Prayudh and begged him to accept 30,000 baht for the copyright fees and to sign his name retroactively. Phra Prayudh would not accept money for his works, and the official from the Ethics Section allegedly went to see him about this several times. Phra Prayudh said that there was nothing he could do to help. (Sathienpong wryly added that this was the official's own *kamma* and that he would have to help himself.) On January 27, 1984, when matters got progressively worse, the Department of Religious Affairs returned 40,000 baht to the government, but its members said they could not recall who put that money in their coffers. The Department claimed that when it saw that money in its accounts and realized something was amiss, it returned these funds to the Ministry of Finance. When a newspaper asked them why they received the money in 1982 but did not return it to the government until 1984, the same official from the Ethics Section said, "I don't know. I just took the money and put it in a drawer. I have a lot of work to do." Sathienpong wrote that if the story had not made the news, the money would still be sitting there or put to some other ("mysterious") use. When I asked Phra Prayudh about this "problem" with the Department of Religious Affairs, he said he had no problem, it was *their* problem.[31]

The Characteristics of *Buddhadhamma*: Placing Phra Prayudh in the Context of Modern Buddhist Scholarship

Phra Prayudh in the Context of Other Major Thai Buddhist Scholars

> **Maha Narong:** In the Rattanakosin period, during the reign of Rama V, Maha Samana Chao [Wachirayanwarorot] was a "modern monk"; later Buddhadasa Bhikkhu was a "modern monk" when the change of government took place. Now, there is Phra [Prayudh] who has given us a "scientific" explanation of Buddhism appropriate for these times.[32]

This statement by a Buddhist monk-administrator represents the opinion of the majority of scholars interviewed about the contributions of Phra Prayudh. Placing him in the company of these monks puts him in the circle of the finest Thai Buddhist thinkers of the modern era.

Curiously, as Maha Narong implied, each of these Buddhist thinkers emerged at a crucial juncture in Thai history. At the turn of the century,

Prince-Patriarch Wachirayanwarorot was one of the key figures involved in the bureaucratic reforms taking place at that time. Wachirayan was the forty-seventh son of King Mongkut (Rama IV), which made him a half-brother to King Chulalongkorn (Rama V), a king credited with carrying out many more liberal and "modern" policies for Siam.

Born of a concubine, Wachirayan did not enjoy princely status.[33] However, when his half-brother, King Chulalongkorn, encouraged Wachirayan to enter the monkhood, telling him his government service would not be wasted, he began to take ordination more seriously. The King had promised that if Wachirayan were to stay in the Order for more than three years (*phansa* or "rainy seasons") he would confer a princely rank and title on him. Wachirayan exclaimed that, "It was beyond my imagination," and this motivation for rank and title played a crucial role in the commitment of this monk-scholar.[34]

After spending the obligatory three years in the Order, princely rank was bestowed upon Wachirayan in 1881, the same year as the ceremonies for the Bangkok centennial.[35] The Prince-Patriarch went on to lead the Thammayut reform order started by his father, and he became a key figure in the reform of secular and monastic education in Thailand, writing many textbooks himself, perhaps the most famous being *Navakovāda* [Instructions for new ordinands], which is still in use today.[36] Steven Zack, writing in 1977, observed that an educated monk in Thailand would probably understand the Dhamma-Vinaya primarily on the basis of Wachirayan's texts.[37] But this is changing. A point of contention between the Elder monks (*thera*) and the younger monks (*yuwasong*) still centers around the appropriateness of the extant Wachirayan curriculum for the modern world—a debate that continues to unfold.

Phra Prayudh's own experience and his concern for education has led him to take note of the tendency for some conservative, Elder monks to cling to the works of Prince-Patriarch Wachirayan. He has stated that there has been a tendency to become "so submerged in the tradition as to be blinded by it"; and he cites the continuing use of certain texts created by Wachirayan as constituting a "Wachirayan cult."[38] Take, for example, *Navakovāda*. According to Phra Prayudh, this book may be useful as a basic reference, but as a textbook it is inadequate and can indicate some of the things that are wrong with the way monks are educated.

A good deal of the monk's education has depended on rote learning, and this has often led monks to study and memorize reference books, such as dictionaries and fixed passages specified for certain Pali examinations, instead of reading works that attempt to give a more holistic presentation of the Dhamma. If we examine the structure of *Navakovāda* we can see that it essentially contains the traditional lists of Dhamma teachings and does not integrate these into any coherent whole. This tendency to learn lists and isolated terms has been an obstacle to a more comprehensive conception of what the Buddha taught. Phra Prayudh has stated that when lists are learned in ascending order according to the number of elements that they contain—for example, the groups of two, groups of three, groups of four, and so on—important concepts are usually not linked according to the proper realization of the Dhamma. According to Phra Prayudh,

> Most Dhamma concepts are separated and not presented in proper sequence. For instance, there are three types of craving; the Four Noble Truths are in the groups of four; the Eight-fold Path in the groups of eight; the Five Aggregates (*pañca-khandha*) of Existence in the groups of five and they are usually separated far from one another and are not put in proper sequence. They should be studied together, because when we study the Four Noble Truths, the first one deals with suffering (*dukkha*), and suffering deals with the Five Aggregates of Existence, and so the Five Aggregates of Existence should come into play here. And then when we study the second Noble Truth, it deals with the three kinds of craving (*taṇhā*), and then we deal with the two kinds of nibbana, but nibbana is now in the groups of two, usually far away from consideration at this point.[39]

And so, the tendency to cling to textbooks that do not go beyond this type of methodology has become an obstacle to improving education and the practical knowledge of Buddhists. While Phra Prayudh feels that many of the works of Wachirayan are good as far as they go, he feels very strongly that it is time to move on. There is much work that needs to be done, concepts need to be expanded upon, and those who have realized some of the inadequacies of these past works should be expanding and improving the curriculum with alternative materials. In this light, Phra Prayudh's *Dictionary of Buddhism* can be seen as an improved and more integrated reference book, and *Buddhadhamma* is a more sweeping attempt to explain and integrate the major concepts found in the Buddha's teachings.

The career of Buddhadasa Bhikkhu is also marked by significant turning points. One is the major event cited by Maha Narong as "the change of government," meaning the end of the so-called absolute monarchy in Thailand, which took place in 1932. Buddhadasa Bhikkhu was enrolled in the ecclesiastical system of education established at the turn of the century until he rejected it, determining that this system went against his nature. In a book recalling his earlier years he wrote,

> I have resolutely determined that Bangkok is not the place to find purity. The mistake I made in enrolling in the ecclesiastical dhamma study is a blessing, because it made me aware that I had made a wrong step. Had I not known this, I would have made many more. . . it would have been difficult to retreat. . . .[40]

At this point in his life, he chose to retreat to a place near his natal village in the South and live a simpler life of contemplation close to nature in the forest.

> Reading the Buddhist Canon in the city was. . .four or five times less profound than in the forest. . .writing is more lively there. . .the crowded environment is full of a mental stream that is directly opposed to that in the forest.[41]

He said that he had found himself going against his true nature: "I acted as a town monk while my true nature was a forest monk."[42] As it turns out, his "retreat"—we could just as easily view his actions at this time as a "charge"—coincided with a major event in the modern history of Thailand.

> I left Bangkok at the very end of 1931. . .and stayed at Wat Mai, Phumrieng [Suratthani, Southern Thailand]. . . .We searched for a good place to stay in that area, and then four or five of us who were good friends pitched in and built some dwellings to move into. We made the move around May, 1932. . . .And later in June, the government system in Thailand changed [from an absolute monarchy to a constitutional monarchy]. Therefore, the starting point in the calendar of [our new spiritual dwelling place called] Suan Mokkh is easily recalled and associated with the phrase: "In the same year as the change of the system of government." We took this change to be a good omen that would lead us into a new era, a period in which we hoped to correct many things as best as we could.[43]

The establishment of one of the most holy Buddhist places in Thailand, Suan Mokkhabalarama ("Garden of Liberation"), is, thereby, associated with this change of government.

Buddhadasa Bhikkhu's works are innovative and deep, and yet they are different from those of Phra Prayudh. Buddhadasa's works have been characterized as topical (*pen kho-kho*), as focusing on or emphasizing a particular point of the Buddhist doctrine, elaborating this point, and then moving on to another. One of the important aspects of this approach is that he dug deeply into the Buddhist canon to find understudied concepts, and then elaborate on them in lectures that were eventually published as books. In this regard, Phra Prayudh has said that he was profoundly influenced by Buddhadasa Bhikkhu's explanations of causality. Buddhadasa Bhikkhu's contribution, then, tends to be more topical than systematic; it is creative theology that takes liberties with certain doctrinal aspects of the tradition and puts less emphasis on offering a comprehensive outline of the whole of the canon.

And it is Buddhadasa's creativity and generous interpretations that have often made him the focus of criticism. His liberal comparisons of Buddhism and Christianity, equating Dhamma with God, raised the eyebrows of many conservative Theravada Buddhists; and in the mid-1960s he had an on-going debate with writer and member of the royal family M. R. Kukrit Pramoj over the nature of emptiness (*chit-wang*) and its potential applications in daily life.[44]

When Buddhadasa Bhikkhu was asked to compare his works with Phra Prayudh's, he offered the following:

> **Buddhadasa Bhikkhu:** (Laughter.) Ah, comparisons! These should not be made in terms of which one is better or worse or more correct; we should look at what direction we are trying to go. Chaokhun Prayudh has put together Pali statements (*kho khwam*) that are beautiful (*phairo*), easy to study and listen to (*na fang*). In this current age, he has done very well. We [at Suan Mokkh] may not have done as well by mainly focusing on certain concepts or ideas (*chapho rüang-chapho rüang*), speaking directly to these concepts. But as to whether people now can accept this or not. . .we speak directly, so this is different. He has paid attention to the artistry of the verse (*roikrong*) that will attract modern people, and this should be of benefit in the future. . . .Chaokhun Prayudh has helped to digest (*yoi*) the teachings,

to make them relate to one another (*samphan-kan*), become linked (*nüang-kan*).[45]

Buddhadasa Bhikkhu's move to the South, his bold criticisms of the superstitious aspects of Thai spirituality, his questioning the thought of established philosophers like the 5th-century monk-scholar Buddhaghosa, and his coining of new terms to evoke the essence of Buddhist principles across schools and disciplines brought a great deal of criticism his way. Even Buddhadasa Bhikkhu's passing in July of 1993 was accompanied by a certain amount of controversy. His wishes for a quiet, natural demise were thwarted by doctors attempting to extend his life by artificial means and a media who would not let him go.

Buddhadasa Bhikkhu and his thought have weathered many storms, his lectures and writings comprise one of the largest bodies of works on the interpretation of Buddhist thought in Thai history, and he remains one of the most important contemporary reformers of Buddhism. Monks like Phra Prayudh recognize the importance of the inspiration they received from Buddhadasa Bhikkhu and the precedent he set.

At the same time, Phra Prayudh's indebtedness to other Buddhist teachers must be tempered with his profound knowledge of Buddhism and his own sense of history. While respectful of the efforts of past figures in Thai Buddhist history, Phra Prayudh has attempted to learn from and build upon their efforts. Part of his "middle" position often involves an acknowledgement and a critique of courses of action taken by early reformers in Thai history. For example, while Phra Prayudh has an appreciation for the spirit of the reforms carried out by King Mongkut, which resulted in the establishment of the Thammayut reform order in the latter 1880s, he does not advocate the establishment of new orders that tend to cause further division within the monkhood. Accordingly, each era in Thai history—especially from King Mongkut's time, to the turn-of-the-century bureaucratic reforms at the time of Prince-Patriarch Wachirayan, to the more liberal period of the "change of government" in 1932, to the modern era—have all had an impact on the monkhood and can provide significant lessons for the future.[46]

This same concern is evident in Phra Prayudh's views regarding some of the more experimental reform movements that have arisen in contemporary Thai Buddhism, such as the Thammakai and Santi Asoke movements. In the early 1970s the Thammakai movement formed around the charismatic leadership of some ordained graduates of Kasetsart University, and the group established an urban center in Pathumthani.[47] This movement gained popularity by offering a "new" form of concentration meditation that depended on focusing on an image of a glass ball and moving it (and other objects of concentration) throughout different sectors of the body. Thammakai organized bus transportation from major landmarks in Bangkok to their spacious center on the edge of the city. At the pristine grounds of their center, around a modern temple structure housing a contemporary-styled Buddha image, people sit in rows focused in group meditation. Photographs of such orderly, aesthetically pleasing images began to appear on postcards, greeting cards, and calendars found in shops and department stores all over Thailand. For many, this peaceful retreat offers a respite from the pollution of Bangkok and the rigors of daily urban existence. In the late 1980s, the growth of the movement slowed somewhat as some disillusioned monks from the movement broke stories about some of the movement's considerable holdings and lucative business dealings. One such report called the Thammakai movement "Phutthaphanit"—a Buddhist business.[48] Aside from some of the questionable "business" practices of this group, Phra Prayudh has been concerned that this movement overemphasizes passive forms of meditation at the expense of applying other (more dynamic) aspects of the Buddhist teachings.

Another modern reform movement formed around a charismatic television host turned spiritual leader, Phra Bodhirak, who was first ordained in 1970. This group, eventually calling itself the Santi Asoke movement with its major center in Khlongkum, Bangkok, distinguished itself by defining an ascetic lifestyle that included strict vegetarianism and observing a hierarchy of moral rules, some which exceed the codes established by the Buddha.[49] In addition, this group questioned traditional Thai Buddhist practices: they do not allow the ritual pouring of holy water; they do not burn incense nor display Buddha images; and ordinands do not shave their eyebrows (a practice not mentioned in the code of ethics or Vinaya). While it is necessary for a monk to be in the Order for at least ten years before he is allowed to ordain others, Phra Bodhirak began to ordain people into the Santi Asoke movement before he had completed this tenure. Eventually, Phra Bodhirak went as far as declaring that he did not want to be under the jurisdiction of the governing body of Thai monks—the Council of Elders. Despite these bold positions, the movement flourished until 1989 when it allegedly became too involved in politics and the establishment of a new party—Phalangtham (Power of the

Dhamma). In May of 1989, legal action was taken against Phra Bodhirak, citing a number of charges, including his improper ordination of monks, his unwillingness to recognize the governing body of the monkhood, and his non-traditional approaches to Buddhist practice and ethics. His trial is still pending.

Phra Prayudh's critique's of the Santi Asoke movement have been more clear and direct. In the spring of 1988, following the parliamentary elections of 2531 [1988], Phra Prayudh took a stand on the Santi Asoke controversy and wrote a booklet, entitled *Karani Santi Asok* [The case of Santi Asoke]. This slim volume criticized the Santi Asoke movement and the status of its leader Phra Bodhirak and included allegations regarding the movement's involvement in politics and Bodhirak's breach of a number of other Buddhist codes of ethics. The introduction to the first version of this booklet states that it was first distributed at a "neutral moment" (*pen wan haeng khwampenklang*) after all votes had been cast and polls were closed; its publication would therefore have no political ramifications.[50] In accordance with his general outlook, Phra Prayudh drew on evidence found in the rules of the Theravada Order to question and even condemn some of the teachings of Phra Bodhirak. This evidence was widely accepted by a group of Elder monks who met at Phuttha-monthon, a national Buddhist park, in May of 1989 to discuss the case of Santi Asoke. Many monks have suggested that Phra Prayudh's book provided the major underlying research that led to the charges made against Phra Bodhirak and his movement.

It is interesting to note, however, that for some scholars, Phra Prayudh had gone a bit too far. They found his criticisms of Santi Asoke too direct and too harsh, and they were concerned about the freedom of religion in Thailand. According to some scholars Phra Prayudh had—borrowing an English term—"lost credit" (*sia khredit*). Phra Prayudh's stated attempt to bring about proper understanding and a quick end to the Santi Asoke controversy ended up causing a certain amount of division of opinion. Currently, in the eyes of some people, Phra Prayudh no longer appears to be "standing in the middle." Nevertheless, he remains firm on what he sees as the canonical principles of Theravada Buddhism.

Building on the Work of Others: The Orderly and Systematic Character of Phra Prayudh's Work

We have already pointed out how Phra Prayudh's major contribution to Buddhist studies took place at a time when, as some people have put it, "Thai society was stood on its head": students took the liberty of criticizing and chastising their teachers and elders and telling them what to do. Out of this ferment, came refinements to the systematic presentation of *Buddhadhamma*, almost as if it were an attempt to establish order in what was to become a very chaotic and tragic era. As the merit of Phra Prayudh's works became more clear, people were brave enough to compare him with the great Thai Buddhist scholars of the modern Bangkok period and incorporate him into this evolution of scholarship. In an interview with Phra Dusadee, the following comparison emerged:[51]

> **Phra Dusadee:** I think that in one sense, you can compare [Phra Prayudh] to Maha Samana Chao [Wachirayanwarorot], because he was thinking of curriculum (*laksut*) when he created his works. You can see that many of Phra [Prayudh]'s works match the latter's works. . . . Sulak [Sivaraksa] once noted that Phra [Prayudh]'s works will help to make the works of Maha Samana Chao more complete, and if we put this more directly, he has improved upon them. Phra [Prayudh] feels that saying this amounts to praising him too much and he does not really want people saying it or soon there might be one group of monks who become fed up with him.
>
> In Thailand, people still cling to their particular teachers. Maha Samana Chao [Wachirayanwarorot] was the pioneer of many important works, and since he did a lot of this himself and it was done a long time ago, there must be some inadequacies in terms of references or translation. Chaokhun [Prayudh] sees that many monks have misunderstandings; they see that Maha Samana Chao was very capable, and that his works are good enough; therefore, they respect him and praise him with an unwillingness to change. He sees this as only preserving the form, but there is no development, no improvement. Phra [Prayudh] feels that what Maha Samana Chao would have wanted is someone to carry on with his intentions. He was trying to prepare better textbooks, make them more beneficial. A hundred years ago, his texts were most modern, to the point that Rama V even commented that they might be too progressive. For example, in his *Navakovāda* he did not use the Pali words but had included translations. Those of the older generation (*run kao*) thought that he should include more Pali words so that they would know what he is talking about.

If he translated it all into Thai, the older monks would not be used to these meanings, so he put in more Pali with the Thai.[52] And Phra [Prayudh] has tried to carry this on.

As already noted, Phra Prayudh's work is seen as building on that of Prince-Patriarch Wachirayan and Buddhadasa Bhikkhu. The creation of *Buddhadhamma* as an authoritative reference, a distillation of the Buddhist canon, is widely perceived as an extension of the contributions of both of these monks. One administrator in charge of graduate-level Buddhist studies at Mahachulalongkorn Buddhist University put it this way:

Maha Prayoon Mererk: [At the turn of the century] the works of Prince-Patriarch Wachirayan revived Buddhist education. We can say that this was the beginning of the age of Buddhist education for Siamese intellectuals. When Maha Samana Chao [Wachirayanwarorot] wrote *Navakovāda, Vinaya-mukha,* and other books on the Dhamma, that was the beginning; but after that there were no works that had an effect until *Buddhadhamma*. Due to the lack of this type of work, different groups could easily arrive at their own mistaken interpretations. And when the intellectuals studied or applied these interpretations, they were not certain if they were correct. They needed a reference source, an "authority," that they could apply or study in the various matters of science or education they were currently studying at the university. *Buddhadhamma* serves these needs. . . .

There was a gap. There were all sorts of minor studies not worth referring to, but something was lacking for those doing research at the graduate level. Buddhadasa has helped quite a bit, but he does not always mention his sources, so his works are not as useful and convenient as *Buddhadhamma*. When *Buddhadhamma* came out, it was as if the atmosphere of Buddhist studies was revived. It was like water that had been held back was released; you can see that many works [on the Dhamma] are coming out now, because people have more confidence.

And this incorporation of the more integrated and applied approach to presenting the Buddhist teaching could be seen in works dealing with teaching methodology—such as the popular work by Sumon Amonwiwat, *Kanson doi sang sattha lae yonisomanasikan* [Teaching methods that build confidence and apply the (Buddhist) principle of critical reflection][53]—and the influential works on public and mental health by the Magsaysay award-winning Dr. Prawes Wasi.

When acclaimed as a unique contribution to Thai Buddhist literature, *Buddhadhamma*'s systemization, clear sources and references, and its evocative section headings are all frequently cited as important, interesting, and new. The volume was different from typical expositions of Buddhism that began with the course of practice based on the fruits of the attainment of enlightenment—such as the Four Noble Truths, the Eight-fold Path, kamma, and a description of nibbana, the final goal of Buddhism. Instead, Phra Prayudh has divided *Buddhadhamma* into two main parts: part one begins with "The Middle Way of Expressing the Truth" (*majjhena dhamma-desanā*), that is, a description of unbiased, neutral, balanced, or natural truths that were the foundation of the Buddha's enlightenment and the Buddhist system of practice as it later developed. A great deal of lengthy explanation is devoted to descriptions of these interrelated natural laws coupled with their ethical importance. It is only after these fundamental principles "to be understood first" are clearly explained, that Phra Prayudh moves on to an elaboration of part two, "The Middle Way of Practicing the Truth" or the Middle Path (*majjhimā paṭipadā*) advocated by the Buddha following his enlightenment.

Even though Phra Prayudh states in the introduction to *Buddha-dhamma* that the work will not get involved in the intricacies of various philosophical debates, he chose section titles that put forth large, stirring philosophical questions: the book begins with sections entitled "What is Life?", which discusses the Five Aggregates (*pañca-khandha*)[54] that make up life; "What is the Nature of Existence?", which discusses the Three Characteristics of Existence (*tilakkhaṇa*); "What is the Life Process?", which offers an extensive explanation of causality or dependent origination (*paṭiccasamuppāda*) that lays out this Buddhist theory literally backwards and forwards; and "How Should Life Proceed?", which explains the ethics of the Eight-fold Middle Path.

Some critics, however, have suggested that the broad philosophical questions the author has posed are too grand and can never be answered. One Buddhist teacher said, "Asking 'What is Life?' is like posing the question 'What is Love?' These questions are too big and ultimately unanswerable. In a sense, these are the same kinds of big questions that the Buddha said do not bear fruit." People holding such opinions remain in the minority, however, and the questions posed by Phra Prayudh continue to be one of the unique and most enticing features of *Buddhadhamma*.

Phra Prayudh's references to canonical material are explicit, consistent, and very carefully prepared. He has set an example or new standard for scholars in general. In the past, most Buddhist publications, which have come out of a largely oral tradition, did not always cite their sources, and if sources were mentioned, there was often a lack of standardization and clarity. This made many of these works of limited use to scholars. Phra Prayudh seems to want to follow rules of international standards in the citation of sources. Later editions of *Buddhadhamma* even include a sample cataloging card on the title page verso to make sure that library cataloging of the volume will be consistent. Such attention to detail has also brought him accolades among Thai scholars who did not find many religious works reliable or well-grounded.

On the other hand, while scholarly circles (*wong wichakan*) praised the form of this work, others, naturally, found it a bit too scholarly and dry, especially the sections dealing with mental practices and meditation. Some members of the Thammakai meditation movement have criticized Phra Prayudh for being too much of a cerebral "theory man"; and, similarly, some members of Santi Asoke have criticized the objective style of *Buddhadhamma* as being too far removed from real life. For many of these critics, Phra Prayudh only cites passages and adds precious little from his own experience. The lack of any discussion of personal experience was, however, a conscious decision on the part of Phra Prayudh.

The systemization of *Buddhadhamma*—Phra Prayudh's distillation of the major principles of the Pali canon into one book—has caused some people to refer to this work as the most "scientific" presentation of Buddhism in Thai history (some say in any language). People would often suggest that if a person does not have the time to read the whole of the canon, then just read this one book—*Buddhadhamma*. Recently, especially for monk-students studying for higher degrees in Buddhist studies, the aura and authority of this text have begun to cause some problems. In an interview with Maha Prayoon Mererk (December 1991), author and administrator at Mahachulalongkorn Buddhist University, some of the same concerns that people have had about Wachirayan's texts are beginning to emerge regarding Phra Prayudh's writings. In place of a "Wachirayan cult," perhaps a kind of "Phra Prayudh-ism" may be surfacing:

> **Maha Prayoon Mererk:** The language [in *Buddhadhamma*] is so beautiful or elegant that it is sometimes hard for the students to get beyond it and develop their own style. This has been a

real problem; sometimes when students are working on their theses, they do not read other books, only *Buddhadhamma*—they think that is enough. Sometimes their bibliography may contain only two sources: for Pali, the Tipiṭaka; and for Thai, *Buddhadhamma*—that's it. One of our students here [at Mahachulalongkorn Buddhist University] just finished a thesis at Chulalongkorn University in philosophy, and it was no different. He cited several works in English, several in Pali, but when it came to Thai, his principal source was *Buddhadhamma*. It seems as if some people feel that, in terms of its "weighty" content, after they have read it they have acquired a deep understanding of the Dhamma.

If a professor is not careful about how he guides and advises his students, [*Buddhadhamma*] can become the new canon to which people cling—it can actually become "Phra [Prayudh]-ism." (Laughs.) And this is especially true for those students who remember that Phra [Prayudh] used to work here, and so they are willing to accept his teachings that much easier. It is easy for them to become attached to his work.

People see [*Buddhadhamma*] as instant Buddhism, as very accessible—it tends to be that way. They do not try to see how *Buddhadhamma* came from the Tipiṭaka; they do not go that far. Part of this is due to the fact that we tend to believe that all that is presented in *Buddhadhamma* is correct and people believe that it is all inclusive. It is these beliefs that make people feel overwhelmed or discouraged [when they see a tome the likes of *Buddhadhamma*]. But actually there are many subjects in *Buddhadhamma* that should be investigated further, but because it is presented in such a systematic fashion (*pen rabop*), people adhere to the framework and do not go beyond it. It is a method of presentation, and if you merely stay within this framework, all questions can be answered. *Buddhadhamma* is really a presentation of a framework, a viewpoint. . . subjects that relate to the application of the Dhamma need to be further elaborated: such as, Buddhism and society, Buddhism and politics. . . [*Buddhadhamma*] explains the way to nibbana, but for those who want to apply Buddhism to education, politics, or economics, they must go deeply into what the Buddha had to say on each one of these topics. *Buddhadhamma* does not answer all of these. . . but if we were to try and answer these [social applications] perhaps a new framework would emerge. . . Phra [Prayudh] has written about

> more social applications of Buddhism in other books. . .and this is one thing that shows us that *Buddhadhamma* itself is not enough. . . .

Buddhadhamma was intended to be an authoritative work and it has become authoritative. Not designed as an introductory text (*nangsü samrap chuan hai süksa*), it presents its information with authority—backed by canonical references and the scholarly attainments of a high-ranking monk, whose stature has made many people reluctant to criticize his works. Its unique organizational structure is a part of its didactic method, but at the same time the author's decision to compile an "objective" presentation limits the impact of the work; the impartial style of *Buddhadhamma* seems to disallow the use of a more engaging, Socratic-type discourse that is often found in the Buddhist texts themselves. The author rarely invites the reader to contemplate particular aspects of modern life or personal experience in the context of Buddhist teachings—with statements, such as, "Have you ever considered that. . .?" or "Have you ever experienced. . .?"—a method that the Buddha himself often employed. In *Buddhadhamma*, this method only becomes apparent when dialogues with Lord Buddha are cited. One Thai scholar noted, "*Buddhadhamma* is especially clear about the importance of the application of a critical method of reflection, but it is not reflexive enough and stops short of inviting the reader to criticize the text itself."

The "scientific" or positivistic nature of Phra Prayudh's works is apparent in especially two aspects of *Buddhadhamma*: his efforts towards systemization and objectivity. Since we have already discussed the structure of *Buddhadhamma*, Phra Prayudh's objectivity should be addressed. His intention was to write a summary of Buddhist doctrine that would be free of the writer; or rather to free the writer from the book (*tham hai nangsü ni pen itsara chak phu khian*).[55] In interviews, Phra Prayudh stated that he perceived his role as a person who would point to the teachings of Lord Buddha, taking a role of non-involvement. Admittedly, a writer makes subjective choices and is the one in charge of the summary; still it is his hope that the essence of the Buddha's message would prevail.[56]

In certain respects, some people have noted that *Buddhadhamma* is a work that is betwixt and between, caught between the author's attempts to be objective and the need to address contemporary subjective experience in the context of modern life. Accordingly, *Buddhadhamma* is not an introductory text that invites the reader to embark on Buddhist studies, nor is it a book that necessarily invites the reader to reflect on his own life.

In many respects *Buddhadhamma* is a modernized presentation of Buddhism, and in other ways it maintains certain traditional aspects of Thai education and means of presenting a subject—with authority. This authority can be viewed as making up some of the strengths and limitations of this work. As one Thai suggested, "He is trying to compile a single-volume Buddhist Bible; and who will dare question such a bible?"[57]

Essentially, Phra Prayudh's various publications are concerned with three main realms: improving education (secular and religious), maintaining meaningful values in the process of development and modernization, and creating high-quality reference books (mainly on Buddhist subjects). His writing of *Buddhadhamma* falls into the last category.

But beyond these categories, Phra Prayudh has described his work more grandly, stating that it actually attempts to deal with the "rediscovery of Buddhist values and the realization of changes and development based on clear understanding and wise use of tradition and the most progressive sciences along with a real understanding of contemporary conditions" (personal correspondence). To this end he has recently published a volume entitled *Toward a Sustainable Science*, which makes an appeal for a science infused with proper values and proper understanding (as it is more broadly understood in Buddhism).[58] This work suggests a unity of knowledge between science and religion in order to achieve a final meeting point of the two "where religion becomes science and science becomes religion, the division between the two gone forever."[59] Without a doubt some of the major contributions that Phra Prayudh has made with the explanations found in *Buddhadhamma*—such as a detailed analysis of causality (*paṭiccasamuppāda*), critical thinking (*yonisomanasikāra*), the rational basis of Buddhist faith or confidence (*saddhā*), and a psychological as well as a physiological explanation of the Buddhist doctrine of no-self (*anattā*)—give clues for a commonground between religion and science.[60]

According to Phra Prayudh, *Buddhadhamma* is meant for those who are brave enough to pursue a difficult subject.[61] For Thais and foreigners alike, reading and studying *Buddhadhamma* presents a formidable yet rewarding challenge.

Notes

1. The title of *Maha* is typically bestowed upon fully ordained monks who have attained at least the basic levels of Pali language studies (*prayok* 3).

2. In official listings of monk's names, often a man's given name followed by the name bestowed upon him at the time of ordination will be noted parenthetically. Many people, however, still refer to him as "Maha Prayudh."

3. Between 1973 to 1976, following the so-called student revolutions of the 14th of October 1973, Thailand experienced a kind of renaissance during which many traditional aspects of Thai culture and society were being questioned by the young. This questioning also extended to the younger Buddhist monk-students (*yuwasong*) at Mahachulalongkorn. See, for example, Somboon Suksamran, *Buddhism and Politics in Thailand* (Singapore: Institute of Southeast Asian Studies, 1982), esp. chapter 3. For details on Phra Rajavaramuni's role in this, see Grant A. Olson, "A Person-Centered Ethnography of Thai Buddhism: The Life of Phra Rajavaramuni (Prayudh Payutto)" (Ph.D. dissertation, Cornell University, 1989).

4. Whose publication by Mahachulalongkorn Buddhist University was not completed until 2523 [1980] in large part due to the slow pace of the government printing house.

5. English translation by Grant A. Olson (Bangkok: Satirakoses-Nagapradipa Foundation, 1987).

6. Pronounced "Thep-way-thi" [Thepwethi].

7. See Grant A. Olson, "Sangha Reform in Thailand: Limitation, Liberation, and the Middle Path" (M.A. thesis, University of Hawaii, 1983).

8. For details, refer to Olson (1989).

9. See especially, Phra Rajavaramuni, *Looking to America to Solve Thailand's Problems,* trans. by Grant A. Olson (Bangkok: Sathirakoses-Nagapradipa Foundation, 1987).

10. For concise biographical information on this prince, see *The Centennial of His Royal Highness Prince Wan Waithayakon Krommun Naradhip Bongsprabandh* (Bangkok: Office of the National Culture Commission, 1991).

11. For information on Dr. Puey see, S. Sivaraksa, *Nai Puai Ungphakon phuyai thi mai kalon* [Puey Ungphakorn: An elder who is not crooked] (Bangkok: Komol Keemthong, 2522 [1979]).

12. Interview with Khunying Krachangsri Raktakanit, April 20, 1987.

13. First published as a cremation volume in 2513 [1970]. Reprinted in Phra Rajavaramuni, *Phutthasatsana kap sangkhom Thai* (Bangkok: Komol Keemthong, 2525 [1982]), 153–162.

14. See Katherine Bowie, *Voices from the Countryside.* Monograph 6 (Madison: Center for Southeast Asian Studies, 1991), introduction, for more on

the context of the era from 1973–1976. The conservative Thanin era, a "dark" age in Thai history, followed this period of openness, inquiry, and creativity; see Benedict R. O.'G. Anderson's *In the Mirror: Literature and Politics in Siam in the American Era* (Bangkok: Duang Kamol, 1985), 39–40.

15. Mattani Mojdara Rutnin, *Modern Thai Literature: The Process of Modernization and the Transformation of Values* (Bangkok: Thammasat University Press, 1988), 75.

16. See Anderson (1985), 25–26.

17. Olson (1989), 230.

18. See Phra Rajavaramuni (Prayudh Payutto), *Buddhadhamma* (Bangkok: Mahachulalongkorn Buddhist University, 2529 [1986]), 925.

19. Olson (1989), 188–190.

20. In certain respects, Phra Prayudh might be seen as a nonfiction counterpart of the new intelligentsia represented in Anderson's sampling of fiction from this era (1985).

21. At this time Phra Prayudh circulated memos about using rational, unbiased thought as opposed to emotional, politically charged appeals; see Olson (1989), 168–170.

22. See Olson (1989), esp. 78–89 and 160–181.

23. Phra Rajavaramuni, *Buddhadhamma* (Bangkok: Khana Radom-tham, 2525 [1982]), (5).

24. Personal conversation.

25. See *Phu tham khunnaprayot to phraphutthasatsana nüang nai okat somphot krung Rattanakosin 200 pi* [Contributors to Buddhism commemorated in conjunction with the Rattanakosin Bicentennial celebrations] (Bangkok: Kansatsana, 2525 [1982]), 19–21.

26. Manas Chitakasem, "Poetic Conventions and Modern Thai Poetry," in *Thai Constructions of Knowledge*, ed. Manas Chitakasem and Andrew Turton (London: School of Oriental and African Studies, University of London, 1991), 37.

27. *Treasury of Thai Literature: The Modern Period* (Bangkok: National Identity Board, 1988), 6. The editorial board of this volume also elected to include an excerpt of Buddhadasa Bhikkhu's "Dhamma Socialism" in this collection of modern literature.

28. Relatively recently the Thais borrowed the word "corruption" from English.

29. The value of the baht can be roughly calculated as 25 baht to $1 (US).

30. The Department of Religious Affairs is under the Ministry of Education.

31. See Olson (1989), 157–158, n. 68.

32. Interview with Maha Narong Cittasobhano, then Acting Deputy Rector for Student Affairs, Mahachulalongkorn Buddhist University; see Olson (1989), 389.

33. Prince Vajirañāṇa, *The Autobiography of Prince Vajirañāṇa*, ed. and trans. by Craig J. Reynolds (Athens, OH: Ohio University Press, 1979), xx.

34. Prince Vajirañāṇa (1979), 37–38.

35. Prince Vajirañāṇa (1979), 52–53.

36. Prince Vajirañāṇa (1979), xxxvi–xxxvii.

37. Steven J. Zack, "Buddhist Education under Prince Wachirayan Warorot (Ph.D. dissertation, Cornell University, 1987), 187.

38. Phra Rajavaramuni, *Social Dimension of Buddhism in the Contemporary World.* Paper no. 15 (Bangkok: Thai Khadi Research Institute, Thammasat University, 1983), 55; see also Grant A. Olson, "Phra Rajavaramuni and the 'Wachirayan Cult': Questioning the Legacy of a Prince-Patriarch," unpublished manuscript.

39. Interview, August 6, 1987.

40. Buddhadasa Bhikkhu, *The First Ten Years of Suan Mokkh*, trans. by Mongkol Dejnakarintra (Bangkok: Dhamma Study and Practice Group, 1990), 51.

41. Buddhadasa Bhikkhu (1990), 15.

42. Buddhadasa Bhikkhu (1990), 17.

43. Buddhadasa Bhikkhu, *Attachiwaprawat nai wai num khong Phutthathat Phikkhu* [The biography of Buddhadasa Bhikkhu as a young man] (Bangkok: Pacharayasan, 2527 [1981]), 1–2 [translation mine].

44. See Buddhadasa Bhikkhu, *Christianity and Buddhism* (Bangkok: Sublime Life Mission, 1967), esp. p. 18; and for his debate with Kukrit, see Arun Wetsuwan, *Wiwatha* (Bangkok: Phræ Phitthaya, 2520 [1977]).

45. See Grant A. Olson, "From Buddhadasa Bhikkhu to Phra Debvedi: Two Monks of Wisdom," in *Radical Conservatism: Buddhism in the Contemporary World* (Bangkok: Thai Inter-Religious Commission for Development and the International Network of Engaged Buddhists, 1990), 262.

46. There is good deal of literature on how the changes of government in Thailand have had a parallel impact on the Sangha Laws imposed on the monkhood: see, for example, Stanley Tambiah, *World Conquerer and World Renouncer* (Cambridge: Cambridge University Press, 1976); Somboon Suksamran, *Buddhism and Politics in Thailand* (Singapore: Institute of Southeast Asian Studies, 1982); and Peter Jackson, *Buddhism, Legitimation, and Conflict* (Singapore: Institute of Southeast Asian Studies, 1989).

47. See Edwin Zehner, "Reform Symbolism of a Thai Middle-Class Sect: The Growth and Appeal of the Thammakai Movement," *Journal of Southeast Asian Studies* 21:2 (Sept. 1990).

48. *Matichon* (*sutsapda*), October 29, 2529 [1986], cover story.

49. For more on this movement see: Olson (1983); Jackson (1989); and Donald Swearer, "Fundamentalistic Movements in Theravada Buddhism," in *Fundamentalisms Observed*, ed. by Martin E. Marty and R. Scott Appleby (Chicago: University of Chicago Press, 1991).

50. Phra Debvedi, *Karani Santi Asok* (private publication as *Ngan raksa phrathammawinai* [Work for the care of Buddhism]), 24 February 2531 [1988], 2.

51. Phra Dusadee holds a degree in law from Thammasat University and a master's degree in comparative religion from Mahidol University; see Olson (1989), 389–390.

52. For more on this see Zack (1977), 193.

53. (Bangkok: Odeon Store, 2530 [1987]).

54. The Five Aggregates are *rūpa* (corporeality), *vedanā* (sensations) *saññā* (perceptions), *saṅkhāra* (mental formations, predispositions), and *viññāṇa* (consciousness).

55. Phra Rajavaramuni (2529 [1986]), 927.

56. Interview with Phra Prayudh, December 7, 1991.

57. Field notes, 1987.

58. Bhikkhu P. A. Payutto, *Toward a Sustainable Science*, trans. by B. G. Evans (Bangkok: Buddhadhamma Foundation, 1993), 142. This is a translation of the Thai publication, *Phutthasatsana nai thana penrakthan khong witthayasat* [Buddhism as a foundation for science] (Bangkok: Mahachulalongkorn Buddhist University, 2535 [1992].

59. Bhikkhu P. A. Payutto (1993), 41.

60. *Buddhadhamma* adds to the work of other scholars who have been fascinated with the "scientific" nature of Buddhist notions of causality: such as, David J. Kalupahana, *Causality: The Central Principle of Buddhism* (Honolulu: The University Press of Hawaii, 1975) and Rune E. A. Johansson, *The Dynamic Psychology of Early Buddhism,* Scandinavian Institute of Asian Studies Monograph Series no. 37 (London: Curzon Press, 1979).

61. Phra Rajavaramuni (2529 [1986]), 929.

BUDDHADHAMMA

Natural Laws and Values for Life

The Things That Should Be Understood First

Various modern presentations of Buddhism often raise the question of whether Buddhism is a religion, a philosophy, or a way of life. When this question arises, it can be the cause of much lengthy discussion. People's views come out differently, often not falling into any single pattern; these views are then the cause of division and never-ending debate. Even though this volume is written in sections suggesting philosophical questions, we will not get involved in this kind of debate at all. The primary intention of this volume is to show what Buddhadhamma has to teach us, what its content is all about. Whether Buddhadhamma is a philosophy or not and whether philosophy can encompass or interpret the whole of Buddhadhamma will remain a problem for philosophy. I want to say that Buddhadhamma is Buddhadhamma and remains Buddhadhamma. There is, however, one restriction: if the principles or teachings related to a quest for truth and wisdom do not reveal ethics and a method of practice that can be applied in daily life, then such principles cannot be considered Buddhism—this is especially true for that which is held to be the original body of teachings of Lord Buddha, which, here, we will call Buddhadhamma.[1]

It is difficult to collect the actual teachings of Buddhism and present a summary of them. Even if we refer to points mentioned in the canon, believed to be the words of Buddha, difficulties still do not disappear, because the interpretations of the canonical teachings are numerous and varied according to the wisdom, intelligence, and biases of different interpreters. In some cases, two people may take opposing sides and both be able to cite statements from the canon to support their ideas. Deliberating the truth of any presentation of Buddhism depends on the accuracy of a person's grasp of the essential meaning and integration of Buddhist principles together with all the evidence that can be shown as a complete, integrated whole. All of the apparent evidence, however, is not broad enough to contain all the points of the doctrine. This predicament is inevitable, and so there is no way to escape the influence of different people's basic understandings of Buddhism on their interpretations of the religion. In this regard, there are other factors that should be considered related to the context of Lord Buddha's life and his practices. Because Lord Buddha is the source of the teachings, biographical information about him can help illustrate the essential objectives of the Teacher better than the teachings expressed in the canon—or at least, they should serve as a supplement for clearer understanding. Even though it can be argued that this information, as well as the teachings themselves, comes from the canon and also depends upon interpretation, we still have to admit that this supplementary knowledge is of great benefit.

From basic canonical and historical information sufficient enough to paint a picture, the situation and social conditions at the time of the Buddha were briefly as follows:

Lord Buddha was born in India (or Jambūdipa, the "continent of rose apples") about 2,600 years ago. He was born into the *khattiya* caste. His previous name was Prince Siddhattha, the son of Suddhodana, who ruled Sakiya, which was located in the northeastern part of India at the foot of the Himalayas. Being the son of the king, and the hope of the royal family, Prince Siddhattha received all services and worldly goods for his pleasure. He lived in the midst of these pleasures until he was 29 years old. In addition, he had a wife and son.

At that time, the politics were such that some states under monarchical rule were gaining power and were trying to make war in order to extend their power and territory. Some states, especially those governed democratically as republics, were conquered and incorporated into other states; the few states that remained strong were in tenuous, tense situations. War could flare up at any time. Even among the larger and more powerful states, economic conflict was common. Trade was increasingly expanding and there was one segment of society that was becoming more and more influential: the rich and wealthy. They had increasingly more influence, even at the royal court. In society, people were divided into four castes according to the teachings of Brahmanism. These people had different rights, prestige, social status, and occupations according to their caste. Even Hindu historians say that the maintenance of castes at that time was not all that strict, but at least the lower-caste *suddas* had no right to hear or cite passages from the Vedas (the sacred canon of the brahmins). There was an extreme punishment stating that any *sudda* violating this restriction would have his body cut in half. Any untouchable (*caṇḍāla*) had no right to education. Caste was determined by ascription, which was used as a tool for dividing people. The brahmins, especially, were trying to upgrade themselves, so they put themselves up as the highest caste. The brahmins, who had handed down Brahmanism from generation to generation, developed a religion based on ritual teachings that became increasingly mysterious, complicated, and grand. At this time, the rituals were increasingly lacking in reason. These rituals not only served the purposes of religion but also served the needs of powerful people who wanted to demonstrate their prestige and greatness. There were also people who hoped for benefits from these powerful people; and so, people were inclined to use these religious rituals for their own gain, as they hoped to receive benefits in the form of wealth and sensual fulfillment. Along with this, troubles were created for the lower-class people, slaves, and workers involved in heavy labor, and numerous animals were cruelly slaughtered in widespread sacrifices.[2]

At the same time, a number of brahmins began to realize that these various ceremonies were not able to give them eternal life. These people started to seriously contemplate the problems surrounding eternal life and the various ways leading to that state. They were even willing to separate themselves from society in order to contemplate, search, and discover the answers to this dilemma. They did this by living in isolation in the jungle. The teachings of the Brahmanism of this era, which was called the Upanishadic period, had many contradictions associated with it. While some parts of the teachings added explanations to ceremonies, other parts condemned certain rituals, and various points of view were expressed concerning the subject of eternal life. The teachings also contained conflicting points of view on the notion of Ātman. Finally, they concluded that Ātman, the source of everything, can be equated with Brahman. There was one state, however, that could not be explained called *"neti-neti"* ("not that-not that"), which was the highest goal of religious effort. These brahmins tried to express the meaning of this state—arguing about the problems related to *"neti-neti"*—at the same time keeping certain aspects of esoteric knowledge to themselves.

At this time, there was another group of ascetics disenchanted with the seemingly nonsensical nature of existence in this world. This group went out to perform their own unique practices with the hope of achieving eternal life or successful, miraculous results. Some of these sages practiced ascetic forms of meditation involving, for example, not eating and even going as far as torturing their bodies in strange ways that were beyond the conception of ordinary people. Some practiced concentration meditation (*samādhi*) to the point of claiming they could perform various miracles. Through meditation some reached states of absorption, attaining both the spheres of form (*rūpa-samāpatti*) and formlessness (*arūpa-samāpatti*).

At the same time, many ascetics, who called themselves recluses (*samaṇa*), gave up family and relations in order to be ordained and seek the meaning of life. They wandered and traveled about to different cities and places to discuss and inquire into problems, and some even established themselves as religious leaders, expressing their attitudes and ideas in different ways. It appeared that there were many different religious groups and doctrines.[3]

We can summarize these tendencies very briefly by saying that at that time, one group of people was prospering due to its power and good fortune, and this group was entertained and intoxicated in the course of its search for wealth and material pleasures. But at the same time, there were many groups of people whose positions and ways of life were declining, and they were largely ignored. Another group of people had taken leave of society in order to seek philosophical truth, without caring for the social situation at this time.

For twenty-nine years, Prince Siddhattha had had all worldly pleasures at his disposal; and not only did he have these pleasures, but he was closed off from seeing or encountering the conditions of suffering (*dukkha*) of the common lay people.[4] But these conditions could not be hidden from him as time went by. The most prominent problems of human suffering and hardship included aging, disease, and death. All of these problems led Siddhattha to consider deeply what their solution might be. He reflected extensively until he was able to perceive the social disparity existing at that time. He noted that people competed, fought, and took advantage of one another. These people continued living blindly in this way; they did not think of the difficulties, suffering, and hardships of others; and they lived like the slaves of material goods. When they were happy, they were intoxicated within the narrowness of their own minds. When they were overcome with suffering, they went crazy, lost their minds, and moped about going to abnormal extremes. Then, they grew old, suffered pains, and died meaninglessly. The underpriviledged people with few opportunities were oppressed and lived in extreme hardship. They too grew old and died meaninglessly. Prince Siddhattha saw these conditions and became bored with his own comfortable lifestyle. He saw all the happiness and entertainment surrounding him as meaningless and nonsubstantial, so he sought for a method that would bring about a kind of happiness (*sukha*) that would be more stable and substantial.[5] Siddhattha tried to come to a solution to this dilemma, but he could not reach it. The condition of his life revolved around arousal, seduction, and confusion; and this situation did not lend itself to fruitful contemplation. Finally, he saw a recluse who had taken leave of society in order to discover various truths. This renunciation was accomplished by living simply, without worry—the most conducive way of life for carrying out a search for knowledge and reason. The Prince came to believe that this way of life might help him reach a successful solution to life's problems, and he thought that perhaps these recluses might have something to teach him.

When Prince Siddhattha reached this point in his life, he went out to lead the homeless life like the other recluses at that time. He wandered about studying and seaching for knowledge, practicing and acquiring as much knowledge as the other ascetics had to offer. He studied methods of concentration (*samādhi*) until he attained the meditative absorptions of the fine-material sphere (*jhāna-samāpatti*) and came to the level of the four absorptions of the formless sphere (*arūpa-samāpatti*), which was the highest state. He practiced yoga until he was capable of performing marvellous feats, and he indulged in austere, ascetic practices to the point of torturing himself and almost losing his life. In the end, he decided that the methods of all of these ascetics were not able to solve the problems he originally set out to overcome. If the Prince's life before he went out to become a recluse is juxtaposed with his life as an ascetic, each of these lifestyles can be seen as extremes. Siddhattha, therefore, turned to search for his own way, until he finally attained enlightenment.[6] The principle that he discovered and later used as a teaching methodology was referred to as "*majjhena dhamma*," the Middle Way of Expressing the Truth; and he called the system of practices that he created "*majjhimā paṭipadā*," the Middle Way of Practicing the Truth or Middle Path.

From the life of Siddhattha, certain Buddhist attitudes can be determined: Living in a society that is blindly enslaved by desire, completely escaping from society and not getting involved in nor being responsible for society, or living by torturing oneself are all considered to be extreme errors that do not help human beings live meaningful and truthful lives.

When the Buddha attained enlightenment, he returned to society and began to seriously teach the Buddhadhamma for the benefit of the world.

teach the Buddhadhamma for the benefit of the world. He worked at this for the latter forty-five years of his life.

Even if we ignore the other aspects of the biography of Lord Buddha and look only at the social side, we can see that he lived for the happiness and benefit of the people at that time, and he was successful because of his role as a renouncer (*pabbajita*). Eventually, Lord Buddha persuaded many higher-class people to forsake their wealth and prosperity and be ordained, study, and attain his Dhamma. Those people participated in Lord Buddha's efforts and devoted themselves to the benefit of all people. They accomplished this by wandering and reaching out to people of all walks of life and castes everywhere they would go. The effects of these beneficial deeds was, therefore, widespread. And, furthermore, the Sangha, or monkhood, was an important starting place for solving the problems of society; no matter what caste people were born into, they could be ordained and all have equal rights. On the other hand, the rich merchants and householders who were not prepared to completely devote themselves to ordination could still have a family and be devout lay people (*upāsaka*); these lay people helped to support the Sangha, and at the same time, these people often shared a portion of their property to help others.

The intentions and comprehensiveness of the religious teachings and practices of Lord Buddha and his followers is apparent in the words attributed to him. The very first time he sent his followers out to spread the religion, he said the following:

> Bhikkhus, you should all wander about for the benefit and happiness of the majority, help the people of this world, support and provide well-being to all deities and human beings.[7]

The aspects of Buddhadhamma that can be applied to society, and the various types of people who can benefit from them, are evident in the *Pāsādika Sutta*. These can be summarized as follows:

The Holy Life (*brahmacariya*) must have all of the following factors if it is to be deemed successful, far-reaching, beneficial to the majority, integrated, and stable by both deities and human beings:

1. The Master [Lord Buddha] is a longstanding Elder (*thera*), a person of experience who has passed through all phases of life;
2. There are bhikkhus and followers who are elders and have expert knowledge, who have received proper training and orientation, and are steadfast and brave; they have achieved the delights of Dhamma

from the practice of yoga, and they can present the Dhamma in a fruitful manner. They can conquer doctrines that dispute or speeches that oppose in a way that is in accordance with the Dhamma. There are also intermediate and newly ordained bhikkhus and followers who have these same abilities;

3. There are bhikkhunī and female followers who are Elders (*therī*), intermediates, or newly ordained, who also have these same abilities;
4. There are male lay devotees (*upāsaka*) without families who lead a chaste Holy Life (*brahmacārī*), and there are those who still have families and engage in worldly pleasures (*kāmasukha*); these people also have these same abilities;
5. There are female lay devotees (*upāsikā*) without families who lead a chaste Holy Life, and there are those who still have families and engage in worldly pleasures; these people also have the same abilities.

If the religion even lacks the female lay devotees who have families, it cannot be said to be progressive, complete, and well integrated.[8]

This statement shows that the teachings of the Buddhadhamma are aimed at all kinds of people; they are for ascetics, monks, and lay people. In other words, they cover the whole range of society.

The general characteristics of Buddhadhamma can be summarized as follows:

1. It explains the principle of the Middle Way of Expressing the Truth, which is called "*majjhena dhamma*," or it can be called by its full name "*majjhena dhammadesanā*." *Majjhena dhammadesanā* is a way of explaining the truth according to pure reason, as a natural process, for the sole purpose of bringing the benefits of practice to people in their daily lives. It does not support efforts to reach the Truth (*saccadhamma*) by way of argument or by setting up, clinging to, and protecting various theories through philosophical speculation.
2. It shows the Middle Way of Practicing the Truth or Middle Path, which is called "*majjhimā paṭipadā*." This is the principle of living for those who seek to train themselves and for those who know what is going on and do not wish to allow themselves to become foolishly caught up in the world. The goal of success for these people can be described as true happiness, purity, illumination, peace, and freedom, which can be realized in this life by practicing

the Middle Way. These aims will be related to other factors, such as the conditions of the lives of ascetics and lay people.

The Dhamma teachings of Lord Buddha aim at practical results; he wants everyone to take charge of life in this world starting from the present moment on, to know the principle of the Middle Way, and to understand how to tread the Middle Path. All of these things can be applied to life no matter what a person's circumstances or status in society. If there is any speculation regarding a life after this one, then seriously set your mind on making this life the way you want your next life to be. Build your confidence to the point that you are not worried about the next life at all. Everyone has equal rights by nature to achieve the fruits of success even though each person has different abilities. Everyone should have the same opportunity to reach success according to his own abilities, and these abilities can be altered and increased. People should, therefore, have the chance to develop their own abilities as best they can. Even though the real fruits of success must be accomplished by your own efforts, by fully realizing your responsibilities, you can be an instrument for helping other people. Therefore, the principle of conscientiousness and dedication (*appamāda*) and the principle of having good, virtuous friends (*kalyāṇamitta*) emphasize two prominent dimensions of the Dhamma—the former being an aspect of personal responsibility and the latter an external factor that is supportive of other people.

If we examine the life of Lord Buddha and the results of his work, we can see certain trends related to important Buddhist practices, for example, doing away with blind beliefs in many nonsensical rituals, especially those related to animal sacrifice. Lord Buddha accomplished this by teaching and emphasizing the damaging results and nonsensical nature of such rituals. All of these rituals made people depend on external conditions, thirst for ambition, think only in terms of material benefits, and increase their selfishness, making them unaware of suffering and the hardships of human beings and animals. Such rituals made people focus on the future and not think of improving present conditions.

Lord Buddha also taught and confirmed the principle of giving (*dāna*), sacrificing and sharing, and helping each member of the community. Furthermore, he tried to do away with belief in an ascribed caste system, which was used to draw lines of rights and opportunities in society and in the minds of people. He set up the Sangha as an ideal community open to all equally, like a sea that is open to receiving water from all rivers, assimilating them all and becoming one.[9] The institution of the temple was created, which became a center for spreading very important cultural values and education. From these ideals, the followers of Hinduism were motivated to set up their own centers for their religion—some 1,400 to 1,700 years after the passing away of the Buddha.[10]

Lord Buddha gave rights to women so that they might benefit from Buddhadhamma and reach the final goal of the teachings just the same as men. Even though granting this right weighed heavily upon his mind and required careful consideration so that the proper procedures might be established for the society at that time, these rights were granted because the Vedas had so limited the education and spiritual training of women that such opportunities almost became completely closed to them. Lord Buddha taught Buddhadhamma with a common tongue so that people of any educational background could benefit from this Dhamma. This accessibility stands in stark contrast to Brahmanism, which attached itself to the sacredness of the Vedas and limited higher knowledge to only a small circle of people by using the classical language Sanskrit, a language only understood and used within their own group for communicating, handing down, and maintaining the scriptures. Later on, even though there were people who asked permission from Lord Buddha to change his discourses and teachings into the Vedic language, he did not allow this and insisted upon using common speech as before.[11] He also refused to waste time speculating about philosophical truths that could not be proved or demonstrated by reason. If people asked about these kinds of philosophical problems, he would stop them and pull them back to the problems that were more directly related to themselves and the practices that could be applied to daily life.[12] For the things that should be known or understood verbally, he would make verbal suggestions; for the things that should be known or understood by seeing, he would make visual suggestions. Lord Buddha taught Buddhadhamma through various indirect methods. There are many levels of teachings for householders, for people who live in society, and for those who lead the homeless life. The teachings aim at material and spiritual benefits so that everyone will receive all of the fruits of Buddhadhamma. Lord Buddha's activities will bear out the preceding summary of Buddhadhamma.

By teaching Buddhadhamma in the midst of the brahmin culture and responding to the beliefs of the various sects of ascetics at that time, Lord Buddha became involved with the language and terminology of those sects. This involvement is a result of his listening, responding, and referring to these sect's teachings. It is clear that Lord Buddha was not interested in condemning the vocabulary and jargon of other religious groups but rather in criticizing the beliefs inherent or latent in their terminology. In other words, he did not deny or argue by means of violent methods. He preferred to alter people's points of views through a subtle dialectic method or by having them acquiesce to his views. Accordingly, he used some of the teachings of those religious groups and attached new meaning to their ideas in light of Buddhadhamma. He created some new values for the old terminology already in use, for example, he used the term "Brahma" to refer to a kind of worldly being who is born and dies, and he used the same term to refer to parents. He changed the belief of paying respect to the six natural directions (north, south, east, west, skyward and earthward), to practicing duties and maintaining relationships in society. He changed the meaning of three things in the sacrificial ceremony of Brahmanism, which involved worshipping sacred fires, to social responsibility towards three kinds of people. He changed the criteria for being a brahmin and an Aryan by birth to being a person who maintains proper conduct and practice. Sometimes he taught by extracting some meanings from the traditional religious teachings and using them in a good and beneficial way. Any teachings in the traditional religion that were good and correct were approved by him; he maintained that correctness and goodness are universal by nature. In the event that a principle of conduct and practice in the traditional religion had various meanings, he tried to explain which one was proper and which one was not. He was tolerant and asked people to conduct themselves in a proper way. Sometimes he pointed out that some of the more disastrous conduct in the traditional religions could lead to the downfall of those groups. He explained that in the past, some of the teachings of those old religions had served a useful purpose, and so he continued to teach the good and valuable aspects of those traditional teachings. Some examples of good teachings from traditional religions were the following: *tapa* (austerity, ascetic practices), *pūjāyañña* (offerings for worship), principles of good government, some Brahmanical folklore, and so on.[13] The statements mentioned above—aside from showing Lord Buddha's broadmindedness, his intention to teach the truth, and his unbiased approach—should serve to remind people to be careful in discriminating the meaning of words prescibed in Buddhadhamma and other religions.

Furthermore, toward the end of Lord Buddha's life, as time passed and his teachings had spread to various places, the understanding of Buddhadhamma had already been transformed from the original teachings.

Naturally, these transformations differed according to the varying backgrounds, knowledge, education, training, and intelligence of the people who passed the teachings on. They interpreted the meaning of Buddhadhamma differently; they took knowledge and older beliefs from other religions, the influence of local religion and culture, and mixed it with Buddhadhamma. Because of different ways of emphasizing and twisting the doctrine according to personal interests, together with the biases and skillfulness of the people who maintained the teachings, some parts of the teachings became prominent while others tended to fade into the background. This resulted in the separation of Buddhism into various sects, the main ones being Mahayana and Theravada, including many subsects within those two main sects. Theravada Buddhism, even though it was deemed the sect that accurately maintained the original system and teachings of the Buddha, was still not immune to transformation. Even some parts of the teachings in the Buddhist canon are still problematic for people today; people still debate, reconsider, and look for evidence to support or refute a basis for determining which parts of the teachings made up the original. These descrepancies are ever increasing and have become even more evident in the knowledge and understanding found in people's beliefs and daily practices today. In some cases these accretions seem to go against the original teachings or almost become another doctrine in opposition to the original teachings of Buddhism. For example, in Thailand, when the word "*kamma*" is mentioned, it is commonly understood to mean a specific act committed in the past that leads to bad results.[14] Reaping the negative results in the present can, therefore, be attributed to improper conduct in the past. In this sense, then, kamma is a force that reveals the ill effects of bad conduct in previous lives. For the most part, this is the current, popular understanding of "kamma." However, when the true principle of kamma is considered, it becomes clear that this kind of understanding is far removed from the real meaning of the term. Even other items found in the Dhamma including such words as *ārammaṇa, viññāṇa, pāramī, santosa, uppekhā, adhiṭṭhāna, parikamma, bhāvanā, vipassanā, kāmalokiya, lokuttara, puññā, icchā,* and so on—have taken on special, cultural meanings in Thai society that are different from the original meanings found in the Buddhadhamma. In studying Buddhadhamma, we must try to put aside the deviating, popular conceptions of common people before we can come to understand the actual meaning of the Buddhist texts.

In explaining the Dhamma, I will try to show the actual Buddhadhamma that Lord Buddha taught and intended. Here, I will not be considering the popular meanings generally understood by many people, because I feel that they are peripheral and not necessary for understanding the actual Buddhadhamma at all. The Buddhist canon will serve as our most important source for the substance and meaning of the Buddhadhamma and, here, I mean the Pali Tipiṭaka only, because it is generally accepted as the most accurate and complete source of Buddhism. Nevertheless, I will try to pick and choose special parts that illustrate the original points and convey the original meaning by employing a principle of integration and agreement. In order to be more certain, I have included the life and deeds of the Buddha to assist us in our consideration and judgment of the direction and scope of Buddhadhamma. When we consider all of this, we can be confident that the essence of Buddhadhamma very close to the original can be revealed. At a fundamental level, however, this presentation will depend upon this writer's powers of intelligence and some inclinations that he may not be aware of. Consider this book, therefore, as an effort—using methods and principles combined with the most conclusive evidence available—to present the most accurate picture of the Buddhadhamma as Lord Buddha taught and intended it.

If we divide the Buddhadhamma into two parts, *saccadhamma* and *cariyadhamma*, and then stipulate the meaning that is to be used here by defining *saccadhamma* as the part that shows the conditions or true characteristics of dhamma, and defining *cariyadhamma* as the rules of conduct, it can be seen that *saccadhamma* in Buddhism refers to the teachings related to the conditions of all things, or nature, and the ordinary course of things, or natural law. *Cariyadhamma* refers to taking advantage of knowing and understanding the conditions and course of things, or knowing natural law and then applying it in an advantageous way. In other words, *saccadhamma* is natural law, while *cariyadhamma* is knowledge pertaining to the application of *saccadhamma*. All of these principles are not related to factors beyond nature, such as a creator god, at all. Presenting Buddhadhamma for the sake of only knowing and understanding theory is inadequate; *saccadhamma* and *cariyadhamma* will, therefore, be presented together, with the teachings coupled in terms of conditions that point to values that can be put into practice. This method of presentation is opposite to the way of the Four Noble Truths (*ariyasacca*), which points primarily at the results and proper outcome of practice. The Four Noble Truths start with problems that initially appear and then move progressively towards the final goal; but here we will start with knowing and understanding the world and life in terms of Buddhadhamma. After that, the meaning or the value of practice will be explained until we reach the final goal of Buddhism.

Notes

1. For scholars of Buddhism, the various meanings of the term *dhamma* can be as difficult to pin down as the meaning of "culture" for anthropologists. The term dhamma can mean truth, phenomena, principles, righteousness, good acts, morality, or the "body" of the teachings of the Buddha. Here, it is used in this last sense. When the term dhamma is used alone to indicate the whole of Lord Buddha's teachings, it has generally been capitalized in this text. Since Phra Prayudh is using the Pali canon as his principal source, throughout this text I will adhere to Pali spellings of Buddhist terminology—in other words, using dhamma instead of dharma. And since the term is used so often, it will not be italicized—trans.

2. See, for example, *Vāseṭṭha Sutta*, Sn. p. 112; *Brāhmaṇa-dhammika Sutta*, Sn. p. 50.

3. Especially the six outstanding ones mentioned in the Buddhist canon. The evidence in the Pali canon that suggests that the doctrines or recluses and brahmins can be divided into sixty-two different views or theories (D.I.13–46). For the state of Jambūdīpa, see G. C. Pande, *Studies in the Origins of Buddhism* (Allahabad: The Indian Press Private, Ltd., 1957), 310–368.

4. The proper translation of the term *dukkha* has remained a point of contention for scholars of Buddhism. While most commonly rendered as "suffering," it can also mean disease (in the broadest sense of the term, that is, lack of ease), discomfort, disorder, conflict, difficulties, unfullfillment, or pain. It has also been rendered as dissatisfactoriness, a term I find very dissatisfactory, since we hardly ever use this word in English and dukkha is something encountered by most people on a daily basis. To begin with, I have translated dukkha as suffering, fully aware of the inadequacies and pessimism that this can entail. As the text unfolds, generally dukkha will be left untranslated and unitalicized, and its wider meaning will become clearer from the various contexts in which the concept appears—trans.

5. *Sukha* is usually paired as an opposite to dukkha. Sukha can mean (spiritual) happiness, ease, joy, comfort, fulfillment, or pleasure. The Thai terms *suk* and *thuk* come from the Pali terms sukha and dukkha, respectively. In the following sections these terms will generally remain untranslated and unitalicized (especially when they are used in more specific canonical references). When used

in a more general sense in Thai, they may be translated as suffering and happiness, respectively—trans.

6. For this segment of the biography of the Buddha, see M.II.211–213.

7. Vin.I.21.

8. See the *Pāsādika Sutta*, D.III.123–124.

9. See, for example, A.IV.202 and D.III.97.

10. See P. V. Bapat, *2500 Years of Buddhism* (1959), 355; and S. Dutt, *Buddhist Monks and Monastries* (London: George, Allen, and Unwin, Ltd., 1962), 210.

11. See Vin.II.139.

12. See, for example, A.V.193–198; M.I.426–432.

13. See A.V.189; A.IV.41; Sn. p. 50.

14. In this text the Pali kamma will be used in place of the Sanskrit karma. Since this term appears so frequently, it will not be italicized—trans.

PART I

The Middle Way of Expressing the Truth (*majjhena dhammadesanā*)

A Balanced Way of Teaching Natural Truth

What Is Life?

The Five Aggregates of Existence (*pañca-khandha*)

Conditions of Reality

Buddhadhamma looks at all things in terms of integrated factors. There is no real self (or essence) in all things. When all of the elements composing one's being are divided and separated, no self remains. A simple example that is often employed is that of the "car":[1] When all parts are assembled according to certain specifications, the result is called "car," but if all of those parts are completely separated, the form of the car cannot be found; there are only parts that can be referred to according to their various names.[2] That is to say, the essence of the car does not exist separately from the composition of its parts; there is only the word "car" for the condition describing the assemblage of those parts. And no self can be found even in parts that consist of the combination of other smaller parts. Therefore, when we say that something exists, we must understand that it exists in terms of a combination of various elements.

When the condition of all things is seen as an integrated form composed of various elements, Buddhadhamma can further inform us regarding the composition of those various elements and their features. Since Buddhadhamma has a special relationship to life, especially in terms of the mind,[3] a presentation of the various compositions must include both the physical and the mental aspects, or *rūpa-dhamma* and *nāma-dhamma*, and especially an analysis of the mind.[4]

This presentation could be done in many different ways depending on a specific goal, but, here, a presentation will be done based on the Five Aggregrates, which is the popular method found in the Buddhist Suttas.

According to Buddhadhamma, dividing the Five Aggregates entails an analysis of the constituent elements of life, which we call "being" (*satta*) or "person," and so on:

1. Corporeality (*rūpa*) is comprised of the elements of the whole *rūpa-dhamma*, body, and behavior of the body, or matter and material energy, including the qualities and behavior of this matter and energy.[5]
2. Feeling or Sensation (*vedanā*) amounts to the impressions of sukha, dukkha, or indifference that occur by contact with the world through the five senses and the heart/mind (Thai, *chai*).[6]
3. Perception (*saññā*) is that which can be established or known. In other words, it is the establishment of knowledge of conditions and the characteristics of the various features of an object that are the cause for remembering that object.[7]
4. Mental formations, predispositions, or volitional activities (*saṅkhāra*)[8] are the psychological compositions, or the various qualities that embellish the mind making it good, bad, or neutral, and they have intention (*cetanā*) as their guide. Put very simply, some of these good and bad thoughts are as follows: confidence (*saddhā*), mindfulness (*sati*), moral shame (*hiri*), moral fear (*ottappa*), loving-kindness (*mettā*), compassion (*karuṇā*), joy (*muditā*), equanimity (*upekkhā*),[9] wisdom (*paññā*), delusion (*moha*), ill-will (*dosa*), greed (*lobha*), conceit (*māna*), perspective (*diṭṭhi*), envy (*issā*), and avarice (*macchariya*), for example.
5. Consciousness (*viññāṇa*) involves being aware of sensations via the six senses (that is, the five senses and the mind), such as seeing, hearing, smelling, tasting, physically touching, and mentally touching.[10]

The Five Aggregates of Existence and The Five Aggregates of Existence as Objects of Attachment, or Life and Life as a Problem

The Buddha's words reveal the meaning of the Four Noble Truths, which serve as a summary of the essence of Buddhism, and there are statements of special interest related to the Five Aggregates of Existence that appear in the Four Noble Truths: The first Noble Truth mentions dukkha or suffering. Very early on, Lord Buddha illustrated the meaning or definition of dukkha by giving examples of various events and occurrences that were readily apparent and common in people's lives. He did this in order to show various types of dukkha. And in the end, Lord Buddha summed this up by saying that when the Five Aggregates are objects of attachment they become dukkha.

> Bhikkhus, the following comprise the Noble Truths of dukkha: Birth is dukkha; the aging process is dukkha; death is dukkha; associating with things that one does not love is dukkha; separation from people or things that one loves is dukkha; desiring something without attaining it is dukkha. In short, attachment to the Five Aggregates is dukkha.[11]

Buddha's words, aside from showing the status of the Five Aggregates of Existence in the Buddhadhamma, also reveal one important point, and that is the meaning of dukkha. In order to make this concept easy to remember and summarize, dukkha simply describes the Five Aggregates of Existence when they have become objects of attachment.

The main thing that must be studied and noticed here is the difference between the Aggregates of Existence and the Aggregates of Existence as objects of attachment. Please note the following words of the Buddha:

> Bhikkhus, I will explain the Five Aggregates of Existence and the Five Aggregates of Existence as objects of attachment.
>
> What are the Five Aggregates of Existence? Body (*rūpa*)... sensation (*vedanā*)...perception (*saññā*)...mental formations (*saṅkhāra*)...and consciousness (*viññāṇa*); any of these that resides in the past, future, or present, is internal or external, far or near, and exists in a crude or refined, inferior or superior manner, are all called the Five Aggregates of Existence.
>
> And what do the Five Aggregates of Existence have to do with attachment? Body, sensation, perception, mental formations, consciousness, any of these that resides in the past, future or present, is internal or external, far or near, exists in a crude or refined, inferior or superior manner, any of these things that are composed of mental intoxications (*āsava*) are grounds for attachment (*upādāna*)....All of these, therefore, are called the Five Aggregates of Existence as objects of attachment.[12]

> Bhikkhus, I will explain the things that cause attachments and comprise attachments; so, all of you listen carefully.
>
> Body...sensation...perception...mental formations...consciousness are the things that can cause attachment. The desire to attach or cling (*chandarāga*) to body, sensation, mental formations, and consciousness constitutes attachment to that thing.[13]

The preceeding statement represents one of the most fundamental and important principles for understanding Buddhadhamma.

The Ethical Importance of the Five Aggregates of Existence

Ordinarily, human beings have the tendency to believe that their true self exists in one form or another. Some people take the mind (*citta*) to be the self; and some people believe that there is yet another self that is hidden in the mind and that that self is the owner and operator controlling all of the functions of the body and mind.[14] The explanation of the Five Aggregates aims to show that the things we refer to as "being," "person," or "self," when separated, are really only the above five components. There is nothing left that can be called the self, and even each one of those Five Aggregates is interdependent and unable to exist alone. Each of the Five Aggregates of Existence, therefore, has no self. In other words, the principle of the Five Aggregates itself illustrates the existence of no-self (*anattā*). And this principle explains the following: life is the conjoining or coming together of different components; the combination of these components is not the self; each component itself is not the self; and there is nothing beyond these components that can be said to be the self.[15] When you can realize this, attachment and clinging to the self can be extricated. The principle of no-self can be seen clearly when you understand the function of the Five Aggregates of Existence in the chain of dependent causation (*paṭiccasamuppāda*), which will be discussed in detail later.

When we see that life is comprised of the interrelationship of the Five Aggregates, we will not misunderstand this to mean nihilism, which is called *ucchedadiṭṭhi*, nor will we misunderstand this to mean eternalism, which is called *sassadiṭṭhi*. In addition, when we come to know that all things have no self or essence and are related to and dependent on one another, then we will understand the principle of kamma correctly and know how it works. This process of relations and the interdependency of all things is explained by the principle of *paṭiccasamuppāda*, or dependent origination, as well.

Furthermore, viewing all things as broken down and composed of various elements, like these Five Aggregates, is often used as a method of mental practice or a way of getting in the habit of applying a method for analyzing the truth. That is, when you come into contact with people or things or establish various relationships, the mind does not become confused and lose its wits, ending up believing something because of its superficial appearances only. This method of perception is a way of getting in the habit of verifying the truth, and most importantly it involves knowing and seeing all things in all their various conditions (that is, being objective). It is a way of seeing things "as they are" that does not lead to attachments based on greed and desire. This type of perception is very different from viewing things according to the way you would or would not like them to be (that is, being subjective). Objectivity leads to an understanding of the aim of Buddhadhamma and the principle of the Five Aggregates, and this understanding entails not clinging or attaching, not relating to all things with craving and attachment, but coming into relationships and handling situations with wisdom.

At any rate, in presenting the Buddhadhamma, the Buddha did not teach the notion of the Five Aggregates in isolation, because the Five Aggregates are only conditions for further consideration; and that consideration tends to go along with other principles of the Dhamma that indicate the nature and function of the Five Aggregates. The Five Aggregates must, therefore, be presented in the context of other principles, such as *anattā* (no-self), which will make the practical importance of the Aggregates much more apparent. Allow me to quit this discussion of the Five Aggregates in order to consider some of these other principles.

Notes

1. In the Pali texts the "car" is a "chariot"—trans.

2. S.I.135.

3. The Thai term for heart and mind is essentially the same (Thai, *chit-chai,* lit. "mind-heart"); therefore, in the minds of the Thai, the Western distinction between the two is usually less clear.

4. These can be broadly defined as mind (*nāma*) and matter (*rūpa*) or *nāma-dhamma* and *rūpa-dhamma*; but the Abhidhamma tends to divide these into three: mind (*citta*), mental factors (*cetasika*), and matter (*rupa*). For further reference, if these are compared to the Five Aggregates, which will be fully explained below, then *citta* = *viññāṇa-khandha, cetasika* = *vedanā-khandha, saññā-khandha,* and *saṅkhāra-khandha*; and *rūpa* = *rūpa-khandha.*

5. According the the Abhidhamma, *rūpa* can be divided into 28 things: 1) The 4 primary elements (*mahābhūta*): solid element/earth (*paṭhavī-dhātu*); fluid element/water (*āpo-dhātu*); element of heat/fire (*tejo-dhātu*); and the element of motion/wind or air (*vāyo-dhātu*).

2) The 24 aspects of derivative materiality (*upādā-rūpa*):
The five sensitive material qualities (*pasāda-rūpa*)

1. eye (*cakkhu*)
2. ear (*sota*)
3. nose (*ghāna*)
4. tongue (*jivhā*)
5. body (*kāya*)

The four mind-objects (*ārammaṇa*)

6. form (*rūpa*)
7. sound (*sadda*)
8. smell (*gandha*)
9. taste (*rasa*)

The three tangible objects are not counted because they are the same as the three primary elements of earth, fire, and air.
The two material qualities of sex (*bhāva-rūpa*)

10. femininity (*itthatta*)
11. masculinity (*purisatta*)

The physical basis of mind (*hadaya-rūpa*)

12. heart-base (*hadaya-vatthu*)

The material quality of life (*jīvita-rūpa*)

13. vital force (*jīvita-indriya*)

The material quality of nutrition (*āhāra-rūpa*)

14. nutriment (*kabaḷiṅkārāhāra*)

The material quality of delimitation (*pariccheda-rūpa*)

15. space-element (*ākāsa-dhātu*)

The two material qualities of communication (*viññatti-rūpa*)

16. gesture (*kāya-viññatti*)
17. speech (*vacī-viññatti*)

The five material qualities of plasticity or alterability (*vikāra-rūpa*)

18. lightness, agility (*lahutā*)
19. elasticity and malleability (*mudutā*)
20. adaptability (*kammaññatā*)

(the latter two are not counted as they are the same as 16 and 17 above)
The four qualities of salient features (*lakkhaṇa-rūpa*)

21. growth (*upacaya*)
22. continuity (*santati*)
23. decay (*jaratā*)
24. impermanence (*aniccatā*)

Please note that the term "*hadaya-vatthu*," which is taken as the seat of the workings of the mind, was only agreed upon in later texts and did not appear in the Tipiṭaka.

6. Sensation (*vedanā*) can be divided into three types: happiness of the body or mind (sukha), physical or mental anguish (dukkha), neither-pleasant-nor-unpleasant (that is, neither-sukha-nor-dukkha, *adukkhamasukha*, or equanimity, *upekkhā*); or it can be divided into five: physical sukha, physical dukkha, delight, grief, and equanimity; or they can be divided according to how they are perceived: via sight, via the ears, via the nose, via the tongue, via the sense of touch, or via the mind.

7. Perception (*saññā*) can be divided into six factors according to the six senses above. Here, the term "*ārammaṇa*" will only be used in its Pali Buddhist sense; that is, meaning the things that the mind perceives or things that are known via the six sense-doors; the term *dhammārammaṇa*, mind-object, will not be used as it is commonly understood in Thai as "emotion" or "mood" (*arom*).

8. According to the principles found in the Abhidhamma commentaries, 52 mental states (*cetasika*) can be found; and if we compare them to the Five Aggregates, all of these states are comprised of sensation (*vedanā*), perception (*saññā*), and mental formations (*saṅkhāra*): that is, feeling is one of these, perception is one, and then there are 50 mental formations, which can be divided as follows:

1) 11 *aññasamānā-cetasika* (mental states that are good and bad)

a) Five *sabbacittasādhāraṇa* (universal mental states): contact (*phassa*), intention (*cetanā*), one-pointedness (*ekaggatā/samādhi*), vitality (*jīvitindriya*), and attention (*manasikāra*);

b) Six *pakiṇṇaka-cetasika* (particular mental states): initial application of thought (*vitakka*), sustained application (*vicāra*), determination (*adhimokkha*), effort (*viriya*), joy (*pīti*), and resolve (*chanda*).

2) 14 *akusala-cetasika* (mental states that are unwholesome)

a) Four *akusalasādhāraṇa* (universal unwholesome states): delusion (*moha*), lack of moral conscience (*ahirika*), shamelessness (*anottappa*), and feeling unsettled (*uddhacca*);

b) Ten *pakiṇṇaka-akusala-cetasika* (particular unwholesome mental states): greed (*lobha*), improper understanding (*diṭṭhi*), conceit (*māna*), ill-will (*dosa*), jealousy (*issā*), stinginess (*macchariya*), worry (*kukkucca*), sloth (*thīna*), torpor (*middha*), and uncertainty (*vicikicchā*);

3) 25 *sobhana-cetasika* (universal excellent mental states)

a) Nineteen *sobhaṇasādhāraṇa-cetasika* (universal beautiful mental states): confidence (*saddhā*), mindfulness (*sati*), conscience (*hiri*), moral shame (*ottappa*), non-greed (*alobha*), non-ill-will (*adosa*), equanimity (*tatramajjhattatā*), tranquillity of the mental body (*kāya-passaddhi*), tranquillity of the mind (*citta-passaddhi*), lightness of the mental body (*kāya-lahutā*), lightness of the mind (*citta-lahutā*), flexibility of the mental body (*kāya-mudutā*), flexibility of the mind (*citta-mudutā*), adaptability of the mental body (*kāya-kammaññatā*), adaptability of the mind (*citta-kammaññatā*), proficiency of the mental body (*kāya-pāguññatā*), proficiency of the mind (*citta-pāguññatā*), rectitude of the mental body (*kāyujukatā*), rectitude of the mind (*cittujukatā*);

b) Six *pakiṇṇaka-sobhaṇa-cetasika* (particular beautiful mental states): proper speech (*sammāvācā*), proper action (*sammākammanta*), proper livelihood (*sammā-ājīva*)—these three together are often called the "abstinences" (*viratī-cetasika*)—compassion (*karuṇā*), joy in the success of others (*muditā*), and wisdom (*paññā*)—these latter three often being called the "faculty of wisdom" (*paññindriya*).

9. *Upekkhā* is an important dhammic principle that often causes confusion and misunderstanding; we should, therefore, study this term carefully. We should at least divide *upekkhā* into two groups, one related to *saṅkhāra*, which can be equated with *tatramajjhattatā* (mental balance) and another related to *vedanā*, which can be equated with *adukkhamasukha* (a feeling of equanimity, neither-pleasant-nor-unpleasant); but this will have to be explained in more detail later on.

10. *Viññāṇa* can be divided in six ways according to how it arises: eye consciousness (*cakkhu-viññāṇa*), ear- (*sota-*), nose- (*ghāna-*), tongue- (*jivhā-*), body- (*kāya-*), and mind- (*mano-*). According to the Abhidhamma, the whole *viññāṇa-khandha* is called "*citta*" and the various *citta* are separated into 89 or 121 spheres:

a) separated according to levels or stages of *citta*: the 54 consciousnesses of the sense-sphere (*kāmāvacara-citta*), the 15 consciousnesses of the form-sphere (*rūpāvacara-citta*), the 12 consciousnesses of the formless-sphere (*arūpāvacarakusala-citta*), and the 8 supramundane consciousnesses (often further divided into 40);

b) separated according to their properties: 12 immoral consciousnesses (*akusala-citta*), the 21 moral consciousnesses (*kusala-citta*, often further divided into 37), the 36 resultant consciousnesses (*vipāka-citta*, often further divided into 52), the 20 functional consciousnesses (*kiriyā-citta*). It is not necessary to our discussion here to explain the details of each of these consciousnesses.

11. Vin.I.10.

12. S.III.47.

13. S.III.166.

14. We may note the following passage from the canon: "Bhikkhus, those who do not know any better will take this body, which is composed of the four elements (*mahābhūta*), as the self. This is still better than taking the mind as the self, because the body that is composed of the four elements can last as long as a year, two years, 3–4–5 years, 10–20–30–40–50 years, or even 100 years or more. But the thing we refer to as the mind (*citta, mano*) or consciousness (*viññāṇa*) is constantly arising and passing away, all day and all night" (S.II.94).

15. See S.III.2–4, 16–18 and so on, and 111–115.

What Is the Nature of Existence?

The Three Characteristics of Existence (*tilakkhaṇa*)
The Three Natural Characteristics of All Things

The Laws or Conditions

According to the basic principles of Buddhadhamma, all things are born of the conjoining of various elements or take form due to the composition of various elements. This does not simply mean gathering separate parts and putting them together to create a form, such as putting various materials together to make tools. Actually, the statement that all things come into being from the conjoining of various elements is simply an expression to facilitate understanding at a basic level. In reality, all things exist in a constant flow or flux. Each and every component part comes into being due to the break up or disintegration of other component parts; and each of these parts does not have its own essence and arises and passes away one after the other in unending sucession, without absolute certainty or stability. This flow continues to evolve or proceed in a way that seems to maintain a form or course because all of the component parts have a connected and interdependent causal relationship and because each component has no essence of its own and is, therefore, in constant in flux.

All of this goes in accordance with nature and depends upon the relationship of combined and dependent effects; there are no other forces coming into play dependent on a creator or mysterious power. For purposes of simplicity, let us refer to this as natural law.

There are two major dhammic principles pertaining to natural law that are believed to have been set down by Lord Buddha: the Three Characteristics of Existence (*tilakkhaṇa*) and dependent origination (*paṭiccasamuppāda*). Actually, these two concepts are the same principle, but they are presented in different ways in order to reveal the same truth.

The Three Characteristics explain the features of all things in order to reveal them as they are (as proceeding in a related and interdependent manner, as connected causal factors following the principle of dependent origination). Dependent origination aims at pointing out the interrelated condition of all things, as the continuous flow of relationships between causal factors, until these factors can be seen as the Three Characteristics of Existence.

These natural laws are *dhammadhātu,* normal conditions (of cause and effect); they are *dhammaṭṭhiti,* enduring; and they are *dhamma-niyāma,* natural restrictions independent of a creator or mysterious power or the existence of any religion or religious teacher.[16] These natural laws show that, according to Buddhism, the role of teacher or adept is one of a discoverer of these various laws, a revealer who can point the way and explain them to the people in this world.

The Buddha has explained the Three Characteristics of Existence in the following way:

> Whether an enlightened Tathāgata[17] were to appear in this world or not, this principle would still prevail as an enduring aspect of the natural order:
>
> 1. All compounded things (*saṅkhāra*)[18] are impermanent. . .
> 2. All compounded things are [subject to] dukkha. . .
> 3. All dhamma are without essence or self (*anattā*). . .
>
> A Tathāgata, having achieved enlightenment, understands this principle. He declares it, teaches it, and sets it down as a model to reveal, explain, and facilitate an understanding that "All *saṅkhāra* are impermanent. . .all *saṅkhāra* are dukkha. . .and all dhammas are without essence or self (*anattā*). . ."[19]

The Three Characteristics of Existence are also referred to as the "Universal Characteristics," or, in other words, common to all things.

To put this more simply, let me state The Three Characteristics of Existence very briefly:

1. *Aniccatā* means impermanence, instability, and uncertainty, a condition, which having already arisen, gradually breaks down and fades away.
2. *Dukkhatā* is a state of suffering, a condition of pressure that arises and passes away, a condition of resistance and conflict, due to the

fact that something that was created or fashioned in one way changes to become something else, making it impossible for it to exist in that incomplete or deficient condition, not allowing for complete fulfillment of desires or cravings and causing dukkha for the person who desires things with attachment.

3. *Anattatā* means that all phenomena are not the self, and that there is no real essence, soul, or self (*anattā*).

All things that exist, exist within this flow or current, which is comprised of various related and interdependent causes arising and passing away in a constant and unending series. Arising and passing away with uncertainty, things exist according to dependent causal factors, experience pressures and conflicts, and exhibit their own deficiencies. With all things proceeding along in this flow, they are really nothing in and of themselves, and they are unable to maintain any kind of personal self or essence.

Living things are distinguished by being composed of merely the Five Aggregates of Existence; there is nothing else besides the Five Aggregates of Existence—and this settles the problem of the existence of an independent self. If you consider each of these Aggregates independently, you will see that each element is impermanent. Being impermanent, they are subject to dukkha. Therefore, anyone who clings to these Aggregates exists in a state of pressure. Conflict or dukkha is not the self; we can say that dukkha is not the self because each of these Aggregates arises depending on causal factors that also have no self or essence, and these Aggregates and factors are not subject to the power nor the ownership of living beings. (If a person were the real owner of the Five Aggregates, then he could exercise control over these elements as he willed and not allow them to veer from a desired course or an ideal form that he would like them to maintain, such as desiring not to grow old nor to ever become ill.)[20]

One prominent example in which the Buddha mentioned the Three Characteristics of Existence in the context of the The Five Aggregates of Existence is the following:

> Bhikkhus, body (*rūpa*). . .sensation (*vedanā*). . .perception (*saññā*) . . .compounded things (*saṅkhāra*). . .consciousness (*viññāṇa*) are without self (*anattā*).[21] If body. . .sensation. . .perception. . .compounded things. . .consciousness were to have a self, then they would not become ill, and furthermore, one could obtain whatever one wished relating to body. . .sensation. . .perception. . .compounded things. . .consciousness saying: "May my body. . .my

> sensation. . . my perception. . . my compounded things. . . and my consciousness all exist according to my wishes and not any other way." But because body. . . sensation. . . perception. . . compounded things. . . and consciousness are not the self, they are subject to illness and disease and no one can have his own way with these things. No one can implore or control these Aggregates.
>
> So, bhikkhus, what do all of you think? Is the body permanent or impermanent? (Lord Buddha asks about each Aggregate.)
>
> Impermanent, Lord.
>
> So, if something is impermanent, is that thing dukkha or sukha?
>
> It is dukkha, Lord.
>
> So, if something is impermanent and is by nature subject to dukkha and change, should we view that thing as our own, or associate ourselves with it, or see it as our self or essence?
>
> We should not view it that way, Lord.
>
> Bhikkhus, because each and every Aggregate—including body. . . sensation. . . perception. . . compounded things. . . and consciousness—whether in the past, the future, or the present, whether internal or external, coarse or detailed, crude or refined, far or near, all of you must view them with proper insight in the following way: "It is not mine; I am not it; it is not my self."[22]

Many Hindu sages and Western philosophers have tried to explain the reason why Lord Buddha did not reject the notion of self (*attā*) or Ātman at the highest level but only rejected some phenomena, such as those found in the above passage. These philosophers suggest that Lord Buddha rejected the Five Aggregates and all other phenomena as the self because the *attā* that really exists is not composed of the Five Aggregates. Accordingly, these thinkers have cited many other statements in order to demonstrate that Lord Buddha only rejected some phenomena as the self, but he did accept a notion of self (*attā*) at the highest level, and they have attempted to explain that nibbana (nirvana) is the same state as this self or Ātman—that is, at the highest level nibbana is *attā*. While this matter may be worthy of a larger philosophical discussion, I would just like to turn to a brief consideration of the ethical importance of this: Common people, especially those who have been educated to believe in Ātman, will have the inclination to cling to or grab at any notion or form of self (*attā*) in order to fulfill a desire that is hidden and deeply imbedded in the mind. When people are introduced to these principles and discover that they must lose the latent sense of a self (at the level of the Five Aggregates), they try to create or build something new to cling to. But according to Buddhist principles, a person should not let go of one thing only to cling to something else—you should not free yourself only to become the slave of something else. In other words, things that have a self do not exist; and things that exist, are without self.

The existence of all things in a state of flux or as a flowing current, all interrelated and interdependent, each the related cause of the other, each impermanent, subject to dukkha, and without a self (*anattā*), must be clarified by an explanation of the principle of dependent origination (*paṭiccasamuppāda*).

The Ethical Importance of the Three Characteristics of Existence

Aniccatā

The principle of impermanence (*aniccatā*) relates to the arising, the existence, and the passing away of all things, including the most minute and detailed matters, as well as physical (*rūpa-dhamma*) and psychological phenomena (*nāma-dhamma*). The impermanence of these small, intricate things—when they appear in a larger or conglomerate shape or form that can be seen—is called change; and people tend to feel as if there were a self behind all of this. This is a kind of false understanding, a cause of clinging and attachment. This way of thinking can lead a person to become tied up with thoughts that do not match the facts. When your life continues in a way that cannot keep pace with the conditions confronting you, then you will be dragged down, disturbed, and grasp at false illusions you have built up, only to deceive yourself in the end. Living like this is called slavery; but if you can keep pace with surrounding conditions, live freely, and take advantage of natural law, then the principle of impermanence can be very useful to ethics and morality.

Impermanence is neutral, neither good nor bad; but when it is related to the existence of human beings, it is designated as one kind of change—progress—and yet another kind—degeneration. Whatever kind of change takes place depends upon the relevant causal factors present. In the case of conduct, the principle of impermanence is used to teach the natural way of understanding degeneration and progress, stating that things that have already developed are also subject to degeneration, and vice versa. Furthermore, things that have already developed may continue to develop depending on various causal factors—and with all of these causal factors human beings can play a very important role as the creator of other causal factors. In this sense, progress and degeneration are not, therefore, things that go whichever way the wind blows; rather they are phenomena made and created through the involvement of human beings according to the progress and degeneration over which they can exercise some control (*yathākamma*).[23] This means that human beings can get involved and play a significant role in various matters without having to wonder about the intervention of other supernatural factors—because other supernatural factors do not really exist. So, in terms of ethics, impermanence or change is a natural law that gives human beings hope. Because natural laws are usually neutral, the outcome of a given situation depends on the causal factors that brought it into being. It is possible, then, for people to alter their circumstances, to bring about improvements in the world. It does not matter if it is material or mental progress, such as making a dull-witted person intelligent, making common people become enlightened beings (arahants), or correcting, transforming, and improving yourself in every way—an understanding of relevant causal factors can lead to enlightenment.

In summary, impermanence, understood at the level called change, teaches us that this progress can degenerate, resulting in a regression. To avoid degeneration, you must be careful to elude and eliminate the causes of degeneration and try to cultivate or nurture the causes that will lead to changes that sustain progress. Those who succumb to regression can correct and improve themselves by throwing off the causes of degeneration and backsliding and creating new causes that will result in further improvement. Moreover, changes for the better that have already taken place are able to promote further progress by increasing progress-related causal factors. At the same time, a person must not be too heedless or overexuberant about this progress to the point of not seeing the likelihood of regression and, thereby, missing the various causes that might reverse this process. At this point, I would like to mention a most important principle that serves as a tool for linking the truth (*saccadhamma*) with ethics (*cariyadhamma*): in order to have wisdom, from the very beginning you must know what real degeneration and progress are all about and understand their root causes. The principle of impermanence, therefore, can play an especially valuable role in terms of ethics: it offers hope for increased progress, supports the principle of kamma (which relates to the effects of human deeds), and emphasizes the importance of education and training in order to bring about wisdom that is able to change things for the better.

In terms of internal aspects or direct psychological benefits, the principle of impermanence helps us to live with a mind that can keep pace with the truth. At the same time, in the external realm, we are able to employ wisdom to avoid degeneration and make various kinds of internal psychological progress, so that we can live with freedom and not fall into the enslavement of *both* degeneration and progress. We can also learn how to take advantage of natural laws and deal with them without feeling as if we are at their mercy and are being pushed around in a drifting and dazed manner. Being helplessly caught in an undertow without knowing the current is of no help to yourself or other swimmers.

A person with a free mind knows and understands all things according to the truth and does not attach or cling to things with craving (*taṇhā-upādāna*). This person, therefore, knows real degeneration and real progress. And here I do not mean the kind of progress that collectively drags people down and binds them to further slavery; the person with a free mind is able to realize the full benefits of this present state of progress and act responsibly to help others.

At the basic levels of ethics, the principle of impermanence teaches us to know the common nature of all things. This knowledge keeps dukkha within limits when degeneration or loss takes place; it also helps to check carelessness and overexuberence related to any progress made. At higher levels, the principle of impermance teaches us to gradually attain truth until the principle of no-self (*anattā*) is reached; it allows us to live with a free mind, free from attachments and dukkha. This is called living with total and true mental health.

The principle of impermanence is often used as a means of calming yourself or others when disaster, suffering, or loss occurs. It can be more or less consoling. Employing the principle of impermanence in this way is somewhat beneficial when the circumstances happen to be right; it may be especially useful for instilling mindfulness (*sati*) in those who have not been very aware of this principle in the past. But if you often employ this principle in this way in daily life, then it becomes more of a danger than a benefit, because you allow yourself to become a passive slave to worldly processes. Using impermanence as a rationalization actually goes against the principle of kamma and runs contrary to efforts toward self-improvement that aim at achieving the goals of Buddhadhamma and bettering your life.

Dukkhatā

In the principle of *dukkhatā,* there are two significant points that indicate the importance of ethics.

As all things arise due to the composition of various small elements—each in flux, in a condition of arising, and changing and passing away according to the principle of impermanence—the composition of each those elements is actually another composition of various changes and conflicts that exists with a latent possibility of breaking down or degenerating at any time. This being the case, in order to control these various small compositions and shape them into something desirable, or to direct these changes in a certain way, a person must apply energy and use a method of organization that will, out of necessity, become a part of these compositions; the greater the number of small elements and the complexity of these elements, the greater the amount of energy and care is required to change them. In order to change the course of something, any action carried out toward it must be done in accordance with the true cause of that thing and with a knowledge of the result of that action and the means by which mistakes, once committed towards it, may be corrected. This is a way of acting toward all things in a free manner, without encumbering yourself and causing dukkha. But contrary to this is acting out of desire and attachment, which will lead to becoming tied up and pressured by those things. Desire and attachment not only result in personal dukkha, they steer you away from positive results.

According to the principles of action put forth in the Noble Truths, responding to dukkha takes exact knowledge (*pariññā*), which means taking note of conditions or coming to understand them. This correct response to dukkha is extremely important but is often overlooked. Buddhadhamma teaches us to react to dukkha with a knowledge of what is what and a knowledge of what constitutes dukkha; this means knowing your own problems, not for the purpose of dukkha but for the purpose of correctly responding to dukkha and eliminating it—or, to put it simply, for the purpose of experiencing true sukha. In yet another sense, the principles for action in the Noble Truths teach that whatever is problematical must first be studied, known, and clearly understood before you begin to solve that problem. Studying a problem does not mean that you create a problem or that you set out in search of trouble—it is a method for alleviating problems. A person who does not know the principles of action in the Noble Truths might react to dukkha in a mistaken, aimless, or distorted way, and this will only increase personal dukkha, resulting in a pessimistic outlook.

When you know these two main points, then, according to the principle of dukkha, the following ethical values can be stipulated:

1. All things are subject to pressure that cause them to arise, develop, and pass away, which results in further pressure, conflict, and an inability to maintain a constant condition. This condition shows that all things have a deficiency, an incompleteness in themselves, and this deficiency or incompleteness will increase according to the amount of time that passes and any external and internal changes that occur. This being the case, all things that try to maintain their condition or expand to a state of completeness have to constantly fight and struggle. Maintaining a good life and directing life towards progress and completeness means that you must be constantly correcting and improving yourself.
2. When conflict and struggle arise (from either internal or external causes) resulting in further change, and there is an ignorant resistance to change (whether on the part of things, people, or institutions), then the result tends to be bad rather than good, as in the case of culture change making a turn for the worst, for example. Knowing how to adjust and improve yourself is, therefore, very important, and once again I want to emphasize the necessity of wisdom, especially in terms of principles of conduct, so that you can keep pace with and manage all things according to their actual causes.
3. Sukha and things that bring about sukha, as they are more commonly understood in this world, fall under this principle of truth as well. These kinds of sukha tend to have an incompleteness about them: any state of sukha or search for sukha must change, and so this state cannot provide complete satisfaction. Mindlessly basing your hopes on this type of sukha is tantamount to making yourself one and the same with that incompleteness or throwing yourself into the current of change and being dragged, oppressed, and pressured in a manner beyond self-control, depending on how things change or how much hope you have invested. When change, flux, or disappointment occur, the power of dukkha will increase

by that amount. Seeking after this kind of sukha is like selling yourself into slavery or putting your life at stake in a bet. Those who seek sukha in a more intelligent way, while still delighted with seeking happiness from things in flux, must still keep pace with the truth and enjoy sukha with clear comprehension (*sampajañña*). The people who really know that the impermanent nature of sukha can instill fear are shaken up the least. To put this another way, whatever happens, you should maintain freedom of mind the best you can.

4. There are two kinds of sukha that can be divided according to their values: one fulfills the needs of the five senses and is a response to various drives or thoughts; the other is the result of a mental condition that is clear, free from difficulties and obstacles, and limitations of thought, such as feelings of anxiety, restrictions, and other impairments that entangle the mind.

   The first kind of sukha depends on external causes, such as material goods and thoughts, for fulfilling various wants. The mind that is caught up in this kind of sukha is a mind that is grasping, struggling, and agitated; secondly, this type of sukha is accompanied by attachments, narrowness, greed, and getting caught up in yourself. All of these symptoms are very important in terms of ethics, because they are related to clinging, desiring, or selfishness, and when these things are not brought under control, various problems arise. These kinds of thoughts and behaviors depend on external causes, therefore, it is common for this kind of sukha to make people overdependent and become the slaves of various external factors. The fluctuation of these external factors, in turn, shakes these people up. According to the Dhamma, this kind of fulfillment is referred to as *sāmisasukha*—a kind of sukha that attempts to fill a lack or feeling of deficiency and is dependent on the allurements of material things (*āmisa*).

   The second kind of sukha is a happiness that does not depend on external causes to fulfill desires. This sukha is a mental condition that allows the mind to be itself—with nothing disturbing it. This condition can be decribed in the following ways: clean, because there are no unwholesome tendencies (*kilesa*)[24] present to stir it up and muddy it; bright, because it is constituted with wisdom that sees things as they really are, far and wide, without limitations, with correct understanding, and is ready to acknowledge and consider things objectively; peaceful, because there is no agitation, worry, frustration, and gullibility, only relaxation and calm; independent, because one is free, since there are no limitations placed on thought, no obstructions, and no attachments—the mind is light, wide open to expressing love, good intentions, and kindness towards humans and animals, acknowledging the suffering of others with compassion, and participating in the happiness, prosperity, and success of others with sympathetic joy; complete, because there is no feeling of a lack or deficiency or loneliness, only freshness and openness. If this mental state is compared with the body it is equivalent to being physically fit. This kind of complete mind has the following important qualities: freedom—there is no attachment or slavery; and wisdom—there is knowledge and understanding according to the truth. These two qualities are visible in a condition of mind called equanimity (*uppekhā*), a condition of calmness and neutrality that allows involvement with things in an objective manner, following pure reason. This kind of sukha has the highest importance for ethics and is called *nirāmisasukha*, a spiritual happiness that is problem-free, allowing a person to assist others with their difficulties; it is a condition that is refined and deep, beyond what we normally refer to as sukha. It is, therefore, simply referred to as being free from dukkha, because it is beyond deficiencies and fluctuations.

Most people are usually caught up in the search for the first kind of sukha; it is impossible for them to fulfill their desires at all times and sustain this type of sukha, because it is subject to external causes and changes in accordance with natural law. It is necessary, therefore, for people to establish a state of mind similar to the second type of sukha, so that this sukha may be a foundation for living in the world with comfort and true happiness, with the least amount of dukkha; and this means knowing how to respond to the first type of dukkha so that it will no longer create problems for yourself or others. This state of mind can be created by seeing things as they are so that you might live without attachments, keep pace with the true principles of nature, and finally attain the level of understanding called no-self (*anattā*).

5. In the search for the first type of sukha that is dependent on external causes, you must accept the fact that this will involve at least a relationship between two sides or elements; for example, if two

people, or one person and one material thing, come into contact and each side has dukkha, conflict, and deficiencies coming along with it, then this can only increase the amount of conflict and violence between them in accordance with their own improper behavior. To give you a very simple example for the sake of convenience, we might say that one side is the consumer of sukha and the other the consumed; both sides have deficiencies and conflicts within themselves already. For example, the consumer is not prepared to constantly consume according to his desire, and, at the same time, the consumed is not prepared to be constantly taken advantage of. In this state of affairs, it is impossible that each side can gain unless they are both willing to give up something. When either side or both sides do not fully realize or accept this truth and only hold on to their respective desires, there will be disagreement and conflict arising between these two sides beginning with a dislike for one other.

Furthermore, when the consumer wants something from the consumed, this often extends to wanting that object of desire forever. But these feelings are opposed to the natural process that flows along according to various causal factors; such feelings, therefore, obstruct the smooth flow of the natural process. When a person lives without understanding this truth, clinging only to craving and attachments—that is, *taṇhā* and *upādāna*—this can be called living with resistance and ignorance that will cause collisions, conflicts, pressures, and repercussions to manifest and create various types of dukkha.

Moreover, aside from two parties being elements relating to one another in a natural process, there may be another factor—a third party—that is involved; for example, there may be another person who wants to share in the consumption. Obstructed desire or attachment will inevitably cause a reaction between each party involving certain kinds of conflict, such as, competition, discord, and fighting—all of which are forms of dukkha. The more problems are resolved with desires and attachments, the more violent the dukkha becomes; but the more problems are solved with wisdom, then the sooner they fade away.

Accordingly, ignorance (*avijjā*) or delusion (*moha*) consists of not knowing things for what they are, and this causes selfish desire or greed (*lobha*). When this desire is obstructed or left unfulfilled and a person does not possess the kind of wisdom that can keep pace with the circumstances, ill-will (*dosa*), frustration, and destructive tendencies arise. From the roots of these three unwholesome tendencies (*kilesa*), other tendencies and habits soon follow, such as developing a miserly disposition, envy, paranoia, irrationality, anxiety, fear, feelings of vengeance, laziness, and so on. This conglomeration of unwholesome tendencies causes conflicts that lead to an obstruction of and separation from the harmony of the natural process. Any conflict with nature will have bad repercussions, resulting in pressures that amount to a form of natural punishment. This form of "natural dukkha" or the natural build-up of dukkha (*saṅkhāra-dukkha*) can be felt for yourself:

- Causing narrow-mindedness, darkness, melancholy, anxiety frustration, and repression;
- Causing mental and physical disturbances, disorders, and disease;
- Causing normal physical suffering, such as pain during sickness, to redouble because of attachment to craving;
- Causing others to suffer conflict, narrow-mindedness, melancholy;
- When the majority of people in society increase their unwholesome tendencies (*kilesa*) and cut themselves off from each other with selfishness, various kinds of conflicts increase; society falls apart and finds itself in trouble because of people's collective (mis)deeds (kamma).

This is a cumulative process that leads to feelings of dukkha (*dukkha-vedanā*) or real dukkha (*dukkhadukkha*). This dukkha is the result of dealing with things in an ignorant manner, resisting the natural process, and letting yourself become a slave to this cycle. In short, all of this can be attributed to clinging and attachment.

The opposite course of action involves living in a way that keeps pace with truth, that is, knowing the way of all things and how to relate to them with wisdom; practicing with the knowledge that dukkha is part of the natural process; knowing that the formation of dukkha is still there but does not create conflict or danger any more than it should; and remembering that you can take advantage of dukkha if you know it for what it is. If you do not cling to dukkha with craving, then you do not become attached, live with resistance, build up unwholesome tendencies, restrict yourself, and become the cause of conflict. You should know how to live in harmony with nature by acting virtuously: with *mettā*—love and good intentions for others; *karuṇā*—helpful intentions; *muditā*—joy in the success of others; *upekkhā*—equanimity and even-mindedness, judging all events according to true causes and conditions; *sāmaggī*—unity and cooperation; helping, bringing benefits to others, sacrificing, being composed, patient, modest, respectful, and having critical faculties that do not make you gullible. All these qualities are related to openmindedness; they are opposite to the unwholesome tendencies that cause conflict and narrow-mindedness: such as hatred, vengence, envy, repression, division, competition, selfish want, self-indulgence, abruptness, stubbornness, pride, fear, paranoia, laziness, indifference, depression, delusion, over-exuberance, and foolish belief.

This is the way to live in harmony with nature, to be able to benefit from natural law or use natural law in a beneficial way without losing your freedom. According to a Buddhist proverb: Living without attachments or living with wisdom is held to be most excellent (*paññājīviṁ jīvitamāhu seṭṭhaṁ*).[25]

Anattatā

The principle of no-self (*anattatā*) has important value in terms of ethics.

At a basic level, when examined in terms of craving (*taṇhā*), the principle of no-self will decrease selfishness. It does not allow you to cling to your own gains and makes you see them in a broader perspective, without having a self as an obstructing or limiting factor.

Furthermore, all things exist in a condition of no-self due to the conjoining of various elements, which exist according to a variety of causal factors. All things, in whatever form they may appear, depend on the make-up and the creation of causal factors that link relationships to a purpose within the scope of their capabilities. Accordingly, it should be emphasized that a person should act with a free mind that is able to respond to the causal factors present. This is the best method for achieving success and avoiding craving and attachments.

At an intermediate level, with respect to a person's outlook or biases (*diṭṭhi*), the principle of no-self will broaden the mind, making it able to get involved, consider, and solve problems by not letting the self, selfish wants, and attachments become obstructions. Instead, the unbiased mind can consider and solve those problems according to their nature and causal factors. In other words, a person can establish equanimity (*uppekhā*), consider things in the light of truth, avoiding autocratic tendencies, and practice "dhamma-cratically."

At a higher level, knowing the principle of no-self amounts to knowing the actual way of all things, that is, knowing the true principles of nature at the highest level. Total knowledge at this level can shake off attachments to the point of attaining complete freedom or enlightenment. This is the final goal of Buddhadhamma. A clear understanding of the principle of no-self, however, depends on an understanding of dependent origination (*paṭiccasamuppāda*) and practicing according to the Noble Eight-fold Path, which will be explained in due course.

In general, the principle of no-self (*anattatā*), together with the principle of impermanence (*aniccatā*) and being subject to dukkha (*dukkhatā*), all attest to the truths that support other principles of conduct, especially the principle of kamma and other practices leading to true liberation (from dukkha and attachments). For example, because all things have no self, their various forms come into being according to a flow of related and dependent causal factors; and because this is so, kamma exists. And because all things have no self, true liberation is possible. At any rate, now all of this must still be considered further in terms of the principle of dependent origination.

Notes

16. In the commentary to the Abhidhamma, *niyāma* or natural law is divided into five types:

1. physical inorganic order (*utu-niyāma*), which pertains to natural laws concerning temperature, weather, the seasons and the environment surrounding human life;
2. physical organic order (*bīja-niyāma*), which pertains to natural laws concerning the continuation of species and genetics;
3. order of act and result (*kamma-niyāma*), which pertains to natural laws concerning human behavior and the progression of the results of actions (the law of kamma);
4. order of the norm (*dhamma-niyāma*), which pertains to natural laws concerning relationships and interdependent causality;

5. psychic order (*citta-niyāma*), which pertains to natural laws concerning the working of the mind (DhsA.272; see also DA.II.11).

17. Another name for a Buddha or enlightened one, literally a "thus-gone one" (or "thus-come one") or, in looser, more modern terms, one who has "gone the [spiritual] distance"—trans.

18. The meaning of *saṅkhāra* can differ according to contexts. In the context of the Five Aggregates of Existence (*khandha*), *saṅkhāra* tends to mean bad thoughts that a person harbors, and so its sense is psychological; but in the context of the Three Characteristics of Existence (*tilakkhaṇa*), *saṅkhāra* tends to mean all compounded things, be they physical or psychological—in other words the whole of the Five Aggregates of Existence.

19. A.I.286.

20. See, for example, Vism.618, 628, 640.

21. Which translates as "no-self" or "not-self."

22. S.III.66–68.

23. Here, the term *yathākamma* is used in its more canonical sense and not according to common Thai usage, which tends to mean fate or chance.

24. In much of Buddhist literature, the term *kilesa* is rendered as "defilements," which I have avoided here; in fact, the author asked me if there were some word other than defilements that we could use to describe this Pali term. I have chosen "unwholesome tendencies" or "bad habits" to express this concept. In other words, practices, behavior, and ways of thinking that are not conducive to accomplishing the goal of Buddhism. More literally, however, *kilesa* can mean a stain, soil, or (mental) impurity. In ethical terms, it tends to refer to vices and behavior that can be attributed to our "lower nature," and in Thai this term has come to bear this more ethical sense, referring to inappropriate wants, desires, and lust—trans.

25. Sn. p. 33.

What Is the Life Process?

Dependent Origination (*paṭiccasamuppāda*), The Principle of the Interdependence of All Things

The Laws or Conditions of Reality

The Basis and Importance of Dependent Origination

Dependent origination is composed of another group of Dhammic principles that Lord Buddha put forth as naturally occurring principles of truth; and these principles do not depend on the arising of the Tathāgatas or enlightened Buddhist teachers in this world.

The words of the Buddha reveal this natural principle of dependent origination in the following way:

> Whether an enlightened Tathāgata were to appear in this world or not, this principle would still prevail as an enduring aspect of the natural order—that is, conditionality (*idappaccayatā*).[26]
>
> The enlightened Tathāgata has attained this principle, spoken of it, explained it, set it down, revealed it and handed it out freely, making it easy to understand—saying "see for yourself."
>
> Because ignorance (*avijjā*) exists, mental formations (*saṅkhāra*) come about, and so on. . . .
>
> Bhikkhus, objectivity (*tathatā*), necessity (*avitathatā*), invariability (*anaññathatā*) constitute the principle of conditionality (*idappaccayatā*) that is called dependent origination (*paṭiccasamuppāda*).[27]

The importance of dependent origination can be seen in the following words of the Buddha:

Whoever sees dependent origination sees the Dhamma; and whoever sees the Dhamma sees dependent origination.[28]

Indeed, bhikkhus, enlightened disciples (*sāvaka*) have knowledge and insight in this matter so that it is unnecessary to believe others, knowing that when this exists, this also exists, because this comes about, then this arises. . . .

Whenever Noble Disciples (*ariyasāvaka*) come to understand the arising and passing away of all things in this world according to this process, then they can be said to be "well-grounded," endowed with "complete vision," having attained the true Dhamma (*saddhamma*), composed of perfect intuition or knowledge. Those who have already realized the process of the Dhamma may be called Noble Disciples, wise and free of unwholesome tendencies (*kilesa*), or they can be considered as dwelling close to the door of the eternal (*amata*).[29]

Any recluses (*samaṇa*) or brahmins who know these Dhammas. . . know their causes, know their passing away, and know the way leading to their passing away, and so on, are recluses among recluses or brahmins among brahmins, and should be known as having attained the benefits of being a recluse or brahmin through their faculties of highest wisdom, dwelling properly in the present moment of this existence.[30]

At any rate, some statements by the Buddha function as reminders to keep us aware of this principle of dependent origination. The texts treat dependent origination as a principle of cause and effect that is not easy to understand. There was one case in which Ānanda approached the Buddha and the following exchange took place:

How marvellous, Lord, this thing that never was before, this principle of dependent origination, which is such a profound teaching that appears to be very deep, yet has occurred to me as simple.

Don't talk about it like that, Ānanda! This dependent origination is indeed a deep doctrine and appears to be something very profound because people do not know, do not understand, have not penetrated through to this principle; humans are, therefore,

> mixed up and confused like a twisted wad of knotted thread or matted grasses, and they are unable to get out of these states of misery (*apāya*) and unhappiness (*duggati*), unable to break free of being born into suffering (*vinipāta*) and the cycles of existence and rebirth (*saṁsāra*).[31]

Those who have studied the life of the Buddha are likely to remember his words just after he attained enlightenment, just before he set out to spread the Dhamma. At that time, the Buddha was inclined not to preach. The Tipiṭaka states the following:

> Bhikkhus, the following thought occurred to me: "The Dhamma that I have realized is deep, difficult to see, difficult to realize, calm and peaceful, subtle, not attainable through mere logic, refined, requiring a wise one to understand.
>
> See, these people are engrossed in external things, are happy to exist with them and to be caught up with them.[32] The principle of conditionality (*idappaccayatā*) and dependent origination tends to be difficult to perceive. These conditions are also difficult to perceive: the quelling of all mental formations (*saṅkhāra*), the severing of all entanglements, the end of all craving (*taṇhā*), lust (*virāga*), dukkha (*nirodha*) and the attainment of the final goal, nibbana. If I were to teach the Dhamma, and others could not fathom its depth, this would be the cause of just plain exhaustion and frustration for me.[33]

These thoughts of the Buddha refer to two principles of Dhamma, dependent origination (*paṭiccasamuppāda*) and nibbana. They emphasize the difficulty and importance of the two as principles that he attained upon enlightenment and subsequently wished to offer as teachings for mankind.

References and Interrelationships Concerning the Principle of Dependent Origination

References to the principle of dependent origination can be divided into two types:

1. General references that do not specify the main factors or elements;
2. Those that single out the names of the various factors or elements and link them together in an ordered progression.

The first type, which tends to be used as an introduction to the second, is a more neutral or general method; and the second, more detailed method is often mentioned in the canon without reference to the first. The second type might be called the explanatory or expanded version, because it shows more details and applies the various factors of the principle, at the same time bringing natural processes to bear on the meaning of the general principle itself.

Furthermore, these two types can each be divided into two parts:

1. Explaining the process of the arising of dukkha;
2. Explaining the process of the extinguishing of dukkha.

These two types each reveal two kinds of relationships. The first part is called the arising (*samudayavāra*) and refers to the process of unfolding called *anuloma-paṭiccasamuppāda*; if compared to the Four Noble Truths, this coincides with the second "Truth," the condition of the arising of dukkha (*dukkhasamudaya*). The second part shows the process of cessation called the extinguishing (*nirodhavāra*); it explains the reversal of the process called *paṭiloma-paṭiccasamuppāda*. When compared to the Four Noble Truths, it coincides with the third "Truth," the extinguishing of dukkha (*dukkhanirodha*).

The two are explained in the following way:

1. The general principle

a. *imasmiṁ sati idaṁ hoti*	when this exists, then this exists
imassuppādā idaṁ uppajjati	because this arises, this also arises
b. *imasmiṁ asati idaṁ na hoti*	when this ceases to exist, this also ceases to exist
imassa nirodhā idaṁ nirujjhati[34]	because this ceases to exist, this also ceases to exist

If we examine this literally, this general principle is in accordance with conditionality (*idappaccayatā*).

2. The specific or applied principle

a. *avijjāpaccayā saṅkhārā*	because of ignorance, mental formations exist
saṅkhārapaccayā viññāṇaṁ	because of mental formations, consciousness exists
viññāṇapaccayā nāma-rūpaṁ	because of consciousness, mind-and-body exists
nāma-rūpapaccayā saḷāyatanaṁ	because of mind-and-body, the six senses exist

saḷāyatanapaccayā phasso	because of the six senses, contact exists
phassapaccayā vedanā	because of contact, sensation exists
vedanāpaccayā taṇhā	because of sensation, craving exists
taṇhāpaccayā upādānaṁ	because of craving, attachment exists
upādānapaccayā bhavo	because of attachment, becoming exists;
bhavapaccayā jāti	because of becoming, birth exists
jātipaccayā jarāmaraṇaṁ	because of birth, decay-and-death exist.

Sokaparidevadukkhadomanassupāyāsā sambhavanti—Sorrow, lamentation, suffering, grief, and distress all arise.

Evam etassa kevalassa dukkhakkhandhassa samudayo hoti—This whole "heap of suffering" arises in this way.

b. *avijjāya tveva asesavirāganirodhā saṅkhāranirodho*	because ignorance has been completely disgorged, mental formations are extinguished;
saṅkhāranirodhā viññāṇanirodho	because mental formations are extinguished, consciousness is extinguished
viññāṇanirodhā nāma-rūpanirodho	because consciousness is extinguished, mind-and-body is extinguished
nāma-rūpanirodhā saḷāyatananirodho	because mind-and-body is extinguished, the six senses are extinguished
saḷāyatananirodhā phassanirodho	because the six senses are extinguished, contact is extinguished
phassanirodhā vedanānirodho	because contact is extinguished, sensation is extinguished

vedanānirodhā taṇhānirodho	because sensation is extinguished, craving is extinguished
taṇhānirodhā upādānanirodho	because craving is extinguished, attachment is extinguished
upādānanirodhā bhavanirodho	because attachment is extinguished, becoming is extinguished
bhavanirodhā jātinirodho	because becoming is extinguished, birth is extinguished
jātinirodhā jarāmaraṇaṁ	because birth is extinguished, [so is] decay-and-death [extinguished].

Sokaparidevadukkhadomanassupāyāsā nirujjhanti—Sorrow, lamentation, suffering, grief, and distress are [thereby] extinguished

Evam etassa kevalassa dukkhakkhandhassa nirodho hoti[35]—The extinguishing of this whole "heap of dukkha" occurs in this manner.

Please note that this summary of dependent origination indicates that it is a process involving the origin as well as the extinction of dukkha. These types of references appear as a summary of dependent origination in various parts of the canon. In some cases, however, they may refer to the arising and disintegration or extinction of the world. The Pali texts state: "*ayaṁ kho bhikkhave lokassa samudayo*—Bhikkhus, this is the arising of the world"; "*ayaṁ kho bhikkave lokassa atthaṅgamo*—Bhikkhus, this is the disintegration of the world"[36]; or "*evam ayaṁ loko samudayati*—Thus this world arises (because of these conditions)," "*evam ayaṁ loko nirujjhati*—Thus this world ceases (because of these conditions)."[37] At any rate, in essence, these two summaries are similar and equal. The problem rests with the wording, and this demands further explanation.

In the Abhidhamma and Commentaries (*aṭṭhakathā*), there is another name for this principle of dependent origination called *paccayākāra*. This translates as the state of all things being causally related.

When the principle of dependent origination is put forth with all of its factors, it is composed of twelve elements. This composition is interrelated in the shape of a circle, without beginning and without end; that is, it has no origin or "first cause." Taking ignorance (*avijjā*) as the first element does not mean that it constitutes a first cause or is the source or all of the rest that follows. Rather, ignorance is named as the first element as a matter of convenience, as an aid to understanding; this is done by dividing the process into sections and choosing an element deemed most suitable to be the first and then counting the others in order from there. Sometimes Lord Buddha guarded against people taking ignorance as the first cause by referring to the arising of ignorance in the following way:

> Ignorance arises because intoxicating impulses (*āsava*) arise; ignorance is done away with because intoxicating impulses are eliminated When intoxcating impulses arise, ignorance arises; when intoxicating impulses are eliminated, ignorance is also eliminated.[38]

The twelve elements of dependent origination are counted from ignorance (*avijjā*) to decay-and-death (*jarā-maraṇa*). The twelve elements are: ignorance [*avijjā*] → mental formations [*saṅkhāra*] → consciousness [*viññāṇa*] → mind-and-body [*nāma-rūpa*] → six sense-bases [*saḷāyatana*] → contact [*phassa*] → sensation [*vedanā*] → craving [*taṇhā*] → clinging [*upādāna*] → becoming [*bhava*] → birth [*jāti*] → decay-and-death [*jarā-maraṇa*]. Sorrow, lamentation, suffering, grief, and distress are simply things that follow as a result. They arise in a person who still has impurities and unwholesome tendencies (*āsava, kilesa*). And so, when decay-and-death comes around, the various feelings of dukkha previously listed are the cause of the accumulation of unwholesome tendencies that lead to perpetuating ignorance and the turning of the wheel and, in turn, they contribute to supporting the continuation of the same old cycle.

When explaining the application of dependent origination, Lord Buddha did not always speak of the various elements in order or as a whole from beginning to end. Usually he spoke of the whole process when he was stating the complete principle, but in terms of practice (*paṭipatti*) he often started with a problematic element, and then explained the process in reverse (decay-and-death ← birth ← becoming ← clinging ← craving ← sensation ← contact ← the six sense-bases ← mind-and-body ← consciousness ← mental formations ← ignorance).[39]

Some explanations of this process of dependent origination may also begin with one of the intermediate elements, until the source of the problem is reached; this problematic element is then held up to careful scrutiny. For example, a text may begin with birth,[40] sensation,[41] or consciousness,[42] and be linked up following the process of dependent origination until decay-and-death is reached (that is, beginning at the middle and continuing to the end); or an explanation may retrace elements in reverse back to ignorance (beginning in the middle and returning to the beginning); or some may begin by citing a different case outside the realm of the twelve elements and then begin to explain this case according to the process of dependent origination.[43] The explanation of dependent origination does not have to include all twelve elements previously mentioned, and it may not always occur according to a fixed pattern.

Another important point is that a "factor" in this list of elements carries the exact same meaning as a cause. For example, the causal factors concerning the germination and growth of a plant do not only indicate the existence of a seed, but also imply that the following elements must be present: soil, water, fertilizer, air, and proper temperature. Each of these is a causal factor, and each is interrelated and does not have to exist in any orderly process according to a certain time and place.[44]

Translating the Meaning of Dependent Origination

The principle of dependent origination is often translated and explained in different senses, which can be summarized in the following ways:

1. Explained according to the evolution of the world and life by interpreting the texts, sometimes according to a literal translation of the word *loka-samudaya* (the arising of the world);[45]
2. Explained as the process of the arising and the extinction of life and the dukkha of human beings, which can be divided into two senses:
   a) As explaining the broader, more general process of movement from existence to existence, that is the crossing over from one life to another life. This is another way of translating the words of the texts, and it is a method generally found in the Commentary texts, in which definitions are described in much more detail, as various patterned processes with definite levels and regulations attributed to them. In some of these texts, this tendency can manifest itself to the point of seeming very mixed up and confusing for those who are just beginning to study causality.
   b) As explaining the cyclical process that is constantly in motion in all realms of life, as a way of translating the meaning hidden in the first sense above related to the evolution of the world. This cyclical explanation offers a deeper sense or an applied

meaning according to what we understand as the Buddha's purpose (the intentions of the principles of Dhamma), which is especially relevant to our modern world. This method of explanation justifies itself by referring to various Sutta texts, such as the *Cetanā Sutta,*[46] *Dukkhanirodha Sutta,*[47] and the *Lokanirodha Sutta.*[48] In the Abhidhamma literature, there are Pali texts explaining the whole of the process of dependent origination that arises in its entirety within the space of a single thought-moment; a certain section of the canon has been set aside for a discussion of this.[49]

Occasionally, people will take the first explanation and use it to interpret the meaning of dependent origination as the basis for the arising of this world, with ignorance (*avijjā*) as its "first cause"[50]—they then proceed from ignorance to the remaining elements. This interpretation gives the impression that Buddhism is similar to other religions or philosophical systems that teach that there was a "first being," such as a creator, who is the forerunner of all other beings and earthly things and has power that transcends nature. The Buddhist texts, however, explain development simply in terms of an evolution of natural causal factors. Interpretations of Buddhadhamma that lead you to believe that there was a first cause are incorrect; any notion of a first cause goes against the Buddhist notion of causality and conditionality (*idappaccayatā*) or the principle of dependent origination. Dependent origination states that all things exist as interdependent factors, arising in an interrelated manner and continuing on according to a perpetual process of cause and effect that is without end. A "first cause" is impossible here, no matter if it exists in the guise a creator or anything else. For this reason, translating the meaning of dependent origination as an explanation of the evolution of the world and life is only acceptable if it allows us to see the unfolding and expansion of a natural process of constant development or dissipation according to relevant causes—continuing in a cyclical fashion, without beginning, without end.

One important way of determining whether or not a translation of dependent origination is correct or acceptable is by examining the intentions of the Buddha when he explained the Buddhadhamma—which we must believe was the purpose of the teaching of the principle of dependent origination, as well. In explaining Buddhadhamma, Lord Buddha intended to teach that which could be put into practice, that which would be of benefit to life and could be related to life and the solution of life's problems.

He did not advocate the attainment of truth (*saccadhamma*) by brooding and arguing nor by looking for reasons based on impractical metaphysics. For this reason, a true understanding of Buddhadhamma is dependent upon accompanying ethical behavior (*cariyadhamma*). Even if we were to accept dependent origination as an evolutionary theory—that is, as a cyclical process without beginning or end—it would still have little value in terms of ethics (in terms of putting the theory into practice in order to reap benefits in daily life). Acceptance of this theory could potentially enrich a person's worldview or outlook on life by providing an explanation of the life process: it is a theory that proceeds according to reason, explains a procession of natural causal factors, does not allow for a creator or supernatural being, and lacks aimless, accidental occurrences. In other words, an examination of this theory can show us that the goal of Buddhism is not attained through hope, desire, imploring a creator, nor through any power transcending nature or by waiting for your accidental fate or destiny. However, the goal of Buddhism is not attained through the passive intellectual understanding of a theory, it is attained by applying yourself to the task. That is, first, people must depend on themselves by creating the causal factors that will allow them to reach their goals; they must create causal factors in order to achieve desired results through correct knowledge and an understanding of the natural process. Wisdom, therefore, becomes an important virtue; so, second, we must relate to and manage everything with wisdom. Third, knowing and understanding the natural process means acting in accordance with the flow or "current" of causal factors. This helps reduce misunderstandings that are the basis for grasping and attachment to things that are often associated with the self. Understanding the natural process makes us relate to all things in a correct manner, in a beneficial and free way in accordance with our aims, not by falling back into a relationship of slavery with those things. The worldview or outlook on life previously mentioned—even if it is correct and has value in terms of the aim of all the points of Buddhadhamma—must still be considered too unrefined, unstable, and imprecise to bring about the three values of self-reliance, wisdom, and an understanding of the natural process in a complete and certain way (and this is especially true for the third value).

In order to make this method of translation or interpretation of meaning more valuable, we must consider the process or cycle of nature in a clearer, more detailed manner; that is, we must develop the kind of understanding that can keep pace with the flux of this process. Regardless of the cirucumstances that appear before us at any time, we must see the current, the interconnectedness and interdependence of all causal things that are present in this manner. The three values mentioned above will all certainly come into play and should encompass the long-term, evolutionary meaning of dependent origination as well.

With the first method of translating the meaning of dependent origination in terms of evolution, we can see that the aim is to look outward and explain the external world; and the second sense stresses looking inward to the internal life of beings, to the things related to the interconnectedness of the life process and the experience of dukkha.

The first section (a) of the second way of explaining of dependent origination—as the transmigration from existence to existence—occurs in many parts of the Commentary texts in detail.[51] The Commentaries contain various additional references in order to more clearly explain this process as a system of ordered steps; but at the same time, this may give people the idea that this is a fixed system, resulting in attachment to these set steps. It may also become something mysterious and confusing for those first beginning to study it. I will devote a separate section to an explanation of this. Finally, the second sense of the meaning of dependent origination has characteristics related to the first, which will now be explained in order.

A Basic Summary of the Meaning of Dependent Origination

At first, we need a basic summary of the explanation of the meaning of dependent origination to facilitate a general understanding.

Such a summary of dependent origination can reveal the whole process of the arising and extinguishing of dukkha; or we might even say that the whole goal of the principle of dependent origination is to explain the arising and extinguishing of dukkha. The word dukkha has a great deal of importance and plays a large role in Buddhadhamma. Even other important aspects of the Dhamma, such as the Three Characteristics of Existence (*tilakkhaṇa*) and the Four Noble Truths (*ariyasacca*), have dukkha as an important element. We should, therefore, come to a clear understanding of the term dukkha first. In the first section of this volume that discussed the Three Characteristics, a short explanation of dukkha was offered. But now, this concept should be discussed in more detail.

If we are to reach an understanding of dukkha in Buddhadhamma, we must look beyond the more narrow meaning it has in Thai.[52] We must consider the word anew in the wider context of the teachings of Lord

Buddha and the Commentary texts.[53] Dukkha can be divided into the following three types:[54]

1. *Dukkha-dukkhatā*—Dukkha that really feels like dukkha, that is, dukkha of the body and mind. This is commonly known in all its various manifestations as the sensation of dukkha or *dukkha-vedanā* (that is, ordinary dukkha that comes about when disagreeable things, *aniṭṭhārammaṇa*, are encountered or when things come into conflict).
2. *Vipariṇāma-dukkhatā*—Dukkha associated with flux and change, or dukkha associated with fluctuations in sukha that bring about dukkha because of change itself. (Our normal state is one of a neutral kind of ease or comfort that does not feel like dukkha at all, but when certain types of sukha are tasted and then these sensations begin to dissipate or fade away, the original condition of comfort changes to dukkha—just as if dukkha were latent and then appears as soon as that sukha loses its flavor or fades away. As sukha increases, so does the strength of dukkha, just as if latent dukkha were spreading out further and further. If that kind of sukha were not to occur, then the dukkha associated with it would also not arise. But if people taste sukha and then realize sukha must come to an end, then dukkha based on fear overcomes them.)
3. *Saṅkhāra-dukkhatā*—Dukkha related to the conditions of compounded things and mental formations (*saṅkhāra*), that is to say, the conditions of compounded things themselves, or all things that arise due to causal factors related to the Five Aggregates of Existence (including the Path [*magga*] and the fruits of higher practices [*lokuttara-dhamma*]) that are dukkha. It is a condition of stress that comes about due to conflicting causal factors that arise and pass away. Nothing is complete in and of itself. Everything exists in a current of causal factors that is able to bring about dukkha (the sensation of dukkha or *dukkha-vedanā*) for those whose knowledge cannot keep pace with this condition or flow and stubbornly resist it with craving and attachment (*taṇhā-upādāna*) rooted in ignorance (*avijjā*). Such people do not wish to acquaint themselves with the principle of causation nor live in accordance with it.

The third type of dukkha is the most important. It explains the condition of all compounded things according to the way they really are. This condition may also have psychological significance in the sense that it may not give a person complete satisfaction and can lead to a constant state of dukkha, especially for those who approach this type of dukkha with ignorance, craving, and attachment.[55]

The principle of dependent origination allows us to see the relationship between all things as interconnected, as the cause and effect of one another, and as a flowing current. The meaning of this current can be expanded in order to explain its various senses:

> All things have a relationship dependent on common factors;
> all things exist in an interrelated fashion;
> all things are impermanent, existing only temporarily;
> all things do not exist unto themselves, that is, there is no real self;
> all things do not have a "first cause" that brought them into existence.
>
> To put it another way, the condition of all things appearing in different forms, progressing and degenerating in various ways, shows that their real state is a fluctuating current or procession;
> existence being a current or procession points to the nature of the make-up of its various constituent elements;
> this current is visible because all of its elements are related in an interdependent manner;
> this current changes because its elements are impermanent and exist only momentarily;
> elements exist only momentarily because they have no real self;
> there is no real self, so we are subject to various causal factors;
> the various causal factors are interdependent and, therefore, a direction of flux takes shape;
> existing as interdependent causal factors shows that there can be no "first cause" for all things.
>
> To state this in a reverse and contrary manner, if all things had a real self, then there must be permanence;
> if all things are permanent, even for a moment, then they cannot exist as related causal factors;
> when they do not exist as related causal factors, then they cannot make up a current;
> when there is no current of factors, then there is no natural process;
> and if there is any kind of real self at the center of this current, then it is impossible to have existence according to real causal factors.

This current of causal factors, which makes all things appear and exist in accordance with natural law, continues along because all things are impermanent, unstable, arising and fading away, without self, and related in an interdependent manner.

The state of impermanence, instability, arising, and fading away is called *aniccatā*. Being subject to the pressures of arising and fading away, experiencing pressures from latent conflict, and having a feeling of insufficiency is called *dukkhatā*. Being without a real self is called *anattatā*. The principle of dependent origination allows us to see these three conditions in all things, and it explains the relationship of interconnected factors in all things and the forms that those factors may take in nature. All aspects of existence follow the principle of dependent origination, including physical (*rūpa-dhamma*) and mental phenomena (*nāma-dhamma*), the material world (*vatthu*), as well as living things composed of both physical and mental phenomena. In the process of observing dependent origination, various natural laws can be discerned, such as *dhamma-niyāma*, the laws concerning relationships between cause and effect; *utu-niyāma*, natural laws concerning physical inorganic matter; *bīja-niyāma*, natural laws concerning organic matter and heredity; *citta-niyāma*, laws concerning the workings of the mind; and *kamma-niyāma*, laws relating to kamma (action and the fruits of action)—all of which have a special relationship with sukha and dukkha in life and also must have a direct bearing on a person's ethics or conduct.

One thing that must be emphasized, because it goes against the feelings of most people, is that what makes kamma—or the process of all causes in nature—possible is that all things are impermanent and without self (*anattā*). If all things were permanent and had a self, then natural law, including the law of kamma, would be impossible. Once again, aside from this, the following law also holds true: There is no first cause, such as a "creator."

All things have no real self because they come into being depending on a variety of other causes and exist in an interrelated fashion. To state a rather simple example: a bed comes from a variety of parts that are put together according to a certain design concept. There is no essence to the bed apart from its parts. When it is disassembled, that's it. There is no longer any bed to be found; there is only the idea of "bed" left in the mind. And even that idea or sense of "bed" does not exist of itself but must depend on relationships with other notions or purposes, such as sleeping, reclining, a place for setting things down, and empty space.

Such ideas are part of the common perception of people and are understood due to the construction of various notions that coexist with pertinent factors and relationships. But when relationships occur to us, we are accustomed to grasping, craving, and attaching to them; and so, we become wrapped up in ideas that give us the feeling of having a definite self. This notion of a self obscures our perception and separates us from our relationship with other things, making us ignorant or blind to our true condition. In this way, ego-consciousness (*ahaṁkāra*; literally, self-making) and self-attachment (*mamaṅkāra*) come into play in full force.

Furthermore, by nature all things are without a first cause. If we take up anything for consideration and unceasingly search back to its genesis, we will not be able to find an original cause for it. But most people have a longing or desire for something that might serve as a first cause, a desire that does not accord with nature. We can call this desire an abnormal longing that is the result of human habit. When a person encounters something and considers what its source might be, thought stops and latches onto something it determines as its only cause, and then inquiry stops. This habit makes most people's consideration of cause and effect come to an abrupt halt and get stuck in a rut in a way that goes against natural law—insisting that there must be some kind of first cause for all things. If we were to think naturally, we would have to inquire further as to what might be the cause of the first cause and beyond, without end. Because all things exist in an interrelated, interdependent manner as connected factors, naturally, there can be no first cause. We should repeat the question: Why must all things have a first cause? Because thought resists nature, which is due to the habits of human beings and is related to the notion of a first cause and the idea that, in the past, there was nothing at all. This idea can be traced to becoming accustomed to and clinging to a notion of self.

So, the belief that all things have a creator, which we often consider a natural way of thinking, actually goes against nature. Belief in a creator comes about because people view human beings as the inventors of tools and the creators of art. And because certain things come into existence due to their creation by human beings, people tend to think, therefore, that all things in the world must have a creator, too. This being the case, human beings deceive themselves by separating the meaning of "creation" from normal causes and effects, which leads them to a false conclusion. Actually, creation is only one portion of the meaning of the term causal factor. When human beings create something, this means that they play a role as a causal factor in a process involving other causal factors in order to bring about the final goal that they envision. But there are some other special considerations apart from this process of causal factors and related materials that come into play. These are mental factors (*nāma-dhamma*) combined with intentions (*cetanā*). Even so, there is a chain of factors combining with other factors that must continue along according to a steady procession of related causal factors in order to achieve a desired result. When people want to construct a building, for example, they must become involved, influencing the various causal factors to proceed along a certain line before their project can reach the point of successful conclusion. If the construction work were a supernatural creation, carried out in some special manner apart from causal factors, then people could live anywhere and create a dwelling or building according to their wish or need, but we know this is impossible. The act of construction does not have meaning outside of or above a certain set of causal factors; therefore, when all things proceed according to a procession of related causal factors, the problem of the existence of a creator should not occur at any step along the way.

At any rate, theorizing about cause and effect in terms of the problem of a first cause and a creator is held to be of little value in Buddhadhamma, because there is no need for it. It does not lead to practical benefits in real life. Although searching for a creator or a first cause might broaden a person's perspective or outlook on life, this search can be overlooked in favor of the value placed on ethics. It is important, therefore, that we should direct our attention to a life of practice.

We have stated all along that life is composed of the Five Aggregates of Existence. There is nothing else outside of or over and above these Five Aggregates; there is nothing hidden in the Five Aggregates or existing separate from them that is the owner or controller of them and makes life continue on. When we examine life, the Five Aggregates comprise the key set of elements, sufficient and complete.

The Five Aggregates are also part of a process that continues on according to dependent origination; they exist as a flow or current of various interconnected and interrelated factors. There is no part of this current that can be fixed or permanent. There is only arising and passing away. And this condition allows this process of related causes and effects to continuously maintain a form (*rūpa*).

The Five Aggregates, or life itself, are, therefore, subject to the laws of the Three Characteristics of Existence: that is, they exist in a state of impermanence (*aniccatā*), instability, are born and then deteriorate; there is nothing at all that constitutes a real self (*anattatā*) to which we can cling, declare ownership, or to use to force order upon the world to make things go as we wish; and there are numerous pressures resulting from the constant arising and passing away of phenomena, so that suffering (*dukkhatā*) is always present for those who deal with the world according to ignorance and attachment.

The process of the Five Aggregates (or life) continues to change at all levels, because there is no permanent self and because things are subject to a variety of related causal factors that move in their own natural way. But in the case of ordinary human beings, there is often resistance to this natural flow or current. This makes humans subject to mistaken views and brings about a tendency towards attachment to the shape of the current, or any part of it, and the mistaken belief that that constitutes a self. A desire is then established for this self to take a consistent shape or form or to continue on in a certain way. At the same time, the cycle of change that naturally comes about with the flow of the current of life ends up coming into conflict with these desires. This creates a pressure that pushes people to even stronger desires. This struggle and the wish for a self in some form or another—whether it be making the self exist as you wish or making it permanent, stable, or eternal within the bounds of a desired form—only escalates desire. As soon as things do not go along as you wish, this pressure only shows itself more distinctly as disappointment. Then, dukkha and distress increase accordingly. In addition, when you catch your first dim glimpse of the truth, you will see that some kinds of change must inevitably take place and that the self to which you are clinging may not actually exist or may even disintegrate. This realization, in turn, may lead you to bury the roots of your attachments and desires even more deeply and hold to them more strongly. Fear and apprehension are emotions that can be deeply hidden and intertwined; these psychological conditions are called *avijjā* (not knowing things in accordance with the truth and believing in a self); *taṇhā* (wanting a self, which you believe you possess, to exist or not to exist in a certain fashion); and *upādāna* (mistakenly attaching the imagined self to various things). These kinds of unwholesome tendencies (*kilesa*) are deeply hidden in the mind and gradually force all human behavior to succumb to them—consciously and unconsciously—until they mold your character and even come to play an important role in your destiny. Generally speaking, this is the background of the arising of human suffering.

The conflict or clash between two processes can be summarized as follows:

1. The life process that continues according to the laws of the Three Characteristics of Existence—which are definite natural laws, that is, impermanence (*aniccatā*), suffering (*dukkhatā*), and no-self (*anattatā*)—explains all conditions from birth to decay-and-death, in both a basic and simple manner and a subtle and deep manner;
2. Not knowing the process of life for what it truly is results in the mistaken belief in a self and causes people to cling to a notion of a self, which is fraught with inherent fears and anxieties.

To put this even more succinctly, the above constitutes a conflict between natural law and attachment to a mistaken notion of selfhood; or to state this even more directly, creating a self obstructs the flow of natural law.

We can call this living according to ignorance, living with attachment, as a slave, in conflict with natural law—or living a life of dukkha.

Living like this, if stated in terms of ethics and conventional truth (*sammuti-sacca*), might be said to consist of two kinds of "selves": one, the flow of life that goes along according to natural law and changes in accordance with causal factors. Although there is no real self, we designate a current or a process apart from other currents and processes that we might call, according to conventional truth, a "self"; in discussions of ethics, this supposition of the self can be useful. And second, the idea of a false self is created and, due to ignorance (*avijjā*), craving (*taṇhā*), and attachment (*upādāna*), is believed to be permanent. The first type of self—while designated out of convenience in accordance with conventional truth, with full knowledge of the true nature of "self"—is not the cause of false attachments nor clinging. But the second type of self—built up and hidden behind the first—is a self based on attachments that eventually clashes with the first type of "self," resulting in dukkha.

Living with fears and anxieties and hiding them in the deepest recesses of the mind, only to have them become motivating forces underlying behavior, puts the life process out of sorts and makes people unwitting slaves. Aside from this, such anxieties have many other adverse effects: they breed selfish desires that only lead to searching for things to fulfill an unending stream of desire without thought for others.[56] This makes people latch onto various opinions or views that they determine to be their self or personal possession; people then cling to and cherish these notions to protect themselves. This kind of attachment builds a wall that cuts you off from the truth. It makes reasoning and critical faculties obstinate and inflexible.[57] This, in turn, makes people's beliefs and behavior naive and irrational; and people cling to such beliefs and behaviors because they see the relationship between cause and effect in only a very dim light or with superstition and self-uncertainty. But at the same time, there is anxiety about the false self that people have built up and to which they are now attached—there is a fear that that self will be lost or disappear. This makes people desperately grab at things to fulfill their hopes, even though this means living in a superstitious and deluded manner.[58] This makes for a "floating" type of self that lacks direction. Furthermore, this self must be coddled, nurtured, and protected against impact or loss. While at the same time, protecting this self amounts to limiting yourself to a very narrow sphere of action, which sacrifices freedom and indirectly conflicts with this created self.[59] In this sense, conflict, pressure, and dukkha do not, therefore, exist only in and for yourself, but also spread out to cause conflict, pressure, and suffering for others in society at large. We can say that this condition constitutes the arising of dukkha and all other social problems resulting from the actions of human beings.

The applied principle of dependent origination reveals the origin of all of life's problems or the creation of a self (that is, living as if one had a self)—an equation for dukkha. When the cycle of dependent origination is broken, this amounts to destroying all dukkha that comes about based on the existence of a self (or existing as if one had a self). This break brings about a condition that is the complete opposite of dukkha: living freely with wisdom, without attachment to a self, and in harmony with nature.

Living with wisdom means being able to keep pace with changing conditions and knowing how to reap benefits from nature. Reaping benefits from nature relates to living in harmony with nature; to live in harmony with nature is to live freely; living freely means not succumbing to the power of craving and attachment; to live without attachments is to live wisely, or to know and relate to all things according to their causal factors.

There is something else that should be emphasized concerning the relationship between human beings and nature: According to the principles of Buddhadhamma, there is nothing higher than nature, or nothing besides nature. If there were anything outside of nature, then it would have nothing to do with nature; that is, it would completely transcend nature. Anything that relates to nature cannot exist outside of nature but must be part and parcel of it. Furthermore, the whole of the natural process continues along according to causal factors; it does not proceed in an aimless manner and it is not subject to supernatural influences apart from causal factors. Strange, fantastic, or incredible occurrences that appear to be due to miraculous powers are all things that come about according to causal factors. In some instances causal factors may come together in a seemingly chaotic manner and we are not able to perceive any rhyme or reason to them. In these instances, occurrences often appear to be fantastic or incredible. The aura of the strange or incredible disappears, however, as soon as the various causal factors that have come into play are completely realized. Terms such as "transcending nature" or "outside of nature," as previously mentioned, are only expressions. There is really no such thing.

Similarly, when considering the relationship between human beings and nature, often the two are split into separate categories, or people say that human beings can "control nature." Again, these are only expressions, just manners of speaking. Actually, humans are merely part of nature, and the human ability to control nature only means that people can become one causal factor applying pressure on other causal factors in nature that proceed in an interconnected fashion until a desired result is achieved. It is only in the case of human beings where there are psychological factors combined with intentions (*cetanā*) that enter into this process. These human factors lead to actions and the fruits of action, which are often called creation or creativity, but they are all completely related to causal factors. Human beings are not able to create something out of thin air, in the sense that they are able to create something without the involvement or consideration of causal factors. Saying that human beings can control nature means that they can come to realize the process of the various causal factors that will lead to a desired result. There are two aspects to this "control": 1) knowledge or understanding, and 2) factors affecting other factors. The first thing that is important and necessary is understanding, in other words wisdom. When you attain wisdom, you are able to be in harmony with the process of causal factors in a way that accords with your wishes. Becoming involved with all things by means of wisdom and intelligence can, in a positive sense, be called taking advantage of the benefits of nature or "controlling nature. " This relates not only to material things (*rūpa-dhamma*) but psychological matters (*nāma-dhamma*) as well. Therefore, in this sense, taking advantage of the benefits of nature is the same as living in harmony with nature. We can say that we are able to control our psychological nature, as well—control our mind, control ourselves—and these figures of speech are all correct in the sense that living with wisdom is crucial if human beings are to reap the benefits of both material and psychological processes.

A life of wisdom can be viewed from two perspectives: First, in terms of internal aspects, such as being peaceful and calm and being free from impediments after having achieved proper understanding, which means being *truly* free. This also means that when you have tasted sukha, you do not succumb to it or get lost in it; and when you lack sukha or are separated from various allurements, you are secure, untroubled, unagitated. You are no longer subject to depression or sorrow, hopelessness or desperation, and do not put yourself in the clutches of those external allurements, allowing them to determine your fate. Second, this can be viewed from an external perspective. People with wisdom appear competent, agile, always ready to be involved or come to other people's assistance in a proper manner, for pure reasons. Such people do not get all caught up in or attached to internal things that become obstacles, hindrances, or barriers that might lead them astray or skew their vision.

Some of the Buddha's words explain the characteristic differences between a life of attachment and a life of wisdom:

> Bhikkhus, people who do not know may feel pleasant sensations (*sukha-vedanā*), unpleasant sensations (*dukkha-vedanā*), and some neither-pleasant-nor-unpleasant sensations (that is, neutral, neither-sukha-nor-dukkha). Noble Disciples who already know may feel some pleasant sensations, unpleasant sensations, and some neither-pleasant-nor-unpleasant sensations. Bhikkhus, in this case, what is special or strange, what is the difference between the Noble Disciples who know and those who do not?
>
> Bhikkhus, the people who do not know, who are subject to the forces of unpleasant sensations are sorrowful, mournful, crying and lamenting until they become deranged. They feel these two types of sensations—the physical and the mental.
>
> It is like the hunter who shoots a person with one arrow and shoots yet another arrow into himself. When this is the case, that person feels sensations due to both arrows—the physical as well as the mental. Those who do not know are just like this. . . . They feel two types of sensations, the physical and the mental.
>
> Furthermore, because unpleasant sensations disturb them, they become angry; when they are angry, then rage erupts due to the existence of latent sensations. They feel unpleasant sen-

sations and resort to indulging in sensual pleasures (*kāmasukha*).[60] Why? Because those who do not know, do not know the way to escape from unpleasant sensations aside from indulging in the pleasures of the senses. People become engrossed in these pleasures or lustful inclinations (*rāgānusaya*) because these sensations are latent in their minds; and when such sensations occur, their minds cannot keep pace with the arising and passing away of these sensations, their good and bad aspects, as well as the avoidance of these sensations. When people do not know. . . sensations for what they are, ignorant inclinations (*avijjānusaya*) appear due to the latent sensation of neither-pleasant-nor-unpleasant (= *upekkhā-vedanā* or equanimity). If people feel sukha, then it is as if they are bound by it; if they feel dukkha, then they feel as if they are bound by it; if they feel neither-pleasant-nor-unpleasant, then it is as if they are bound by it. Bhikkhus, these people, then, are called people who do not know. Those who are composed of[61] birth, death, sorrow, lamentation, suffering, grief, and distress—we call them people composed of dukkha.

Bhikkhus, for those Noble Disciples who already know, when they feel the pangs of unpleasant sensations, they are not sorrowful nor mournful, they do not wail, lament, nor beat their breasts crying, nor do they become deranged. They feel only physical sensations, not mental torment.

It is like the hunter who shoots a person with an arrow and shoots yet another arrow that misses. When this is the case, that person will feel the sensations of only one arrow. The Noble Disciples who already know are like this. . . .They only feel physical pangs and remain unscathed by the mental ones.

Furthermore, those who know will not harbor anger based on those unpleasant sensations. When this anger no longer exists, then tendencies towards anger (*paṭighānusaya*) related to unpleasant sensations are no longer latent. These people may feel unpleasant sensations, but they do not resort to indulging in sensual pleasures. Why? Because the Noble Disciples who already know also know the way to escape from these unpleasant sensations, which lies beyond sensual pleasures. When passionate tendencies are no longer latent in the mind, people do not indulge in sensual pleasures or lust. At this point, knowledge can keep pace with the arising, the passing away, and the good and bad

> aspects of these sensations. When a person realizes the nature of these sensations, the escape route is also clear. When people know. . .them for what they are, then ignorant tendencies related to those pleasant sensations are no longer latent. If pleasant sensations are felt, they are felt without being bound by them; if unpleasant sensations are felt, they are felt without being bound by them; if neither-pleasant-nor-unpleasant sensations are felt, they are felt without being bound by them. Bhikkhus, these people are called Noble Disciples, people who know, people who are free from birth, decay, death, sorrow, lamentation, suffering, grief, and distress. We call them people free of dukkha.
>
> Bhikkhus, this is what is special, strange, and different about the disciples who know and those who do not.[62]

The above should serve to explain what is what and what should be done away with. When you have certain sensations and attachments, what can you expect? And what should you do? And once that has been done, what can you expect? What must be done to get rid of certain things and make other things happen? This is where proper conduct comes in, and so this is what will be explained next.

A Diagrammatic Explanation of Dependent Origination

The following type of explanation is very detailed, subtle, and comprehensive. It constitutes an especially scholarly approach. Those who study it must depend on a certain foundation of knowledge of Buddha-dhamma and technical terms from the Pali language. There are also some texts that explain directly the principle of dependent origination.[63] Therefore, only a summary of the principle will be offered here.

The Names of the Elements and their Framework

All of the names of the elements have been explained in a previous chapter, therefore, in this section the elements will be pulled together and summarized for easier understanding.

> (1) ignorance (*avijjā*) → (2) mental formations (*saṅkhāra*) → (3) consciousness (*viññāṇa*) → (4) mind-and-body (*nāma-rūpa*) → (5) six sense-bases (*saḷāyatana*) → (6) contact (*phassa*) → (7)

sensation (*vedanā*) → (8) craving (*taṇhā*) → (9) clinging (*upādāna*) → (10) becoming (*bhava*) → (11) birth (*jāti*) → (12) decay-and-death (*jarā-maraṇa*). . . sorrow, lamentation, suffering, grief, and distress = the arising of dukkha (*dukkhasamudaya*)

The extinguishing of the whole process of dukkha, or *dukkhanirodha*, follows according to these same elements.

Furthermore, the dhammic process of dependent origination revolves in a cycle of rounds of existence or rebirths. There is no beginning point nor end point. Let us look at the following diagram so there will be no misunderstandings about this.

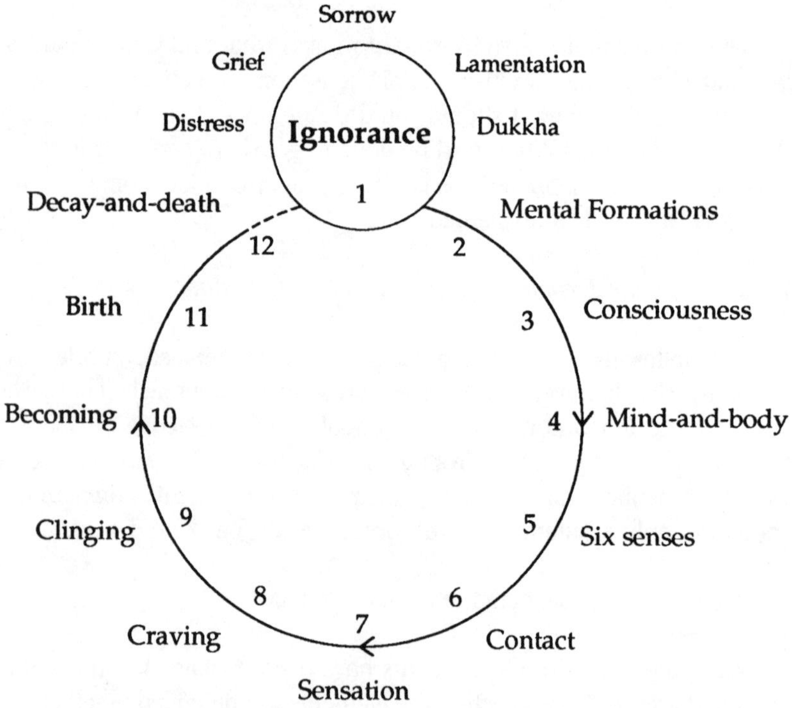

Terms Limiting the Meaning of the Elements or Headings in Order[64]

1. Ignorance (*avijjā*) = not understanding dukkha, its arising (*samudaya*), its passing away (*nirodha*), the path (*magga*, the Four Noble Truths) and (according to the Abhidhamma) not under-

standing the past, future,[65] both the past and future, and dependent origination (*paṭiccasamuppāda*);

2. Compounded things, mental formations, or predispositions (*saṅkhāra*) = physical (*kāya-saṅkhāra*), verbal (*vacī-saṅkhāra*), mental (*citta-saṅkhāra*)[66] and (according to the Abhidhamma) the formation of merit (*puññābhisaṅkhāra*), formation of demerit (*apuññābhisaṅkhāra*), and formation of the faultless (*āneñjābhisaṅkhāra*);[67]
3. Consciousness (*viññāṇa*) = eyes (*cakkhu*), ears (*sota*), nose (*ghāna*), tongue (*jivhā*), body (*kāya*), mind-consciousness (*mano-viññāṇa*)—the six senses;[68]
4. Mind-and-body (*nāma-rūpa*) = mind (sensation [*vedanā*], perception [*saññā*], intention [*cetanā*], contact [*phassa*], attention [*manasikāra*]; or according to the Abhidhamma: sensation [*vedanā-khandha*], perception [*saññā-khandha*], mental formations [*saṅkhāra-khandha*]) + body or form (the four primary elements—water, air, earth, and fire—and forms that depend on these);[69]
5. The six senses or sense-bases (*saḷāyatana*) = eyes, ears, nose, tongue, body, and mind.
6. Contact (*phassa*) = contact with the eyes, ears, nose, tongue, body, or mind (six senses);[70]
7. Sensation (*vedanā*) = feelings arising from contact via the eyes, ears, nose, tongue, body, or mind—the six senses;[71]
8. Craving (*taṇhā*) = craving for bodily form (*rūpa-taṇhā*), craving for sound (*sadda-taṇhā*), craving for smell (*gandha-taṇhā*), craving for taste (*rasa-taṇhā*), craving for physical contact (*phoṭṭhabba-taṇhā*), and craving for mental stimuli (*dhamma-taṇhā*)—the six cravings;[72]
9. Clinging (*upādāna*) = clinging to passions of the body, taste, smell, sound, sight, and other types of contact (*kāmupādāna*), clinging to views, such as opinions, doctrines, and various theories (*diṭṭhupādāna*), clinging to mere rules and rituals as the only true way (*sīlabbatupādāna*), and clinging to a self and mistakenly creating a self to cling to (*attavādupādāna*);
10. Becoming (*bhava*) = sensual becoming (*kāma-bhava*), physical becoming (*rūpa-bhava*), formless becoming (*arūpa-bhava*), and, in another sense:

= kammic becoming (*kamma-bhava*)—*puññābhisaṅkhāra, apuññābhisaṅkhāra, āneñjābhisaṅkhāra* (see number two); and birth (*upapatti-bhava*)—*kāma-bhava, rūpa-bhava, arūpa-bhava, saññā-bhava, asaññā-bhava,* the realm of neither-perception-nor-non-perception [*nevasaññānasaññāyatana,* the fourth immaterial *jhāna*], *ekavokāra-bhava, catuvokāra-bhava,* and *pañcavokāra-bhava.*[73]

11. Birth (*jāti*) = the appearance of all the aggregates (*khandha*) that come from the various sense-bases (*āyatana*), or the birth or arising of those various phenomena;
12. Decay-and-death (*jarā-maraṇa*) = growing old, the aging of the senses and the deterioration of the aggregates, the stopping of the life functions, or the degeneration of various phenomena.[74]

Examples of the Most General Types of Explanation

In order to provide the shortest and simplest explanation of dependent origination the following succession or cyclical example should be cited:

(*Āsava* →) Ignorance (*avijjā*): Believing that being born into heaven is the highest happiness; believing that killing this or that person will bring happiness; believing that killing yourself will bring happiness; believing that attaining the Brahma-state exempts you from birth and death; believing that by performing sacrifices or propitiatory offerings you can attain heaven; believing that you can attain nibbana by severe ascetic practices and self-mortification; believing that this very self can be reborn in a particular state depending on your actions; and believing that after death there is nothing, only a void, and so on.

→ Mental formations, predispositions, or volitional activities (*saṅkhāra*): Thinking, establishing moral habits or intentions based on certain understandings and thoughts; devising means to do various things (kamma) according to your intentions, thinking that this is good kamma (*puñña,* meritorious), bad kamma (*apuñña* or *pāpa,* demeritorious), or faultless (*āneñja*).

→ Consciousness (*viññāṇa*): Most importantly, it is coming to realize and sense various kinds of ideation, especially those that accompany certain kinds of intentions or volition. To put it most simply, it is the mental state or consciousness that is embellished with certain properties, which arises in various ways and takes various forms. When we die, the force of our *saṅkhāra*—that is, our accumulated kamma—causes the birth of another consciousness that has the same properties as that force. The birth of this consciousness comes into being in keeping with its nature.

→ Mind-and-body (*nāma-rūpa*): This is the process of birth and progress that creates a form, which springs to life ready for action (kamma). This form—born complete with corporeality (*rūpa-khandha*), sensation (*vedanā-khandha*), perception (*saññā-khandha*), and psychological predispositions (*saṅkhāra-khandha*)—is, therefore, made up of properties and various deficiencies according to the force of the *saṅkhāra* that has composed it. This force is affected by a person's kamma and the realm of existence into which that person is subsequently born—be it the realm of human beings, animal beings, or divine beings.

→ Six sense-bases (*saḷāyatana*): This is the aspect of life that responds to needs and is prepared to act or confront the external world in order to inform this process about its progress. The senses depend upon mind-and-body for support and the life process continues along according to the power of kamma, to the point that the six sense-bases come into being, that is to say the nervous system—eyes, ears, nose, tongue, body and the sense that sends information about internal objects of ideation, that is, the mind.[75]

→ Contact (*phassa*): This is the process that can inform the life process through the contact or convergence of three groups of factors: one, the internal sense-bases (eyes, ears, nose, tongue, body, and mind); two, the external sense-bases (form, sound, smell, taste, tangible objects [*phoṭṭhabba*] and intangible mind-objects); and three, consciousness (eye-consciousness, ear-consciousness, nose consciousness, tongue-consciousness, body-consciousness, and mind-consciousness). This process takes place whenever a person becomes aware of something.

→ Sensation (*vedanā*): This is the feeling of having "tasted" emotions that have arisen in one form or another, such as happiness or pleasure (*sukha-vedanā*), discomfort, pain, suffering (*dukkha-vedanā*) or neutrality/equanimity (*adukkhamasukha–vedanā* or *upekkhā–vedanā*), and depending on our character, this process is not likely to stop here; therefore, we have. . .

→ Craving (*taṇhā*): If we are comfortable, happy, attracted to something and want it, or progressively want more and more of it, there is an increase of desire and different kinds of seeking. If we experience dukkha, are uncomfortable, disturbed, and resentful, then there is the desire for things to disappear or go away either by destroying them or escaping from them. This causes anxieties and the struggle to break free from disturbing mind-objects. This may make us seek out and focus on other mind-objects that will bring us pleasure or at least return us to a state of equanimity and calm (*upekkhā*). This is a subtle kind of feeling akin to pleasure because there is no feeling of being disturbed, but it is really only a mild form of comfort.

→ Attachment (*upādāna*): This is a stronger feeling of desire that becomes grasping, clinging, or being engrossed in something. When we do not have something, we crave it; and when we get it, we attach ourselves to it. Once we have attached ourselves to something, this is not only linked up with the object of desire (*kāmupādāna*), it is also linked up with attachment to various opinions, theories, and biases (*diṭṭhupādāna*). Attachment to certain patterns of behavior or courses of action that allow us to fulfill our desires (*silabbatupādāna*) and attachment to a self (*attavādupādāna*) are involved. This attachment leads to the following.

→ Becoming (*bhava*): This is the will (*cetanā*), purposeful action that leads to existence and continuing on according to our attachments. This brings about a whole course of action (*kamma-bhava*) that may include good behavior, bad behavior, and faultless behavior (*āneñja*). Becoming is linked with craving and attachment; for example, we may wish to go to heaven and continue to believe that we are headed in that direction due to certain deeds that we have performed. In this way, actions are determined by wants. These actions also determine the conditions of life—that is, the Five Aggregates of Existence—which take shape according to the kamma that we have performed and accumulated (*upapatti-bhava*). When the process of the forces of our kamma reach this point, even if our life has come to an end, the collective force of his kamma (*kamma-bhava*) pushes on, bringing about the next level in the cycle.

→ Birth (*jāti*): This begins with rebirth-consciousness (*paṭisandhiviññāṇa*), which has properties linked up with the force of the above kamma. Rebirth brings us into an existence befitting our kamma. The Five Aggregates converge, beginning the life process, which continues on its way. That is, mind-and-body, the six sense-bases, contact, and sensation arise and are perpetuated once again. Once birth takes place, the next cycle is certain.

→ Decay-and-death (*jarā-maraṇa*): This is the decline, degeneration, and breakdown of the life process. Decay-and-death constantly threatens and pressures most of us both explicitly and implicitly (existing deep within the mind). In the cycle of ordinary human life, therefore, decay-and-death goes together with sorrow, lamentation, suffering, grief and distress—all of which can simply be called dukkha. And this leads to our previous summary of dependent origination: "This whole heap of dukkha arises according to these factors."

At any a rate, at this point there is no end to this cyclical state. Actually, these factors become another important step that contributes to the perpetuation of this cycle, leading to sorrow (*soka*), lamentation (*parideva*), suffering (*dukkha*), grief (*domanassa*), and distress (*upāyāsa*), which are the apparent symptoms of unwholesome tendencies (*kilesa*). These bad habits exist as stagnant and fermenting states of mind and are called mental intoxicants (*āsava*). The mental intoxicants are interested in sustaining various opinions, attachments, and things that respond to the desires of the six senses (*kāmāsava*): such as believing that our bodies are our selves or that they belong to us (*diṭṭhāsava*); taking psychological enjoyment that this or that condition in life is the best, most excellent, and most pleasurable, such as believing that being born a god or celestial being is the highest pleasure beyond words (*bhavāsava*); and not knowing things according to their true nature (*avijjāsava*). Decay-and-death is an indicator of the degeneration and breakdown that runs counter to these mental intoxicants. For example, in the case of the mental intoxicants that respond to the senses (*kāmāsava*), decay-and-death gives people the feeling that, "I am disintegrating and am losing all hope for the things I enjoy or desire." In the case of believing that our bodies belong to us (*diṭṭhāsava*), if a person is attached to the idea that the body is the self, then as soon as the body changes, there is sorrow. As for seeking psychological enjoyment in higher states of being (*bhavāsava*), decay-and-death may make people feel as if they will be disappointed or miss out on the opportunity to assume a life form that they will enjoy. Not knowing things according to their nature (*avijjāsava*) is to lack fundamental knowledge and understanding of important questions: "What is life?", "What is old age and decay?", and

"How should we act in the face of old age?" When people lack knowledge and a correct way of thinking, then when they think about or come face to face with old age, various foolish, cowardly, and depressing feelings and symptoms arise. Mental intoxicants (*āsava*) are, therefore, seeds that instantly grow into the sorrow, lamentation, suffering, grief, and distress to which decay-and-death is related.

Furthermore, sorrow, for example, points to "dark" symptoms in the mind. Anytime dukkha occurs, the mind will become distorted, hot, and overloaded and lack wisdom.[76] When these symptoms occur, it is the same as hitching up with ignorance (*avijjā*). As it is stated in the *Path of Purification* (*Visuddhimagga*): "Sorrow, suffering, grief, and distress cannot be separated from ignorance; and, normally, lamentation occurs with the person who is lost. For this reason, when sorrow, for example, has succeeded in taking over, ignorance also triumphs."[77] Also, "As for ignorance, you should know that it triumphs over those who are sorrowful (and so on)."[78] In another passage, "Ignorance continues to exist when sorrow, for instance, continues to exist."[79] In this sense, the Buddha stated that, "Because mental intoxications (*āsava*) exist, ignorance comes about."[80] This can be summarized as follows: ordinary human decay-and-death, which is linked with sorrow, lamentation, suffering, grief and distress, tends to be the cause of ignorance that continues on in an endless cycle.

While making this type of cyclical explanation, there are some points that should be given special consideration:

First of all, according to this type of explanation, the cycle of dependent origination is more popularly referred to as the "cycle of becoming," which may be translated as the "wheel of becoming" (*bhava*) or the "wheel of *saṁsāra*," that is, the cycle of death and rebirth. It can be seen that these explanations are linked with three phases of life: one, ignorance (*avijjā*) and mental formations or predispositions (*saṅkhāra*); two, consciousness (*viññāṇa*) to becoming (*bhava*); and three, birth (*jāti*) and decay-and-death (which is linked with sorrow and so on). If we take the middle phase, consciousness to becoming, as being our present life, all three phases of life that are composed of the twelve elements of dependent origination can then be divided into the following periods of time:

Past—ignorance, mental formations or predispositions
Present—consciousness, mind-and-body, the six sense-bases, and becoming
Future—birth, decay-and-death (plus sorrow and so on)

When these are divided into three phases, we can take the middle phase—our present life or birth—as a basic reference point. When we do this, we can see the relationship between causes in the past to effects in the present (past causes → present conditions). As for the future, we can trace from present causes to see what kinds of results may come about in the future (present causes → future results). In this sense, the middle phase—the present—has *both* effects and causes that can be shown in four phases (and are called *saṅgaha* or *saṅkhepa*):

Past causes—ignorance, mental formations or predispositions
Present effects—consciousness, mind-and-body, the six sense-bases, contact, sensation
Present causes—craving, attachment, becoming
Future effects—birth, decay-and-death (plus sorrow and so on)

If an explanation of each element of the cycle of dependent origination is given, the meaning and interrelationship of some elements can be seen. The elements, therefore, have been arranged in the following groups.

Ignorance (*avijjā*), craving (*taṇhā*), and attachment (*upādāna*). From an explanation of ignorance, we can clearly see that craving and attachment exist, especially attachment to the notion of a self. These are hidden in all instances when a person does not know life as it truly is. A person may think he has a self and then has craving for and attachment to things that will be of benefit to that self. It is said that, "When mental intoxication (*āsava*) occurs, ignorance arises"; the intoxication of sensuality (*kāmāsava*), intoxication of becoming (*bhavāsava*), and the intoxication of ideas, opinions, and thought (*diṭṭhāsava*) are also related to this same craving and attachment. So when we speak of ignorance, it is always linked with or tied to craving and attachment.

The same is true for the explanation of craving and attachment; we can see that when ignorance is hidden or involved in the creation of a self, people crave and become attached for the sake of that self. Because people do not understand things according to their true nature, they get involved with them by means of craving and attachment, considering these things to be "theirs" and wanting them for themselves. This is a matter of selfishness. The more people crave and cling in this way, the more they overlook pertinent causes and effects. They cannot see all things according to their conditions and they increasingly neglect to treat them with mindfulness and intelligence, according to reason. This is why, when we speak of craving and attachment, we must see that they are linked with and have a bearing on ignorance as well.

In this sense, placing ignorance in the category of past causes and placing craving or attachment in with present causes amounts to the same thing. Putting ignorance in the past phase and clinging and attachment in the present phase is done to point out the main factors that are related to other elements in this "wheel of becoming."

Mental formations or predispositions (*saṅkhāra*) and becoming (*bhava*). Mental formations and becoming are explained in terms of this cycle in a very similar way. Mental formations exist in the past phase of life, while becoming is related to the present phase. Each is important in embellishing life to the point that it is born into various existences. The meanings of these two factors, therefore, are very similar, which almost makes them the same thing, but they remain different in terms of emphasis. Mental formations point to intentions (*cetanā*) that accompany actions; they are the leading instigators in the creation of kamma. As for becoming, it has a broader meaning that can be divided into the active process of becoming (*kamma-bhava*) and the passive process of rebirth (*upapatti-bhava*). Even if the active process of becoming has volition as its principal force—as is the case with mental formations—it still has a more all-encompassing sense that extends to the whole process of human behavior. As for the passive process of rebirth, this refers to the Five Aggregates of Existence that come into existence due to the active process of becoming. So, in this way, mental formations and the active process of becoming can be grouped together.

Consciousness (*viññāṇa*) to sensation (*vedanā*) and birth (*jāti*), to decay-and-death (*jarā-maraṇa*) plus sorrow and so on. The portion of the cycle of dependent origination that extends from consciousness to sensation relates to the present life, which is the result of causes in the past. This part of the cycle seeks a broader awareness of the process and conditions of the various components of life, which are the results of the effects found in the present moment. When these components meet, they bring about other factors that become present causes and will, in turn, lead to future effects.

Birth to decay-and-death is shown as an effect in the future in order to point out that when sufficient present causes still remain, future effects will follow. We simply use the words birth and decay-and-death—which refer to the arising and passing away of the elements of the cycle from consciousness to sensation—as a summary, but they must be emphasized in light of the arising of dukkha, which is linked up with and leads back to the same old cycle again. Therefore, following this principle, the portion of the cycle from consciousness to sensation and birth to decay-and-death are one and the same and can be spoken of interchangeably.

When we follow this line of thinking, according to the four phases of causes and effects, we can further divide the elements into phases and assign five to each:

1. Five past causes = ignorance, mental formations, craving, attachment, and becoming;
2. Five present effects = consciousness, mind-and-body, the six sense-bases, contact, sensation (= birth, decay-and-death);
3. Five present causes = ignorance, mental formations, craving, attachment, and becoming;
4. Five future effects = consciousness, mind-and-body, the six sense-bases, contact, sensation (= birth, decay-and-death).

When you count up the number of elements, you get twenty, and these can be called the twenty "symptoms."[81]

From the previous explanation, which divided the twelve elements of the cycle of dependent origination into three parts according to their functions, we can discern what we will now call the three rounds of existence:

1. Ignorance, craving, and attachments are unwholesome things (*kilesa*). These things drive people to embellish their actions in various ways; and this is called the cycle of unconducive tendencies (*kilesa-vaṭṭa*).
2. Mental formations and becoming (*kamma-bhava*) are kamma. The process of activities, or all kamma that embellishes life and makes it proceed in various directions, is called the cycle of kamma (*kamma-vaṭṭa*).
3. Consciousness, mind-and-body, the six sense-bases, contact, and sensation are the results or consequences (*vipāka*). These consequences constitute the condition of a person's life, which is the result of the embellishments of kamma, and they come to be factors that can contribute to further unwholesome tendencies. This is called the cycle of consequences (*vipāka-vaṭṭa*).

These three cycles or "rounds" continue their courses, interconnected with factors supporting one another. This makes the cycle of life proceed in an unending, uninterrupted fashion that can be expressed with the following diagram.

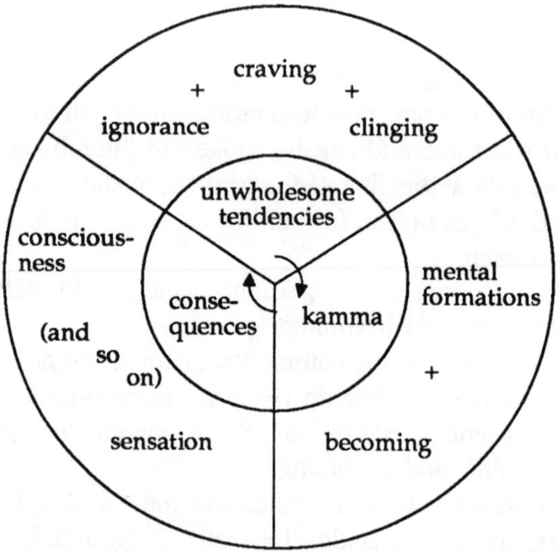

Because unwholesome tendencies (*kilesa*) are the root cause of various actions (kamma) that will embellish life as it continues in a certain direction, they have been indicated as the starting point in this circle. When these unwholesome things are indicated in this way, there are two starting points in this circle, ignorance and craving. Ignorance is the starting point in the past that brings about effects in the present, finally arriving at sensation. Craving is the starting point in the present that continues from sensation and sends its effects into the future all the way to decay-and-death. These can be called the two roots on the wheel of becoming.

The reason for putting ignorance in the first section and craving in the latter is clear from what was stated earlier: that is, ignorance is linked to sorrow, lamentation, and so on. But craving is linked with sensation when ignorance and craving are the major unwholesome factors (*kilesa*) present in certain cases.[82]

The following explanation will show the difference between the case in which ignorance is the major unwholesome factor and the case in which craving plays a major role when birth into a new existence takes place.

Ignorance is a special factor that causes beings to be born into a state of unhappiness (*duggati*), because those who succumb to ignorance do not understand the difference between good and bad, right and wrong, benefits and detriments, and the true causes of degeneration and ruin. Ignorant people act in a deluded manner that lacks principles and, therefore, they have plenty of chances to perform kamma that is way out of line.

Craving for becoming (*bhava-taṇhā*) is a special factor that makes a being achieve rebirth into a state of happiness (*sugati*). In the case that craving for becoming is the leading force, people often hope for or become enamored with a state of existence that is very good. If these hopes are projected into the next world, then these people dream of being born in heaven or the Brahma-world, for example. If these hopes are focused on the present existence, then these people dream of being rich or owning property, being a person with title or status, along with having a reputation for being a good person. When a person has these kinds of desires, he thinks of and performs various kinds of kamma that lead to that goal. For example, in order to be born as a brahmin, a person may practice meditation (*jhāna*); if he wants to go to heaven, he gives gifts (*dāna*) and maintains the moral precepts (*sīla*); if he wants to be rich, he is tireless in his search for wealth; and if he wants to be a person with status, he tries to establish himself as a good person, and so on. Such motives make people stop and think, keep people attentive, and help them to channel their efforts in a good way. People who are motivated in this way have more opportunities to do good than those dwelling in ignorance.

Putting ignorance and the craving for becoming (*bhava-taṇhā*) as the initial elements in the round of existence, still does not make them the "first cause." The Buddhist texts mention the following:

> Bhikkhus, the very first appearance of ignorance cannot be traced. "Before this, ignorance did not exist; since it appeared later, it exists." Regarding this, I say, "Because this is a factor, ignorance appears."[83]

And there is a similar passage related to the craving for becoming.[84] The following passage also shows how ignorance and the craving for becoming come together:

> Bhikkhus, this body is born complete as it is, for the fool. . .and for the wise person, for those who are imprisoned by ignorance, and for those tied up with craving. This very body and the external aspects of mind-and-body—these two things—have contact with the world through the six sense-doors. Fools. . .and sages have contact world with the world via these same sense-doors and, thereby, experience sukha or dukkha.[85]

The elements in the chain of dependent origination exist as interrelated factors and proceed according to various relationships or other factors involving various relationships, which are known as the "24 factors" according to the [Abhidhamma] "Book of Causal Relations" (*Paṭṭhāna*).

Furthermore, each element has its own details and range of meaning. For example, consciousness (*viññāṇa*) or mind (*citta*) can be further divided into categories of good or bad. A number of considerations can help determine these categories: What kinds of properties does the mind have? How many levels? What type of mind will be born into a particular existence (*bhava*)? These are important considerations. And as for form or the body (*rūpa*), there are many other considerations: How many kinds of forms are there? What properties does each one have? Given certain conditions, what kinds of forms may come into being?

Whether we are talking about the "24 factors" or the small details of each of the elements, I feel that it is not yet necessary to explain all of this here. Those who are really interested in this may refer to the Abhidhamma literature on this subject.

The Meaning of Dependent Origination in Daily Life

The explanations that we have just reviewed can be called traditional explanations, in the sense that they are explanations that are found in the Pali canon and Commentaries and have been passed down through the ages. You can see that these more popular explanations emphasize *saṁsāra*—the cycle of birth and death from existence to existence—allowing us to see the interrelatedness of life throughout the "three lives"—the past, present, and future—and yield a circular diagram that can be viewed as a system with a fixed and definite pattern.

Some people do not completely agree with this explanation and have sought an explanation that can cover all aspects of daily life. Some of these interpreters have cited parts of the Abhidhamma that explain the complete cycle of dependent origination as taking place within the space of one thought-moment (*cittakkhaṇa*). Other interpreters concerned about reifying the notion of dependent origination have been able to cite some of the same passages in the Buddhist texts referred to by those who explain dependent origination in traditional ways and make them fit their own unique purposes.[86] In addition, these interpreters are able to provide reasons and canonical evidence to substantiate and strengthen their

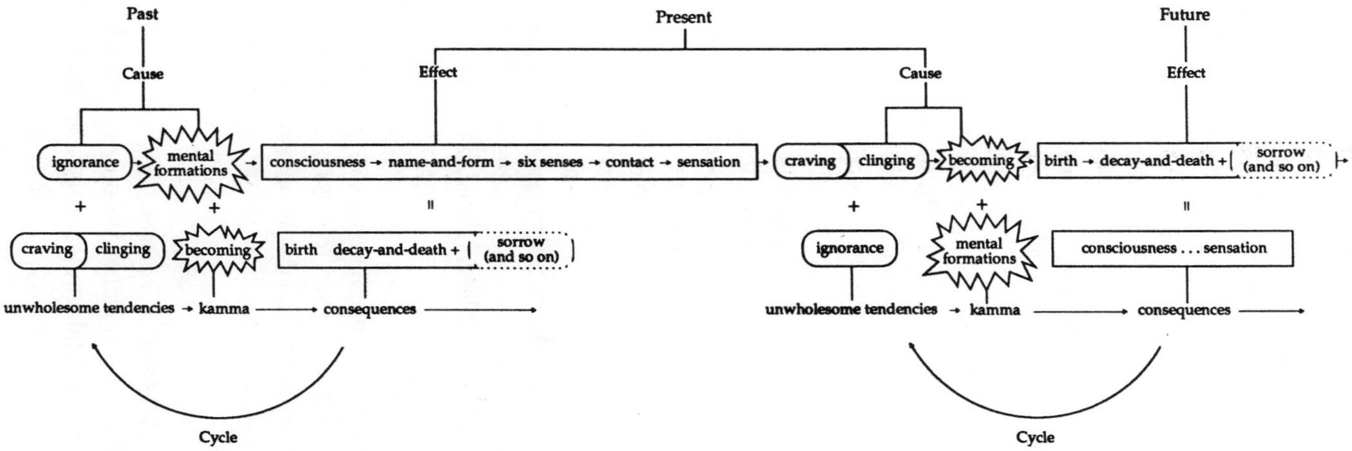

Note: We can compare this diagram with the Four Noble Truths and refer to the section of "cause" as the arising of dukkha (*samudaya*), because it brings on dukkha; and we can call the section of "effect" dukkha. Or we could refer to the section of "cause" as kammic becoming (*kamma-bhava*), because it is part of a process leading to other causes; and we could call the section of "effect" coming into being (*upapatti-bhava*), because it is part of a process leading to other results.

position. This type of argument is especially interesting, and that is why a separate section has been devoted to it here.

There are many points that can be used to support this type of explanation. For instance, maintaining that the extinguishing of dukkha and leading the life of an enlightened arahant can be realized in the present lifetime. You do not have to die first in order to escape rebirth; you do not have to suffer decay-and-death, and eliminate sorrow, lamentation, suffering, grief and distress in a future life. Sorrow, lamentation, and so on can be done away with in the present life. The circle of dependent origination—in terms of the arising of dukkha or the extinguishing of dukkha, for that matter—is completely related to this very life that we are presently living. You do not have to look to a past life or wait and see what a future life may bring. In addition, when you clearly understand this potential in your present life, you can also see it in your past and in your future, as well.

We may refer to the following statement by Lord Buddha:

> Truly, Udāyī, anyone who recalls aggregates (*khandha*) that existed before in numerous and various forms. . .should, therefore, ask me about problems in the past (past lives),[87] or I should ask that person about his problems in the past. That person will thereby assist me in solving past problems, or I can assist that person with his past problems. Anyone who sees all creatures, including those who have died and those who are born with divine eyes (*dibbacakkhu*) [eyes that can see through time]. . .that person should inquire about problems related to the future (the next life),[88] or I should ask that person about problems related to the future. That person will thereby assist me in solving future problems, or I can assist that person in solving his future problems.
>
> So, Udāyī, refrain from discussing the past and the future. I present the Dhamma in this way: when this thing is present, then this thing also exists; when this thing is no longer present, then this thing ceases to exist; because this is extinguished, then this also is extinguished.[89]

> A village headman named Bhagandha seated himself in the proper place and said to the Lord Buddha, "I would like to ask the Accomplished One to please explain the arising and passing away of dukkha."

The Lord Buddha said: "Headman, if I explain the arising and passing away of dukkha to you by referring to the past saying, 'In the past, such as such was like this,' you may still have uncertainty. If I explain the arising and passing away of dukkha by referring to the future saying, 'In the future, things will be like this,' you may still have uncertainties about this. Headman, I am sitting right here, so I will explain the arising and the passing away of dukkha to you, the one who is sitting here right now."[90]

Truly, Sivaka, different kinds of sensations (*vedanā*) arise; bile may be the cause. . . phlegm or mucus may be the cause. . . gas or air (in the body) may be the cause. . . the convergence of various factors. . . these feelings may be due to a change in the weather. . . they can come from not paying adequate attention to yourself. . . you may be the victim of violence. . . or some feelings may be the result of your actions (kamma). The point is that we can know for ourselves the feelings that arise due to (the above possible) causes—this is something widely accepted as the truth.

As for this, any recluses and brahmins who assert or believe that, "People have sensations—be they sukha or dukkha—due to past kamma,"[91] go beyond the things that we can know for ourselves; they go beyond the things that worldly people can determine to be the truth. I can say, therefore, that this is the fault of those recluses and brahmins.[92]

Bhikkhus, when people set their minds on a task, become absorbed or engrossed in something, that thing becomes an object of the mind in order to make the impression (*viññāṇa*) of it last. When this mind-object exists, consciousness has a dwelling place. When this consciousness is established and progresses, the process of becoming (*bhava*) begins anew. When the process of becoming has worked itself into a new existence, birth, decay-and-death, sorrow, lamentation, suffering, grief, and distress will, therefore, follow. The arising of the whole heap of dukkha comes into being in this way.[93]

The meaning of dependent origination according to this trend—even if it requires some special understanding—does not disregard the older explanation according to the tradition. Therefore, before we proceed with explanation of dependent origination and its application in daily life, we should review the explanation of dependent origination according to the tradition.

The Simple Meaning

1. **Ignorance or lack of knowledge** (*avijjā*) = not knowing, not seeing according to the truth, not understanding nor keeping pace with conditions, getting tied up with conventional assumptions, not understanding life and the world according to the truth, not knowing various hidden thoughts and beliefs, a state lacking wisdom, ignorant of causal factors, not applying wisdom or having wisdom fail you at the moment.
2. **Mental formations, predispositions, or volitional activities** (*saṅkhāra*) = embellished thought, intentions, aims, decisions, and showing intentions through action; a thought process that proceeds according to inclination, habit, and various properties of the mind that have been stored up.
3. **Consciousness** (*viññāṇa*) = Perceiving various mind-objects, that is, seeing, hearing, smelling, tasting, and contacting according to the objects in the mind, and this includes knowing the origin of various states of mind.
4. **Mind-and-body or the animated organism** (*nāma-rūpa*) = the perception of physical (*rūpa-*) and psychological factors (*nāma-dhamma*), the condition of all the physical and mental factors existing in an interconnected state and performing all their functions in response to the flow of consciousness (*viññāṇa*), and the various parts of the body and mind (Thai, *chit-chai*) that progress or change depending on a person's state of mind.
5. **The six sense-bases** (*saḷāyatana*) = the state of the senses that are related to the performance of duties and are related to the circumstances at hand.
6. **Contact** (*phassa*) = linking knowledge with the external world, perceiving mind-objects or various experiences.
7. **Sensation** (*vedanā*) = feeling pleasure and comfort, having wishes fulfilled, or experiencing dukkha and discomfort or equanimity (that is, neither-sukha-nor-dukkha).
8. **Craving** (*taṇhā*) = an ambitious, over-eager desire to find things to fufill a need for pleasurable sensations (*sukha-vedanā*), avoiding things that cause unpleasant sensations (*dukkha-vedanā*); it is

being divided by a desire to get, to have, to exist in a continuous state and wanting to avoid, to annihilate, and destroy.

9. **Attachment, clinging** (*upādāna*) = clinging to feelings of like and dislike, manipulating various things and conditions in order to sustain certain feelings, inflating the value and importance of various conditions and things in a way that responds to or increases craving.
10. **Process of becoming** (*bhava*) = the whole behavioral process that reveals itself in response to craving and clinging (*kamma-bhava*, the active process) and the conditions of life that exist for a "self" or for a "self" to occupy (*upapatti-bhava*, the passive process) depending on attachments and the behavior associated with them.
11. **Birth** (*jāti*) = coming to the realization that you exist or do not exist in a certain state, have or do not have certain things, are or are not a certain way.
12. **Decay-and-death** (*jarā-maraṇa*) = being conscious of a lack of or a separation from the above life-state; feeling that you are threatened by final disintegration or separation from that life-state, which includes having certain things and being a certain way. This brings about sorrow, lamentation, suffering, grief, and distress linked with feelings of despair, loss, irritation, frustration, depression, sadness, disappointment, restlessness, and various other miserable feelings.

Examples Showing Basic Relationships between the Elements of Dependent Origination[94]

1. Ignorance (*avijjā*) → mental formations (*saṅkhāra*):[95] Because we do not know the truth and do not have clear understanding, thoughts embellish other thoughts painting various pictures. This is like a person who, on a dark night, sees light reflected in the eyes of an animal; and because this person already believes in ghosts and spirits, he takes this reflection to be a ghost or spirit, experiences fear, and may run away in flight. Or it is like the person who is asked to guess what is hidden in another's closed fist and looks for some evidence on which to base his guess or claim. Or it is like smiling at a person and when he does not happen to return your gesture you are taken aback without investigating the matter any further. You do not consider that that person may

not have seen your smile. He may have been nearsighted, or he is holding onto some other feeling and may have been distracted by his own anger, hurt, or confusion. Or you see someone else smile and you wonder what he is smiling at: you have a "knot" in your mind and conjure up a scenario in which he is looking down at you, and so you think of taking revenge. And there are still other people who believe that the gods will be happy and will supernaturally create something for them if they flatter them and implore them with ritual offerings made to heaven.

2. Mental formations (*saṅkhāra*) → consciousness (*viññāṇa*): When you have the intention or goal of getting involved with something, the consciousness that senses, for example, comes into being. But if you do not intend, do not get involved, even though you are in a position to know, consciousness does not arise. It is like being focused and absorbed in work, such as being absorbed in reading, with the mind taking in only the reading matter. If there is a noise nearby, it is heard, but it does not register. If a mosquito bites, it goes unnoticed. You may be searching for something and you do not see the people or other things that pass before the scope of your perception. You may look at the same thing at a different time with different intentions and perceive the object according to those intentions. For example, you might look at an open plot of land as a child seeking a playground and get one perception and sense of space; or you may see this land another time with the thought of building a house there and come to an entirely different conclusion; or you may view it with the eyes of a farmer or manufacturer and reach yet another conclusion. Different people can look at the same thing and different thoughts will arise. When you think about something that is very good, your mind experiences a good feeling and receives meaning in terms of that feeling. The opposite, of course, is also true. And naturally, these thoughts and feelings are interconnected. Say, for example, that in a grouping of objects existing within a person's range of perception, there is a knife and some flowers. The person who likes flowers will tend to notice them first; this person will perceive only flowers and this perception of "only-flowers" continues repeatedly to the point of not seeing the other objects placed nearby. As this interest in flowers continues, the perception of the flowers also quickens and the perception of other things

decreases. But if a person in search of a weapon happened upon this scene, his mind would only perceive the knife and maintain it as the prominent mind-object. Depending on a person's thoughts and intentions, the knife could be viewed as a weapon, a useful kitchen utensil, or simply as a piece of metal, perhaps depending on whether that person is a thief, a cook, or a metal dealer.

3. Consciousness (*viññāṇa*) → mind-and-body (*nāma-rūpa*): Consciousness and mind-and-body depend on one another like, as disciple Sāriputta put it, "two bundles of straw that can stand because they lean against one another, so mind-and-body exists allowing consciousness to come into being. Because consciousness exists, there is mind-and-body. . . . If one of those two bundles of straw is, therefore, pulled away, the other will fall. If mind-and-body is extinguished, consciousness will also be extinguished; if consciousness is extinguished, then mind-and-body will also be extinguished. . . ."[96] In this sense, when consciousness arises, mind-and-body is able to come into existence, in fact must come into being. In the event that mental formations (*saṅkhāra*) are the cause of the arising of consciousness, this is also the cause of the arising of mind-and-body. Here, we may divide the conditions of consciousness as a cause of mind-and-body in the following way:

a) When I said that the mind receives information from certain mental stimuli, such as seeing something or hearing a sound, actually this is perceived via mind-and-body (here meaning the *rūpa-khandha, vedanā-khandha, saññā-khandha,* and *saṅkhāra-khandha*). Whatever a person has is what that person perceives at a given moment, or it is the mind-and-body that is perceived by consciousness at that time. For example, the rose that exists is only the rose that is presently perceived by the eyes or the mind at that moment. And this "rose-ness" is inextricably tied to and does not exist outside of its mental "concept"; and this concept is tied to sensation (*vedanā*), perception (*saññā*), and mental formations (*saṅkhāra*) that come into play at that moment. So, in this sense, when consciousness is present, mind-and-body also comes with it and exists in an interdependent way.

b) The mind-and-body that is related to consciousness has the quality of being linked with that consciousness as well, especially with the psychological factors that comprise the properties of the mind.

When thought embellishes itself (creating mental formations or *saṅkhāra*) in an excellent way, then this brings about a consciousness that perceives excellent mind-objects and flows in the direction of excellence. With this comes a clear and bright mind along with excellent manners and behavior. When a person thinks in a bad way, then negative mind-objects tend to be perceived; the mind is in a cloudy and gloomy condition, and behavior also reflects these bad thoughts. The various psychological and physical elements act in accordance with these mental formations (*saṅkhāra*) and state of mind (*viññāṇa*); when a person feels love and friendliness (*saṅkhāra*) and perceives excellent mind-objects (*viññāṇa*), the mind is fresh and joyful (*nāma*), the complexion is rosy and bright—which also includes other aspects of physical well-being (*rūpa*)—and that person is ready to act in an excellent manner. As soon as a person becomes angry or annoyed, these bad feelings are perceived and the mind becomes gloomy and upset; that person's features appear sour and serious and he is ready to act according to these same tendencies. As with the athlete in the field, as soon as the competition begins, his various thoughts and goals will throw him right into the game. Various perceptions begin and end within the context of the sport at an increasing or decreasing rate according to the strength of the athlete's goals and the various drives and interests that send him into the game. All related parts of the mind and body are in state of readiness to do their duty to perform a continuous set of actions. A person's course of action at this point constitutes an important part of the kammic process that will bear kammic fruit in the cycle of rebirth that spins within a small sphere (ignorance [*avijjā*]: unwholesome tendencies [*kilesa*] → mental formations [*saṅkhāra*]: kamma → consciousness [*viññāṇa*] and mind-and-body [*nāma-rūpa*]: consequences [*vipāka*]) and is incessantly starting over. This process is an integral step in building character, habits, knowledge, experience, and personality.

4. Mind-and-body (*nāma-rūpa*) → sense-bases (*saḷāyatana*): In order for mind-and-body to continue to carry out its functions, it must depend on knowledge of the external world or extracting knowledge that has been previously stored away. It can then use this knowledge as a bridge to decision-making, for deciding how or in what direction it will proceed in the future. The aspects of mind-

and-body that have a role to play are put on alert, or we can say that there is a line of communication between them and the various mind-objects and sensations. That is, all senses that come into play in a particular situation are in a state of readiness to carry out their duties according to the ordered procession of effects that have led up to this event. Take the case of the soccer player on the field, the important senses that come into play are the eye-sense and ear-sense; these will remain on alert to receive sensations that are related to the sport and the special type of coordination required for the game. At the same time, the senses that do not come into play in achieving the aim of soccer are not placed on alert. To put this very simply, some senses relax their duties; such as, the sense of smell and the sense of taste may hardly arise at all when the athlete is completely absorbed in the action of the game.

5. Sense-bases (*saḷāyatana*) → contact (*phassa*): When the six senses carry out their functions, sensations take place through the meeting of three constituents: internal senses (via any of the following: eye, ear, nose, tongue, body, or mind), external sense objects ([*ārammaṇa*] via any of the following: forms, sounds, smells, tastes, tangible objects, or mind-objects), and consciousness ([*viññāṇa*] via any of the following: eyes, ears, nose, tongue, body, or mind). Sensations occur through this link with the senses.
6. Contact (*phassa*) → sensation (*vedanā*): When contact or sensation occurs, a sensation of sukha or dukkha occurs. One of three things arises: comfort and absorption as sukha (*sukha-vedanā*); discomfort and pain as dukkha (*dukkha-vedanā*); or else equanimity or neither-sukha-nor-dukkha (*upekkhā* or *adukkhamasukha-vedanā*).

   The cycle of dependent origination from the third to the seventh element—that is, from consciousness to sensation—constitutes the part of the process relating to consequences (*vipāka*) or the fruits of kamma, and this is especially true for the fifth, sixth, and seventh elements, which are neither meritorious nor demeritorious, neither good nor bad in and of themselves, but can be the future cause of good or bad results.
7. Sensation (*vedanā*) → craving (*taṇhā*): When you receive pleasurable sensations, you are satisfied, happy, attracted to these sensations, and desirous of more and more happiness. When you

receive unpleasant sensations, you are upset, want them to go away, to destroy them; you want to transcend the unpleasant and search and struggle to find something else that will give you pleasurable sensations. When you feel at peace (*upekkhā-vedanā*), you may experience a neutral feeling of equanimity that invites the possibility of feeling absorbed, of becoming engrossed in this sensation in a deluded way; this sensation is a mild kind of pleasurable sensation that can be addicting and become a seed that grows into a desire for further pleasurable sensations.

This craving (*taṇhā*) can be clearly divided into three types:

a) Craving for sense-pleasure (*kāma-taṇhā*): Desiring things to satisfy the needs of the five senses.
b) Craving for self-existence (*bhava-taṇhā*): Wanting to have various things by relating yourself with a condition of life or wanting a condition of life that can provide everything you wish. In a deeper sense, this involves a desire for a self that can continue as it is or exist in a self-determined manner.
c) Craving for non-existence or self-annihilation (*vibhava-taṇhā*): Wanting yourself to pass away, disappear, or separate from the things or conditions of life that are undesirable. This kind of craving manifests itself in some of its more obvious forms as boredom, loneliness, or even being bored with yourself, fed up with yourself, or taking pity on yourself.[97]

Craving, therefore, has many faces and takes many forms. It may be wanting your life to evolve in a certain way, such as wanting to be rich, have status, or be a god so that you may have everything you desire, or wanting to escape from undesirable conditions of boredom, hopelessness, or suicidal tendencies. Craving shows itself externally when you are upset and do not get what you want. This is sufficient reason for the arising of anger (*paṭigha*), ill-will (*dosa*), violent emotions, and thoughts about hurting other people and other things.

8. Craving (*taṇhā*) → attachment (*upādāna*): As soon as you want something, you fiercely cling to that idea and become tied up with it. As desire increases, so does the force of attachment. When you receive unpleasant sensations, you try to avoid them while harboring strong feelings of dislike towards the cause of these

feelings. Along with the increasing rate of attachment to the things you are struggling to obtain comes attachment to the things that respond to various needs and the conditions of life that will continue to provide the objects of your desire: such as, attachment to a self that can become this or that, attachment to views, conclusions, theories, and rules that respond to craving, including attachment to plans and strategies for achieving personal goals.

9. Attachment (*upādāna*) → becoming (*bhava*): Attachment becomes involved in various conditions of life. Attachment shows a relationship between two things. People want to link themselves to a condition of life that will continue to satisfy wishes and desires. At the same time, when people feel they have the life they want, there are undesirable things that will inevitably accompany it. The condition of life to which people cling is called *upapatti-bhava*.

   Once there is attachment to a particular condition of life, people aim to perpetuate it. They do various things—brainstorming, plotting, and searching—to find ways to proceed according to their aims. But all of those thoughts and actions are under a certain pressure to flow in a particular direction, in a way determined by attachment. That is, they flow according to the strength of people's beliefs, views, understandings, theories, methods, and feelings. This clinging reveals itself in the behavior and actions that are associated with a particular attachment. Let me offer a simple example of this: Let us say that a person wants to be born as a god, so he clings to his faith in the teachings, customs, rituals, or a model of behavior that he believes will allow him to attain this birth. That person thinks, plans, and performs various actions according to that belief, to the extent that if his attachment is strong enough, it will alter his behavior. For example, if a person desires status, he will cling to the values that bring him status. While being attached to a certain notion of status, that person will cling to a model of behavior that is connected to those values. His intentions and activities are aimed in a certain direction based on the model to which he is attached. The behavior that he exhibits will have characteristics related to this attachment.

   On the other hand, that person may desire others' valuables and is attached to the idea of being the owner of those things; he clings to habits or strategies that will bring him those things, unaware of the offences and shortcomings of his misguided methods. This person, therefore, thinks, plots, and acts according to habit or the ways to which he has become accustomed. He becomes thieving and dishonest. He is just another clinging owner, which eventually makes him a thief. Accordingly, in order to obtain their wishes, people perform either demeritorious and bad actions or meritorious and good actions based on the strength of their (mistaken or correct) beliefs and attachments. The quality and motivating force of behavior proceeds in a certain direction depending on the strength of attachment. This is the kammic process, the active process of becoming (*kamma-bhava*). The conditions of life that follow this kamma, such as actually becoming a god, a person with status, or an owner and a thief, are known as rebirths (*upapatti-bhava*). This may be referred to as becoming (into a condition of life, *bhava*) in accordance with desire or even finding yourself in an undesired or unanticipated form or condition.

This portion of dependent origination is an important step in creating kamma and receiving the fruits of kamma. It is also crucial to creating habits, dispositions, and character.

10. Becoming (*bhava*) → birth (*jāti*): Based on the foregoing, a self develops along with the realization of an "I" that is existing in way that may or may not accord with your desires. In Buddhist terms, the self comes into being (*bhava*), with an "I" as its owner, an "I" who is a thief, an "I" who has no status, an "I" who is a loser, and so on. In daily life, birth, or the birth of a self, can be clearly seen in cases of conflict, such as arguments, especially in arguments that become irrational. If a person uses prejudice (*kilesa*) and not wisdom, a self clearly arises in one form or another: "I" am the master; "I" am the one with status (along with the notion of the "other" who is the underling, at a lower level). This is the view of "I." And when this "I" comes into conflict with the world, its definition can decrease or even disappear. And the self becomes more apparent when threatened by decay-and-death.
11. Birth (*jāti*) → decay-and-death (*jarā-maraṇa*): Once a self has been defined, there is also an aspect of the self that does not exist according to that definition. This aspect of the self lacks something and is not in accord with a person's self-definition. This created self is threatened by the feeling of a lack or a

separation from self-definition. This self then encounters clashes, obstacles, and conflicts that keep it from reaching its goal; in the process, a person's self-definition may decrease to the point where it lacks enough definition for it to achieve its goal. Once a notion of a self has already arisen, there is the desire to have it continue on according to certain wishes; but once this self arises, it can also disintegrate. And even if this self does not completely disappear, it will be threatened by deficiencies and losses that occur. This fear of loss results in tying the self ever tighter to a certain condition of life. Fear of self-loss coexists with a fear of death; this is something that is deeply and subtly hidden in the mind at all times and gradually affects the general behavior of human beings, making them anxious and causing them to madly grasp at the conditions they feel they need. Fear of loss serves to make people upset and disappointed when they experience unpleasant sensations (*dukkha-vedanā*), and it causes them to frantically seek and consume pleasant sensations (*sukha-vedanā*).

In this sense, when the self arises in an unwanted condition or arises in a desirable condition that fades away or is threatened by loss or separation, various types of dukkha occur, such as sorrow, lamentation, suffering, grief, and distress. In this state of dukkha, there tends to be a lack of knowledge or understanding of various things according to the way they are. People resist this condition, lack clarity, become misguided and blind, and suffer the symptoms of ignorance. This brings about an ignorant struggle for a way out of a continuing cycle.

To put it simply, in daily life, when there is competition and a winner emerges, this is not always determined by common goals and social conventions (*sammuti*). There are also "winners" who cling to some special meaning or benefits for themselves (*bhava*). In some instances, especially in the case of arrogant people or when an upset occurs, the feeling arises that, "I am a winner" = I am a born winner (*jāti*). But the complete meaning of "winner" here must include status, acclaim, benefits, popularity, and prestige, including the acceptance of others. So the birth of "I" as a winner occurs along with the need for acceptance and acclaim, making someone else lose out, being able to do something that is highly desirable. At the same time the "I" as winner (in all its senses) is born, a feeling of fulfillment or unfulfillment arises. When a feeling of fulfillment occurs, the strong feeling of needing to link yourself to the idea of being a winner also follows. This is due to a fear of losing this status. There is a fear that the acceptance, popularity, and acclaim that you have received will not remain, will decrease, or may be completely lost. As soon as you meet another person who does not afford you the consideration and status you desire or are used to receiving, you tend to be disturbed, gloomy, and left with a feeling of despair, because the self and its self-defined status of "winner" is being pressured by the possibility of a loss of status. In other words, it is threatened with disintegration (*jarā*) and loss (*maraṇa*) of being the winner and all of the valuable benefits that go along with the status to which you have become attached (*bhava*). When the course of existence proceeds in this manner, all the feelings of anxiety, worry, and disappointment that take place, which have not been eliminated by the practice of mindfulness meditation (*sati*) or clear insight (*paññā*), will stack up as innate bad habits (Thai, *sandan*). These, in turn, will have an effect on your character and behavior. According to the wheel of dependent origination, this can be called the consumption of sensations that engross or bind.

Let me cite a simple point for consideration. When a self exists (that is, according to a person's feelings), it tends to take up space. Once it has taken its place, it tends to occupy a designated area or a defined and limited space. Once there is limitation, there is separation. Once this separation has occurred, there is a division of what is and is not yours. When the self of an "I" has arisen, it begins to extend itself, flowing out and swelling with the desire to have, to do, and to show itself to others. But a self and its desires are not able to expand freely, without limitation; they are subject to the resistance and forces of other people. If you have the idea of presenting yourself to others as a good person, or you completely let yourself go revealing yourself as a show-off, there will be clashes with the outside world. Even if you allow yourself to show off completely, this is difficult to sustain and will eventually wear down your internal strength, resulting in a desire for more energy and a further loss of vitality as time goes by. This increases the chances of encountering greater conflict, which constantly dissipates any sense of acting naturally, of "being yourself" (Thai, *pen tua khong tua eng*). Complete fulfillment of desire does not exist. Conflict, clashes, and pressure occur every time this premise is tested.

At any rate, this example attempts to make the relationships between the elements of the cycle of dependent origination easier to understand. The explanations of some parts remain a bit superficial and are not clear nor deep enough, especially the more difficult concepts such as ignorance (*avijjā*) as the cause of mental formations (*saṅkhāra*) and the sorrow and lamentation that start the cycle all over again. The examples used in the previous section on ignorance are things that may not commonly occur. Some people who read this may conclude that people are able to carry on with their daily lives without having ignorance arise at all; or they may conclude that dependent origination is not really a dhammic principle that explains the truth about life. Understand, therefore, that the deeper meanings of some of the more difficult concepts relating to this principle still require more detailed explanation.

The Deeper Meaning of Some Dhammic Concepts

Ordinarily, when people encounter something or are confronted with a certain situation, they interpret information, make decisions, determine meanings and establish goals—all of which are manifested in terms of behavior and action—according to the tendencies and pressures that arise. Certain pressures may lead people to do the following:

1. Take an interest in responding to the needs of the five senses (*kāma*);
2. Take an interest in having a constant self, determining the nature of that self, and maintaining that self in a constant condition forever (*bhava*);
3. Cling to habits, beliefs, conclusions, theories, or any train of thought based on certain teachings and habits (*diṭṭhi*);
4. Foster delusions or misunderstandings that prohibit you from seeing the arising and passing away of causes and effects, as well the meanings, values, properties, relationships of various things or circumstances according to their own natural states; mistakenly thinking that there is a self that enters into action and is subject to the actions of various things; not seeing all relationships as a process of causes and effects. Put very briefly, this amounts to

not seeing things as they are and then taking them for what you think they are or make them out to be (*avijjā*).

We can see, especially with points 3 and 4, that they are interrelated, interdependent conditions. When people are not attentive and lack concentration, they tend to do things according to habit, established beliefs and concepts, and previous training.

Furthermore, points 3 and 4 have a very broad meaning that even covers character and disposition (Thai, *nisai*), habits, outlook, plans, and various behaviors that may be the result of education and training, a social system, and the influence of culture and tradition, for example. These things show the influential relationship between points 1 and 2. This relationship is responsible for establishing and controlling human feeling, determining likes and dislikes, needs, behavior patterns and the direction of responses to needs. These responses become deeply imbedded in people, gradually directing their behavior without them being aware of it. According to ordinary understanding, people feel that they are acting according to their own needs; really, they are totally mistaken. If we clearly trace this process, we might ask the following: What do they feel they really need? Why do they need these things? Why do they do the things that they do? Why do they behave the way that they behave? If we examine these questions, we can see that there is nothing that is theirs at all. Their pattern of behavior has been received, handed down to them through their education and training, their culture, religious beliefs, and the preferences of their society. People merely choose and act within the confines and trends of these acquired ideas. When people do something strange or different, it is only strange in the context of these acquired ideas. The "self" that people cling to is nothing other than the things mentioned in points 1 through 4. These points constitute a force beyond people's control, as well; so there is no way at all that these points could comprise a self.

In dhammic terms, the above points are called *āsava* (inflowing impulses, influxes, biases, or intoxicants); number 1 is called *kāmāsava* (sense-gratification); number 2 is called *bhavāsava* (existence, self-centered pursuits); number 3 is called *diṭṭhāsava* (views, opinions); number 4 is called *avijjāsava* (ignorance). Sometimes number 3 is cut out entirely, leaving only three types of *āsava*.[98]

It can be seen, therefore, that these various *āsava* are the source of human behavior, they are the factors responsible for people becoming misguided and taking other things to be the self. It is ignorance (*avijjā*) at its most fundamental level that forces people to conjure up and embellish thoughts, exhibit various behaviors and actions, and not know themselves for what they are—all of which develops according to the power of ignorance. Once again, ignorance is the first step in the cycle, that is, whenever *āsava* occur, ignorance arises; and when ignorance arises, it is the cause of mental formations (*saṅkhāra*). We can express this condition of misguided behavior by saying, "People are not themselves," because their behavior is being controlled by mental formations and predispositions, an utterly thoughtless driving force.

Let me summarize in order to complete this section with clarity. This state of ignorance amounts to not seeing the Three Characteristics of Existence, especially the aspect of no-self (*anattā*). According to the cycle of dependent origination, ignorance means not realizing the condition we take to be a being, a person, a self, the "I," or the "other" is only a flowing stream of various detailed aspects of corporeality (*rūpa-dhamma*) and mentality (*nāma-dhamma*)—in other words, body and mind. The aspects of this stream are interrelated and interdependent; they are part of a continuous chain of causes and effects and conditions of birth and disintegration, which, in turn, put this process in a constant state of flux. To put this even more succinctly, people are the final result of all feelings, thoughts, wishes, habits, inclinations, opinions, knowledge, values, and beliefs (ranging from those at a basic level of mistaken beliefs that lack reason to those of a more subtle level that are based on reason). When people are not aware of what they have inherited from their culture, education, and training, and they do not understand various internal reactions they have in response to the constant procession of occurrences around them, then they may take these things to be the self. When these phenomena are held to be the self, they become delusions, and people fall under the power of their spell thinking that the self is in charge of many things and that it is acting out its own needs.

What I have said so far can be considered a deeper explanation of what could be put under the heading of "ignorance as the cause of mental formations or predispositions (*saṅkhāra*)." As for the elements of dependent origination that follow, which go up to and include sensation (*vedanā*), they are not very difficult to understand, as you can see from the preceding explanations. I will, therefore, skip over them in order to move on to the important section on craving (*taṇhā*) as the cause of attachment (*upādāna*). This is a section that deals with unwholesome tendencies (*kilesa*).

The three kinds of craving already mentioned are the same three symptoms that are common in the daily lives of all people, but we can see from our analysis of the mind at a deeper level that humans do not know, do not understand, or are unfamiliar with viewing all things as a process of relationships between various naturally occurring causal factors.[99] People are, therefore, living obscured lives, under the impression that they have a self that takes a certain form. And these people maintain a fundamental desire for existence that hopes to extend the life of this self.[100] But the wish to determine a certain course of existence relates to desire. It is the desire to exist in order to partake of or consume the things that yield pleasurable feelings and continue to respond to needs. It can be said, therefore, that people desire to exist out of want, and when they want, desire for existence becomes even stronger.

When desire for existence is strong, then case number 1 may occur. In other words, people do not attain the things they desire fast enough and so a reaction takes place: existence (*bhava*) or life at that time is unattractive, unpleasant, unbearable, and there is a wish for it to pass away. This feeling sticks with a person, but at the same moment, desire shows itself again asking, "If I pass away, then how can I continue to partake of all these pleasurable sensations?" Desire and want, therefore, continue to follow. In case number 2, a person does not get what he wants. In case number 3, he does not completely get what he wants or the situation does not match his desires. In case number 4, he gets what he wants and then wants this situation to continue. The process goes on in the same direction, but the most fundamental aspect, which covers all cases, is that there is increasing desire.

As soon as people get what they want, they begin searching for a way to make this happiness constant. They brush away or forsake the present moment every time. Each present moment is a condition of life that these people cannot bear; they want it to go away or they wish to pass beyond it in their search for a condition that will respond to their increasing desires. Craving, desire for existence, and desire for extinction, continually whirl around in the cycle of daily human life; but this is a subtle and detailed phenomenon occurring in each thought-moment in such a way that most people are not aware that from moment to moment their lives are engaged in a constant struggle to pass beyond the conditions of the previous moment in a search for things that respond to the needs of the new conditions of life that are perpetually arising.

If we go into this further, we can see that these kinds of craving come from ignorance itself. That means that because people do not know things for what they are—as a process of interrelated causal factors—they tend to see all things as having a self, as separate entities, as certain, as eternal,[101] or they tend to view all things as coming to complete extinction or annihilation.[102] Because all people have these mistaken ideas subtly embedded in their minds, the three types of craving exist. That is, because people harbor the misunderstanding that all things have a separate, eternal self, a desire for life arises, or clinging to existence (*bhava-taṇhā*) comes into being. And, in another way, believing that things are destined to eventual annihilation or extinction can bring about a desire for non-existence (*vibhava-taṇhā*). Both of these incorrect views open opportunities for the arising of craving. If you already undertand that life flows along like a current, as a process of interrelated causal factors, then there can be no self that is eternal or separate and there is no separate self that can be annihilated either—and craving, therefore, cannot stir you up. And sensual craving (*kāma-taṇhā*) can also be related to these two incorrect views; fearing that the self or pleasurable sensations (*sukha-vedanā*) will disappear, a struggle is mounted to sustain them.

In a very fundamental way, struggling and seeking to respond to various needs is symptomatic of craving. This also includes being bored with what you have or who you are, along with experiencing despair and depression, which are conditions that become unbearable because there is nothing present that responds to growing needs. What becomes abundantly clear is that craving does not allow human beings to be at peace. If they separate themselves from the things that respond to the needs of the five senses, they are left with boredom or unbearable loneliness. They feel as if they must get out and move about seeking things that respond to the constant flow of new needs in order to escape their boredom. If people do not get what they want at any particular time, they are disappointed, depressed, bored with themselves, or detest themselves; therefore, sukha and dukkha arise only according to external factors. When people have free time, they may rekindle feelings of ill-will and become a danger to human beings—both personally and socially. Boredom, sadness, loneliness, and dissatisfaction all increase even though needs are being increasingly met and the search for sensual fulfillment and the need for contact with various things becomes more crass and heated. Whether this may manifest itself as becoming addicted to something or teenagers using their free time to get into trouble, if we go deeply into the mind, we can see that the essential reason for these social problems is that people find life unbearable, boring, and want to escape from the existence into which they were born.

Craving, however, can also be put to use in a good way. In a positive sense, craving can be channeled towards seeking educational training, suggestions, or religious teachings, and maintaining correct beliefs and holding to various worthy ideals. In other words, this could entail performing good acts in order to become a good person, being tireless and dedicated in order to reap future benefits, doing beneficial things to attain status or to be born in heaven, or putting free time to good use—all of which can be accomplished by using craving to get rid of craving.

There are four kinds of unwholesome tendencies (*kilesa*) related to attachments (*upādāna*) that are the result of craving:

1. **Clinging to sensuality** (*kāmupādāna*):[103] Whenever people struggle to gain something, they become attached to the object of that desire. When it is attained, there is more attachment and increasing desire along with a fear of being cut off or separated from the object of attention. Even if people are disappointed or deprived, they become more determined due to their dependence. People's attachments increase because the things that respond to their needs do not make them feel "full" or do not result in the conditions they seek, and so these people may try to become full by doing any number of things. And because things do not belong to them, they must attach themselves to a feeling of ownership, persuading themselves that they are the owners of the things around them, and so these people's thoughts become further attached to the things that respond to their desires. In this situation, it is difficult for people to be free, clear, and neutral.
2. **Clinging to views** (*diṭṭhupādāna*): Requiring things to proceed or not to proceed in a certain way results in biases and attachments to views, theories or philosophical principles, and doctrines or teachings that accord with a particular need. When people are attached to certain opinions or thoughts, they take them to be the self. Whenever theories or opinions appear that conflict with an established set of beliefs, they are felt to be a threat to the self, as constituting a pressure or something destructive to the self, which will cause it to disintegrate, lack something, or disappear. People must fight, therefore, to maintain these views—often for the honor of the self, for example. This brings about a conflict that reveals itself externally: people become narrow and build

obstacles that block the development of their own wisdom; and this makes people unable to properly apply and share knowledge.[104]

3. **Clinging to mere rules and rituals** (*sīlabbatupādāna*): This category involves wanting to get, wanting to exist. It involves fearing the loss of a self due to a misunderstanding about the actual process of natural causal factors. Attachment to certain views makes behavior and actions foolishly proceed according to things believed to be magically potent, sacred, or personally fulfilling. This also includes not understanding relationships according to cause and effect, wanting the self to exist and be permanent, and clinging to a notion of selfhood. This clinging becomes apparent externally or socially in the form of various attachments, established forms of behavior and associated actions, rules of order, traditions, customs, and rituals. This also includes various established institutions that make certain demands on people without understanding the meaning of values, goals, and relationships to other things according to cause and effect. In the end, people then continue to construct more ideas and found new institutions that cut them off from reaping the benefits of their relationships with other people.

   This "clinging to mere rule and ritual" has been explained by Buddhadasa Bhikkhu in a way that will make its meaning clearer:

> Those who act according to a moral rule (*sīla*) or a point of the Dhamma without knowing its aim, without reason, are merely assuming it to be sacred (Thai, *saksit*); and when these people act according to what they believe to be sacred, they feel that this will bring good results. These people, therefore, accept moral rules or follow the Dhamma by merely following a model or form—only by the letter, by custom, and examples that have been handed down. These people do not get at the true reasons for practice, because they depend on certain overt forms of behavior and have become accustomed to strictly adhering to determined codes. This kind of attachment is difficult to correct. . . . And the second kind of attachment above, clinging to views (*diṭṭhi*) or incorrect thoughts and opinions, amounts to clinging to the superficial aspects of practice or external, overt actions.[105]

4. **Clinging to belief in a self** (*attavādupādāna*): Believing that you possess a constant self or ego is a fundamental error. There are many factors that can reinforce this feeling, such as certain aspects of conventional speech that may encourage people, at least those who cling to convention, to see things as divided, separated, and unchanging selves. But this feeling leads to attachment when craving comes into play; that is, when people want something, they cling to a self that is the recipient and consumer of desire. There is believed to be a self that is the owner of these goods. When there is a desire for existence, there is also a desire for the existence of a certain kind of self. When there is desire for non-existence, there is attachment to a self that you would like to eliminate. And this persistent pursuit of a self only increases, becoming more and more enveloping. What is significant is that desire is related with the feeling that there is an owner or controller, in other words, a self that is the master who controls things and makes them go according to its desires. And it just so happens that attempts to control the fulfillment of wishes often meet with some success; people then mistakenly believe that there is a self responsible for this success. Actually, however, this control only extends to certain aspects of life and is only temporary. The things assumed to be the self are only particular elements in a procession of causal factors, and we are not able to constantly control other things according to our desires. The feeling of being able to at least partially control things—though naturally this cannot be completely accomplished—tends to continually reinforce the notion that there is a self. When people cling to a self, they do not know how to work in accordance with existing causal factors to reap a certain result. They come to view relationships incorrectly and elevate the self to the status of a controller of the world whose powers function according to its desires. When people do not act according to the process of cause and effect, and things do not go as they wish, the self comes under the pressure of its own deficiencies and succumbs to the possibility of decrease and dissolution. It must be emphasized again that this attachment to a self is considered a very important point—it is the basis of all other attachments.

To summarize, attachments make people's minds dull and cloudy; thinking according to cause and effect becomes an onerous task. Attachments make people unable to interpret the meaning of life and unable to perform various tasks with "pure" reasoning according to existing causal factors. Instead of living in accordance with the natural flow of life, there is blockage, bias, narrowness, conflict, and a feeling of continual pressure. Pressure occurs because of clinging to notions of "I" and "mine." When there is "I" and "mine," people feel that things ought to go according to their desires; but all things proceed according to a host of causal factors, not according to personal desires. When desire cannot contain various causal factors, then people are subject to pressure. Whenever the things to which they are attached come under fire, they are also under fire, and this increases with the strength of attachments. This predicament not only brings about dukkha, but also affects behavior that proceeds according to the power of desires and attachments—which is just the opposite of living according to wisdom and causal factors.[106]

After attachments, the process proceeds further to the levels of existence (*bhava*), birth (*jāti*), decay-and-death (*jarā-maraṇa*) to the arising of sorrow and lamentation, for example, according to the trends I have already explained. Once sorrow and lamentation have already arisen, people will not escape these through the thoughts, conclusions, and opinions to which they have already become attached. Nor will they be freed by actions based on habits, inclinations, biases, or certain opinions they have accumulated. None of these will lead to seeing the conditions they are confronting at the moment and seeing things the way they truly are. The cycle begins at ignorance (*avijjā*) and continues on in the same old way.

Even though ignorance is a fundamental type of unwholesome tendency (*kilesa*) that stirs up other kinds of bad habits, when these things appear as specific behaviors, craving tends to be the instigator, the dictator. Its role is very clear. In terms of practice (*paṭipatti*), such as in the Four Nobles Truths, craving is stated as the cause of dukkha.

When ignorance proceeds blindly without direction, craving is also unprincipled, out of control, continuing on in response to the need for success, opening the way for the creation of more bad kamma than good. But when ignorance is set right by means of correct beliefs and proper understanding based on reason, craving is pulled in line with correct aims and is controlled and refashioned so that it can hit the target. Overcoming ignorance brings about good kamma and reaps great benefits. If craving receives the proper inducement, it can be a tool for getting rid of ignorance and craving in the future. Blind ignorance is bad and demeritorious (*pāpa*; Thai, *bap*), transforming ignorance is good and meritorious (*puñña*; Thai, *bun*). Good people and bad people will still experience dukkha depending on themselves, but it is only by proper means that people are able to put an end to dukkha, become emancipated and free.

The correct and beneficial application of craving has been supremely expressed in the following way:

> Sister, a monk hears it said that such and such a bhikkhu has attained liberation of mind (*cetovimutti*) and liberation through insight (*paññāvimutti*) that is untainted. . .and it occurs to him that whenever you are going to attain liberation of the mind and liberation through insight. . .you will depend upon craving to sever craving. I say this body was born of craving and depends on craving to sever craving—this is what we depend on.[107]

If you are unable to do anything else, choose craving that aims at the good, which, in turn, will have an effect on your actions. But if possible, refrain from both good and bad craving and choose the way of wisdom, which is pure, liberating, and does away with dukkha.

Dependent Origination Expressed as a Middle Truth (*majjhena dhammadesanā*)

A proper understanding of dependent origination can be called *sammādiṭṭhi* or correct view. This proper understanding can be referred to as a neutral (Thai, *klang*) position, not inclined in any particular direction. Dependent origination is, therefore, a principle or law that expresses a neutral truth, which is called "*majjhena dhammadesanā*."

The neutrality of this principle of truth can be ascertained by comparing it with other extremely biased doctrines or theories. Any correct understanding of dependent origination must be separated from these extreme theories. And now, we will show these theories in pairs based on statements made by the Buddha, with minimal additional explanation:

Pair 1

1. *Atthikavāda*[108]—the doctrine that all things actually exist (extreme realism);
2. *Natthikavāda*—the doctrine that all things do not actually exist (nihilism).

> Only you, [Lord Buddha] the Accomplished One, say, "Proper understanding, proper understanding (*sammādiṭṭhi*)."[109] To what extent can we take this as the proper understanding?
>
> Kaccāna, this world mainly depends on two conditions (of personal theory), having (*atthitā*) and not-having (*natthitā*). When you see the source of dukkha in this world as it is with proper wisdom (*sammāpaññā*), there is no not-having in this world. When you see the extinction of dukkha in this world as it is, with proper wisdom, there is no having in this world. This world mainly clings to systems and is bound up with dogma (*abhinivesa*). The Noble Disciples do not seek out, latch onto, nor cling to systems, narrowminded determination, dogma, biases (*anusaya*), or an idea of a "personal self." They do not doubt that, "When dukkha arises, it really arises; and when dukkha is extinguished, it is really extinguished." The Noble Disciples have gained insight into this without having to depend on others. When we refer to proper understanding, this is what we mean.
>
> Kaccāna, "everything exists" is one extreme, and "nothing exists" is another extreme. The Tathāgata expresses the Middle Way that does not adhere to these two extremes, saying, "Because ignorance (*avijjā*) is a factor, mental formations (*saṅkhāra*) occur, and because mental formations occur, consciousness (*viññāṇa*) comes about. . .and because ignorance is disgorged, extinguished without a trace, mental formations are also done away with, and because mental formations are extinguished, consciousness is extinguished. . ."[110]

A brahmin, who was a metaphysician, came to see Lord Buddha to ask a question: "Lord Gotama, the Accomplished One, do all things exist?"

Lord Buddha answered, "Saying that all things exist is the most popular metaphysical theory."

Question: "You mean that nothing exists?"
Answer: "Saying that 'Nothing exists' is the second most popular metaphysical theory."

Q: "All things are separate (*puthutta,* plurality)?"
A: "Saying that 'Everything is separate' is the fourth most popular metaphysical theory."

> Brahmin, the Tathāgata does not become attached to either of these extremes and reveals the Dhamma in a middle way by saying that, "because ignorance is a factor, mental formations arise; because mental formations are a factor, consciousness arises. . .and because ignorance is completely disgorged and extinguished, mental formations are extinguished, and because mental formations are extinguished, consciousness is extinguished."[111]

Pair 2

1. *Sassatavāda* (eternalism);
2. *Ucchedavāda* (annihilationism)

Pair 3

1. *Attakāravāda*—the belief that you are the cause of your own sukha and dukkha (self-generationism or karmic autogenesisism);
2. *Parakāravāda*—the belief that sukha and dukkha come about due to external causes (other-generationism or kammic heterogenesisism).

The third and fourth pair are very important to the principle of kamma. When they are studied and understood well, they will help protect against misundertandings about the principle of kamma. We should, therefore, take note of the following statements made by Lord Buddha:

Question: "Am I the maker of my dukkha?"
Answer: "It should not be put that way."

Q: "So, other things are the cause of dukkha?"
A: "It should not be put that way."

Q: "So, I am the maker of my own dukkha along with other things?"
A: "It should not be put that way."

Q: "So, I do not cause my dukkha, it is not caused by other things, but just comes about on its own (by chance)?"
A: "It should not be put that way."

Q: "If that is the case, then is there any dukkha at all?"
A: "We cannot say that there is no dukkha; there is dukkha."

Q: "So, Gotama, we cannot know, cannot perceive dukkha?"
A: "It is not as if we cannot know, cannot perceive dukkha; we know and perceive real dukkha."

Q: ". . . then, Venerable One, please tell me, please reveal dukkha to me."
A: "When you say that 'I make my dukkha,' as you said at first, this is the same as saying that, 'One and the same person acts and experiences [dukkha].' This amounts to eternalism. When you say that, 'Other things are the cause of dukkha,' this is like a person who has a sensation jab his feelings and then says that 'One person did something and another felt it.' This becomes annihilationism. The Tathāgata does not become attached to either of these two extremes and reveals the Dhamma in a middle way by saying that, 'because ignorance is a factor, mental formations arise; because mental formations are a factor, consciousness arises . . . because ignorance is completely disgorged and extinguished, mental formations are extinguished; because mental formations are extinguished, consciousness is extinguished . . .' "[112]

Q: "So, I am the maker of my own sukha and dukkha?"
A: "It should not be put that way."

Q: "Then, sukha and dukkha are caused by other things?"
A: "It should not be put this way."

Q: "So, sukha and dukkha are caused by me and by other things?"
A: "It should not be put this way."

Q: "So, I do not cause my sukha and dukkha, they are not caused by other things, but just come about on their own (by chance)?"
A: "It should not be put this way."

Q: "[If this is the case,] then there is no sukha or dukkha?"
A: "We cannot say that there is no sukha or dukkha; there is sukha and dukkha."

Q: "So, Gotama, we cannot know and cannot perceive our sukha and dukkha?"
A: "It is not as if we cannot know and cannot perceive sukha and dukkha; we know and perceive real sukha and dukkha."

Q: "... then, Venerable One, please tell me, please reveal sukha and dukkha to me."
A: "Because at first you understand there to be a sensation and a person who feels this same sensation, attachment to the notion that you have caused your own sukha or dukkha follows—I maintain that this is not the case. Because you understand that sensation to be one thing, and the one who has this sensation another, there arises an attachment, as in the case of the person who has a sensation jab at his feelings and then thinks that this is caused by other things. We hold that this is not the case. The Tathāgata does not attach to either of these extremes and reveals the Dhamma in a middle way by saying that, 'because ignorance is a factor, mental formations arise... because ignorance is completely disgorged and extinguished, mental formations are, therefore, extinguished...' "[113]

> Ānanda, we maintain that sukha and dukkha depend upon the arising of causal factors. And what do these depend upon? Contact (*phassa*).
>
> Once we have a physical body, depending on the intentions of that body, we will experience sukha or dukkha. When there is speech, depending on the intentions of that speech, we will experience sukha or dukkha. When we have a mind, depending on the intentions of that mind, we will experience sukha or dukkha.
>
> Because ignorance is a factor, people embellish their own physical predispositions (*saṅkhāra*), which become the cause of sukha and dukkha. Because of other things (the influence and persuasion of other people and things), physical predispositions are embellished and become factors in the arising of internal sukha and dukkha. This embellishment of physical predispositions takes place, both consciously and unconsciously, and becomes a factor in the embellishment of predispositions of speech (*vacī*)... mental (*mano*) predispositions arise on their own... due to others... consciously... unconsciously becoming factors for the arising of internal sukha and dukkha. In these cases, ignorance is already deeply imbedded.[114]

Pair 4

1. *Kārakavedakādi-ekattavāda*[115]—the belief that the doer and the receiver of action are one and the same (the extremist view of a self-identical soul or the monistic view of subject-object unity);

2. *Kārakavedakādinānattavāda*[116]—the belief that the doer and the receiver of action are disparate (the extremist view of individual discontinuity or the dualistic view of subject-object distinction).

Question: "Is the doer and the receiver [of the results] of actions one and the same?"
Answer: "Saying that the doer and the receiver of action are the same is an extreme view."

Q: "So, the doer is one thing and the receiver another?"
A: "Saying that the doer is one thing and the receiver of actions is another is the second extreme view. The Tathāgata does not attach to either of these two views and reveals the Dhamma in a middle way, saying that 'because ignorance is a factor, mental formations arise. . . because ignorance has been completely disgorged and extinguished, mental formations are, therefore, extinguished. . .'"[117]

Q: "Accomplished One, what is decay-and-death? Whose decay-and-death is it?"
A: "You have not correctly addressed the problem. 'What is decay-and-death? Whose decay-and-death is it?' or saying that 'Decay-and-death is one thing, and the one who experiences decay-and-death is another,' mean the same thing—only the wording is different. When someone holds the view that, 'Life is one thing and the body is something else' and has dedicated himself to the Holy Life (*brahmacariya*), this cannot be the case. Once you believe that, 'Life is one thing and the body is another,' then there can be no leading the Holy Life. The Tathāgata does not attach to either of these views and reveals the Dhamma in a middle way, saying that, 'because birth is a factor, decay-and-death exist.' "

Q: "Developed One, what are birth. . . becoming. . . clinging. . . craving. . . sensation. . . contact. . . sense-objects. . . mind-and-body. . . consciousness. . . mental formations (kammic-formations)? And to whom do they belong?"
A: "You are not addressing the question properly [the following response is the same as for the element of decay-and-death]. . . because ignorance has been disgorged and completely extinguished, any kind of deluded, scattered, or conflicting views that wonder 'What is decay-and-death? Whose decay-and-death is it?' or say that 'Decay-and-death is one thing, and the

one who experiences decay-and-death is another,' or 'Life is one thing and the body is another,' all of these views are to be driven away, torn out by the roots, completely done away with, until they can no longer be found and no longer arise."[118]

Q: "Who receives contact (*phassa*)?"
A: "You still have not posed the question correctly. I do not say, 'receive contact.' If I were to say 'receive contact,' then I could correctly state the problem as, 'Who receives contact?', but I do not put it that way. So, since I do not put it that way, whoever asks 'What is the reason for the existence of contact?' has correctly stated the problem. In this case, the correct explanation is, 'Because the six sense-bases (*saḷāyatana*) are factors, contact exists; because contact is a factor, sensation (*vedanā*) exists.' "

Q: "Who experiences sensations? Who has craving? Who has attachments?"
A: "You still have not posed the problem correctly. . . .Whoever asks, 'What are the factors that bring sensations into existence? What are the factors that bring craving into existence? What are the factors that bring attachment into existence?' has stated the problem correctly. In this case, the explanation is, 'Because contact is a factor, sensation arises; because sensation is a factor, craving exists. . .' "[119]

> Bhikkhus, this body is not ours nor does it belong to others. Just take note that this old kamma is a factor that we have created, it is determined [that is, created through intention or with intention as its cause] and is the basis for sensation (*vedanā*).
>
> Bhikkhus, regarding this, the Noble Disciples who have studied the way reflect on this process (*yonisomanasikāra*) to the point that they see the interrelatedness of all things (*paṭiccasamuppāda*) saying, "When this exists, then that exists; because this thing has been extinguished, that thing is also extinguished. That is, because ignorance is a factor, mental formations exist; because mental formations are a factor, consciousness exists. . .because ignorance has been completely disgorged and extinguished, mental formations are extinguished; because mental formations are extinguished, consciousness is extinguished. . ."[120]

The principle of dependent origination reveals the natural truths that all things are impermanent (*aniccā*), subject to suffering (dukkha), and are without self (*anattā*). These Three Characteristics of Existence (*tilakkhaṇa*) follow a continual process of cause and effect. There is no problem concerning whether things really exist or are eternal or subject to extinction; but those who incorrectly understand dependent origination also tend to misunderstand the Three Characteristics of Existence, especially the principle of *anattā*. These people tend to hear the superficial aspects of these principles and then interpret *anattā* to mean that nothing exists, which leads them to espouse a nihilistic view (*natthikavāda*)—an extremely distorted understanding of reality (*micchādiṭṭhi*).

Those who already understand the principle of dependent origination have gone beyond the various misinterpretations that are the result of the theories stated, such as believing that all things have a root or "first cause" and believing that there are things that exist outside of the natural order (supernatural). The following words of the Buddha will serve to further illustrate this:

> Bhikkhus, when the Noble Disciples clearly see dependent origination and the interrelatedness of things according to this principle with proper wisdom (*sammāpaññā*) it is not possible to pursue questions, such as, 'In the past, did we exist or not? In the past, what were we? In the past, what were we like? In the past, what was it that made us the way we are now?' or pursuing questions to the other extreme, such as, 'In the future, will we exist or not? In the future, what will we be? In the future, what will we be like? And once we have attained that, what will we be like?' or even wondering about the present asking, 'Do we exist or not? What are we? How are we? Where do we come from and where will we go?' Why is it these are improbable questions? Because the Noble Disciples with proper wisdom have already clearly seen dependent origination and the interrelatedness of dependent origination as it is.[121]

In this sense, those who have seen dependent origination do not sit and speculate about the various problems of 'higher philosophy,' and this is the reason for Lord Buddha's resolute silence on these matters. When anyone came to ask about such matters, he would call them unexplainable problems or deem them unpredictable; because once someone sees dependent origination and understands that all things are linked in a process of cause and effect, these questions do not make much sense.

Allow me to give an example of Lord Buddha's reason for not responding to these kinds of problems.

Question: "Gotama, the Accomplished One, why do various wandering mendicants when asked the following questions,

1. Is the world eternal and everlasting?
2. Is the world not eternal?
3. Does this world have an end point?
4. Does this world have no end?
5. Are life and the body one and the same?
6. Is life one thing and the body another?
7. After death, does a being (*satta*) continue to exist?[122]
8. After death, does nothing exist?
9. After death, do beings both exist and not exist?
10. After death, is it impossible to say that something exists and nothing exists?

respond by saying that 'The world is eternal,' 'The world is not eternal'... 'After death, we cannot say that something exists and nothing exists.'? Why is it when asked such questions Gotama does not respond that 'The world is eternal' or 'The world is not eternal'...?"

Answer: "Vaccha, some of these medicants who adhere to various doctrines tend to believe that the body is the self; some say that the self has a body; some say that the body dwells within the self; some say that the self dwells within the body; some understand sensation... perception... mental formations... to be the self, and so on; some take consciousness to be the self; some say that the self has consciousness; some say that consciousness dwells within the self; some say that the self dwells within consciousness. Therefore, these mendicants who adhere to various doctrines, when they are asked these questions, explain by saying that 'The world is eternal.' ...

As for the Tathāgatas, the fully enlightened arahants, they do not understand the body to be the self or say that the self has a body, or say that the body dwells in the self or that the self dwells in the body... therefore, when they are asked these questions, they do not offer the explanation that 'The world is eternal' or that 'The world is not eternal.' "...[123]

There are other aspects and notions concerning the theory of kamma that conflict with the principle of dependent origination, and we will wait to deal with these in more detail.

Two Principles of the Dhamma Related to Dependent Origination

Actually, the various principles of the Buddhist teachings, although different in name, are one and the same thing, because they all point to or are related to truth (*saccadhamma*)—their common aim. These principles are the same truth in different forms, focused in different directions and suited to different purposes. For this reason, some points of the Dhamma are only detailed aspects of larger principles, while some points are more grand principles encompassing the entire meaning of the teachings.

Dependent origination is one of the more grand principles that covers the whole of the Dhamma. When dependent origination is explained, we can see that we should refer to other more general and recognizeable principles of the Dhamma, as well, to see how they are related. These related principles will improve our understanding of certain points of the Dhamma along with our understanding of dependent origination. Therefore, the two principles that will be discussed in the following sections are kamma and the Four Noble Truths.

1. Kamma (*Skt., karma; Thai,* kam)

A. The Law or Condition of Kamma

Kamma is only one part of the process of dependent origination. This is easily seen when we divide this process into three parts: unwholesome tendencies (*kilesa*), kamma, and the fruits of action (*vipāka*). The principle of dependent origination explains the complete process of action and the fruits of action, starting from the unwholesome tendencies that bring about kamma to the fruits received. When you clearly understand dependent origination, then you also understand kamma. For this reason, there is no need for a separate discussion of the law of kamma at this point.

At any rate, there are certain important points that should be mentioned to avoid serious misunderstandings about kamma.

First, Lord Buddha stated that "Because ignorance is a factor, people, therefore, embellish their physical predispositions[124]. . .verbal predispositions[125]. . .mental predispositions[126]. . .some of which is brought on by themselves. . .some of which is due to other things. . .some of which is done consciously. . .some unconsciously."[127] We have noted that the Buddhist texts refute the theory that sukha and dukkha are brought on by yourself—the view held by the "self-generationists" (*attakāravāda*). The texts also refute the theory that sukha and dukkha are due to other things—the view held by the "other-generationists" (*parakāravāda*).[128] Such texts emphasize that kamma is a process of causes and effects that will have varying effects and must be properly considered in terms of causal relationships, not as isolated incidents.

The proper consideration of such causal relationships guards against a very mistaken belief about kamma that whatever has happened is solely due to what a person has done. This results in not considering all of the surrounding factors and conditions that come into play.

At any rate, we have to distinguish between the principle of kamma as a law or condition and the ethical importance of kamma. I have already mentioned the law of kamma, which is related to a natural process of causes and effects influencing everything. But in terms of ethics, that is the teachings dealing with more concrete practices, we must realize that the people who will come to feel the need to practice will be those who will have had the opportunity to be exposed to the teachings. In other words, emphasis is placed on the recipient. Accordingly, responsibility falls on the shoulders of the practitioner. When becoming involved in various activities and working towards established goals—even when it comes to the Lord Buddha's recommendation to "be a refuge unto yourself"—the practitioner must still maintain a responsible course of action. Seeking this refuge cannot be a selfish endeavor: in its broader sense, it suggests that not only must you help yourself, but in order to help others and be helped by others you must demonstrate a certain amount of self-reliance. Self-reliance can help sustain the kind of cooperation necessary to attain the final goal of Buddhism. For this reason, the aspects of the principle of kamma—whether stated in terms of a natural law or human ethics—do not conflict. Instead, these two dimensions support one another. Let us try to come to an even better understanding of this.

The second important point is that there are three mistaken doctrines relating to human sukha and dukkha that we must be careful not to confuse with the true teachings about kamma:

1. *Pubbekatahetuvāda* (past-action determinism)—believing that all sukha and dukkha are related to past kamma (or *pubbekatavāda*, for short);
2. *Issaranimmānahetuvāda* (theistic determinism)—believing that all sukha and dukkha are related to the will of gods (or *issarakaraṇavāda*, for short);

3. *Ahetu-apaccayavāda* (indeterminism or accidentalism)—believing that all sukha and dukkha go according to uncontrollable luck, good fortune, or fate (or *ahetuvāda,* for short).

According to the words of Lord Buddha:

Bhikkhus, when those who hold to these three heretical doctrines are questioned and examined by pundits, they tend to refer to hand-me-down knowledge relating to a theory of the inefficacy of action [or believing that there are no aftereffects of action, *akiriyadiṭṭhi*], such as,

1. One group of recluses and brahmins asserts or believes that, be it sukha or dukkha, non-sukha or non-dukkha, all of this is experienced due to past kamma (*pubbekatahetu*);

2. One group of recluses and brahmins asserts or believes that, be it sukha or dukkha, non-sukha or non-dukkha, all of this is due to the will of a supreme diety (*issaranimmānahetu*);

3. One group of recluses and brahmins asserts or believes that, be it sukha or dukkha, non-sukha or non-dukkha, all of this is beyond any cause and effect that can be determined (*ahetu-apaccaya*).

Bhikkhus, if I were to call upon (group 1 of) these recluses and brahmins and ask them, "I understand that all of you hold to this view. . . is this true?" and then they respond that this indeed is true, I can then say the following: 'If this is the case, then you have taken life (*pāṇātipāta*) because some of your past kamma made you do it; you took things that were not given to you (*adinnādāna*) because some of your past kamma made you do this; you must have stepped off the path of the Holy Life (*abrahmacariya*). . . lied (*musāvāda*). . . reached improper conclusions (*micchādiṭṭhi*) because your past kamma made you do it.

Bhikkhus, when people take the kamma that they have done as the essential cause, then proper resolve (*chanda*), effort, and "this should be done—this should not be done" do not exist. When what should and should not be done are not established with seriousness and certainty, then it is as if these recluses and brahmins have lost their mindfulness, their control. The words of these recluses are not in accord with the Dhamma. According to the Dhamma, I can reprimand this first group of recluses and brahmins who make these assertions and hold such views.

Bhikkhus, if I call upon (group 2 of) these recluses and brahmins. . .and state that, "You have taken life, because a supreme diety has willed it; you took things that were not given to you, because a supreme diety willed it. . .you stepped off the path of the Holy Life. . . lied. . . reached improper conclusions all because a supreme diety has willed it."

Bhikkhus, when people cling to the will of a supreme diety as essential cause, then proper resolve, effort, and "this should be done—this should not be done" do not exist. . .

Bhikkhus, if I call upon (group 3 of) these recluses and brahmins. . .and state that, "You have taken life without cause; you took things that were not given to you for no reason. . .you stepped off the path of the Holy Life. . . lied. . . reached improper conclusions without cause or reason."

Bhikkhus, when people take lack of reason as the essential cause, then proper resolve, effort, and "this should be done—this should not be done" do not exist. . .[129]

The first doctrine, *pubbekatahetu*, is a doctrine of the Jains. The Buddhist texts state the following:

Bhikkhus, one group of recluses and brahmins asserts or believes that, "All kinds of sukha and dukkha experienced by people due to past kamma can be done away with through the practice of austerities (*tapa*); new kamma is not created and you will no longer be under its control; because you are no longer under its control, this is the end of kamma, and, therefore, the end of dukkha and sensation (*vedanā*); because sensation has come to an end then you have completely sloughed off all dukkha." Bhikkhus, the Jains (*Niganṭhā*) make these kinds of assertions.[130]

Aside from this, there is another section cited earlier emphasizing the same thing:

Truly, Sivaka, some sensations arise having goodness as their place of origin. . .some arise from the fluctuation of the seasons. . .some arise from a lack of consistent behavior. . .some arise

> from being the victim of bad deeds. . .some arise from the fruits of kamma. . . . If any recluses and brahmins assert or believe that, "People have sensations—be they sukha or dukkha, non-sukha or non-dukkha—due to past kamma,". . .I can say that this is the fault of those recluses and brahmins themselves.[131]

These words of the Buddha protect against overly extreme views that tend to see kamma only in terms of past kamma, portraying people as if they were passively lying around waiting for the fruits of their kamma to come knocking and determine their future. If this were the case, people need not think about improving or changing themselves. And this would be a most terrible mistake. Aside from the message conveyed in the textual examples already cited, we can also clearly see that in these passages Lord Buddha pointed out that procrastination is also a crucial factor in the ethical ramifications of kamma.

These texts, however, do not deny the existence of old kamma, because past kamma is partially related to the process of cause and effect and certainly has an effect on the present. But conditions in the present are related to cause and effect, not any power that transcends nature or can be attributed to luck or fate. Those who understand dependent origination and know the process of cause and effect have no problem with this. It is like a person who ascends a three-story building: when he has reached the third floor, it is certain that his rise to the top is due to his actions—his walking each flight—this cannot be denied. And when he has reached that height there are certain things that he cannot do: he cannot stretch his hand and slap it on the floor of the first story, nor can he get into a little car and drive around on the top floor as if it were a superhighway. These things are not possible. These limitations are all due to the fact that he has made it to the top floor of the building, a predicament that cannot be denied. If he is tired and out of breath after the climb and cannot climb any higher nor go back down, this, too, is related to having climbed the stairs of the building. This also cannot be denied. Climbing to that place and moving within that realm are all related to being there. Attaining this level may also involve further thoughts about taking a new course of action and considering what the fruits of that action might be. And the past may even have a bearing on this. For example, a person's strength may be insufficient to work up to full capacity, because of being worn out from previous efforts. Even so, a person must decide if he should give up in the face of his weariness or find a way to overcome his condition.

All of this is tied to a process of cause and effect. We should, therefore, understand past kamma only as it comes to play in that process, in light of conduct. A person who understands dependent origination can take advantage of past kamma and use it as a lesson, as a firm measure of reason, as a part of understanding himself and the surrounding circumstances. This understanding of past kamma serves as a basis for understanding the present, for making plans and setting goals for present action. It serves as a way of changing and improving ourselves.

One Buddhist text states,

> Bhikkhus, anyone who says that, "This person has performed this kamma and so now he is subject to this and that kamma," leaves no room for leading the Holy Life (*brahmacariya*), because he is blind to the way that leads to the complete elimination of dukkha.
>
> But whoever says that, "This person has performed kamma, which is the basis of sensation (*vedanā*), so he feels the effects (*vipāka*) of that kamma," still leaves room for leading the Holy Life, because the way leading to the complete elimination of dukkha is clear.
>
> Bhikkhus, some people perform a small amount of bad kamma and this kamma can lead them into hell. Other people perform a small amount of bad kamma and have finished reaping its effects in the present. Petty kamma may go unnoticed, while substantial kamma is much more apparent.
>
> If any person performs even the smallest amount of kamma, can this kamma lead him into hell? Some people have had no (physical) training, no moral training, no mental training, no training in wisdom (*paññā*), have few good qualities (*guṇa*) and little character. They are usually suffering due to various insignificant difficulties (*vipāka*). These people perform petty kamma and that is enough to lead them into hell (like putting a chunk of salt in a small vessel of water).
>
> What kind of person performs the same small amount of bad kamma and realizes its effects in the present and only realizes the effects of kamma after they have accumulated? Some people have (physical) training, moral training, mental training, training in wisdom, they have many good qualities, are of great character, and have the Dhamma as an invaluable tool. Such people perform

the same amount of bad kamma, but reap its effects in the present. Petty kamma goes unnoticed, while only the build-up of substantial kamma may affect them (like putting a chunk of salt in a river).[132]

Headmen (*gāmaṇī*), some teachers assert or hold the view that those who kill animals must all go to hell; those who steal must go to hell; those who perform sexual misconduct (*kāmesu micchācāra*) must all go to hell; those who tell lies must all go to hell. The disciples who become devoted and believe in these teachers think that, "Our teacher asserts and holds the view that those who kill animals must all go to hell." They, therefore, believe that, "The animals we have killed are dead and gone, so we must go on to suffer the punishments of hell." They do not let go of their teacher's words and view; so, they are willing to go to hell as if they were arrested and carried off. . . .

As for the Tathāgata, the Enlightened One, he came into this world to find fault with the taking of life (*pāṇātipāta*). . . taking what is not given (*adinnādāna*). . . sexual misconduct (*kāmesu micchācāra*). . . false speech (*musāvāda*) through the use of lengthy discourses and saying that, "Everyone should stop taking life. . . taking what is not given. . . sexual misconduct. . . lying." Disciples who become devoted to and believe in these teachings tend to notice that, "Those who point out the faults of taking life [and so on]. . . through the use of lengthy discourses, say that everyone ought to stop taking life [and so on]. . . . There is so much taking of life, and all this taking of life is not good, is not a proper thing to do. We will have a troubled mind because of this action; it will be the cause for other problems, and we will not be able to deny that we have performed bad kamma." When they have seen this, they will stop taking life and give up killing for good. They will have given up their bad kamma by taking this decisive action. . . .

They have given up the taking of life [and so on]. . . lying. . . malicious speech (*pisuṇāvācā*). . . harsh speech (*pharusavācā*). . . frivolous talk (*samphappalāpa*). . . covetousness (*abhijjhā*). . . ill-will (*byāpāda*). . . improper understanding (*micchādiṭṭhi*) and have become people with proper understanding (*sammādiṭṭhi*). The Noble Disciples have freed themselves from covetousness, ill-will; they do not digress, have clear comprehension (*sampajañña*),

> unwavering mindfulness, and they live with a mind emanating loving-kindness in the six directions [that is, the four compass points including up and down], throughout the world, for all beings, in all places. When a person is composed of boundless loving-kindness without measure, has done away with animosity and malice, then the liberation of the mind (*cetovimutti*) through loving-kindness can do astounding things. Any reasonable amount of kamma that a person has performed will cease to exist; it will not be able to co-exist with the freedom of the mind attained through loving-kindness. . . .[133]

These Buddhist texts have been cited to link certain points about the principle of kamma and allow us a more detailed understanding. It is a way of preventing us from coming to conclusions about kamma that may be too simplistic, and this is only one example; there are many other passages that could be cited.

B. The Ethical Importance of Kamma

The following is a summary of the ethical values that can be associated with the principle of kamma:

1. Be a person with solid reasoning. View action and the fruits of action according to a process of cause and effect. For example, do not believe in things blindly, shallowly, such as the holiness of rivers.
2. See that the fruits and goals that you aim for come from applying yourself to the task at hand. You must, therefore, depend on yourself. Do not wait for your lucky day or hope for help from external powers.
3. Be responsible for putting an end to your own bad kamma, and be responsible for others by acting properly towards them.
4. All people have an equal, natural right to do things to change and improve themselves. Everyone has the capacity to improve, to become even more excellent than the gods and brahmins.
5. Believe that good qualities, abilities, behavior, and practice are the measuring sticks of human inferiority or perfection. There should be no dividing people along the lines of race or caste.
6. As for past kamma, use it as a lesson; know and understand yourself according to reason. Do not blame others. Look at the essential nature of yourself that exists at the present moment,

and use this as the basis for change and self-improvement. Make plans for steady progress that is headed in the right direction.
7. Have high hopes for the future of all humanity.

These values can be seen in a general way in the following Buddhist texts:

> Bhikkhus, we call intention (*cetanā*) kamma. People have intentions and then perform physical, verbal, or mental kamma accordingly.[134]

> All beings have personal kamma, kamma that is handed down to them, kamma that they are born with, kamma that is genetic, and kamma that they depend on; kamma divides beings according to those who are inept and those who are skillful.[135]

> However people sow their seeds determines their fruits: those who do good, receive good; those who do evil, receive evil.[136]

> Those who perform kamma will usually be troubled by it later. Having performed bad kamma, their faces are soaked with tears as they cry. Having performed kamma and not been troubled by it later, that kamma is good kamma.[137]

> Fools have inferior intelligence. They treat themselves as enemies; they perform bad kamma and receive searing results. Having performed kamma, people are generally troubled by it later. Their faces are flooded with tears as they receive the fruits of their kamma—this kind of kamma is no good at all.
>
> The person who has performed kamma and is not troubled by it later, and receives its fruits with a cheerful and joyous mind, has performed good kamma. People can recognize beneficial kamma; and they should waste no time in doing just that.[138]

Be a person with solid reasoning; do not believe in things blindly:

> Fools have 'black' kamma. Even if they went to [the holy rivers of] Bahukā, Adhikakkā, Gayā, Sundarikā, Sarassatī, Payāga, Bāhumatī, they would not be able to wash this kamma off. What can the rivers Sundarikā, Payāga, or Bahukā do? They cannot

cleanse people with animosity, people who perform crude and evil kamma; they cannot make these people pure at all. But for the pure person, the most auspicious occasion is any time; for the pure person, every day is a holy day; for those who are untainted and work with clean hands, each moment is a moment for religious observance. Brahmin, you should bathe in our teachings and make all beings happy. If you do not tell lies, do not oppress others, do not take what is not given, have confidence and lack greed, then why do you need to go to the river Gayā? If you can live like this, then even your drinking water will be like the river Gayā.[139]

If people are going to overcome demerits and kamma by bathing [washing away their demerits], then frogs, turtles, serpents, crocodiles, and other water animals will all certainly go to heaven! . . . If these rivers can wash away your demerits, then they can also wash away your merits.[140]

Cleanliness does not come from this (holy) water that so many people go to bathe in. Anyone who has truth, has Dhamma, that person is clean, is a brahmin.[141]

Those who do not cling to the excitement generated by auspicious practices, do not hold to visions and dreams, and do not look for good and bad signs, they can be said to have gone beyond the faults related to the excitement generated by auspicious signs—the kinds of auspicious signs that can overpower people in this existence. These beliefs are like a trench that blocks your way. If you overcome these obstacles, you will not be born again.[142]

While waiting for the proper astrological moment, benefits pass you by. Any time that benefits appear, that is the time to seize the day—what can the stars do?[143]

Whenever a person acts properly, that moment is called the proper moment, the auspicious moment, the best time. For the person who has performed devotions by behaving properly, bodily activity, verbal activity, and mental activity all become auspicious observances. Once a person has done these auspicious things, he will achieve the most auspicious aims.[144]

Apply yourself to the task at hand; do not wait with hopes based on supplication:

We should not turn back and cling to things that have already passed; we should not dream about things that have yet to come. The things of the past are already gone, and we have yet to come upon the things of the future. Anyone who can clearly see the present—the things that are certain and stable—should tirelessly seek to practice and complete the task at hand, should get to work today without hesitation. Whoever comes to know that he will die tomorrow should live a life of ceaseless effort and shun laziness during the day and at night—because according to the Lord of Death and his Great Army we all have no way of postponing this. The Peace-Attaining Sage has said that even if this person lives a single night and makes the best of it, this will be most excellent.[145]

Householders, there are five things worth hoping for, desiring, and being satisfied with; and they are things very difficult to come by in this world—longevity, status, happiness, rank, and heaven. These five things. . .cannot be had simply through supplication or by making a wish. If we cannot get these five things through wishes and supplication, then what is the degeneration of worldly being attributed to? Householders, the Noble Disciples who hope for (long) life do not do this through supplication or blind absorption in the idea of life or because they simply long for more life. The Noble Disciples who hope for life observe the points of the practice that favor life; the points of practice that favor life lead to furthering life. These Noble Disciples are those who have life. Whether superhuman or human. . .those who hope for status. . . happiness. . .rank. . .heaven should observe the points of practice that lead to status, happiness. . .rank. . .heaven. . . .[146]

Bhikkhus, any bhikkhu who is not steadfast and hard working concerning his mental training such that he wishes, "Please free my mind from its impurities," will not be able to free himself from impurities. . . .This is like a mother hen with 8, 10, or 12 eggs, who decides not to sit on them and assist with their incubation but instead stands by wishing, "Please let my chicks use their claws and beaks to break the egg and get out [on their own]." The unhatched chicks will not use their claws and beaks to crack through the shells at all![147]

Do not use status and class as a measure of people, observe their behavior instead:

Vāseṭṭha, you know that among humans, those who make a living as cowherds are farmers, not brahmins. Those who make a living through the arts are known as artists, not brahmins. People who make their living by selling and trading are known as merchants, not brahmins. Those who make a living by serving others are known as servants, not brahmins. Whoever makes his living stealing is known as a thief, not a brahmin. . . .Whoever governs the land is known as a king, not a brahmin.

I do not refer to people as brahmins according to their birth. Those people still have unwholesome tendencies (*kilesa*) and should be addressed with "bho" [a customary address for brahmins]. I refer to those free of unwholesome tendencies and attachments as brahmins.

Established names and clans are just worldly words that have come into useage at certain times and have been perpetuated due to the long accepted conventions of unknowing people. Those who do not know, say that people are brahmins by birth; but people are not brahmins by birth. Actually, people should be dubbed brahmins or non-brahmins by their actions (kamma), should be dubbed farmers by their actions (by the way they make their living[148]), should be dubbed artists by their actions, should be dubbed servants by their actions, are dubbed thieves by their actions. . .are dubbed kings by their actions. All learned people who see dependent origination and know actions and the consequences of actions clearly, see these actions according to the truth: that this world proceeds according to actions (kamma), beings proceed according to actions, and beings are bound together in action like the bolts that hold a vehicle together as it rolls along![149]

Brahmin, I do not call a person excellent because he is of high birth; and I do not call a person lowly because he is of high birth. I do not call a person excellent because he is high class; and I do not call a person lowly because he is high class. I do not call a person excellent because he has great wealth; and I do not call a person lowly because he has great wealth. Actually, some people, while of high birth, still enjoy killing, stealing, engaging in sexual misconduct, lying, provoking people, using crude language, speaking nonsense, being covetous, and causing conflict, which all constitute improper understanding (*micchādiṭṭhi*).[150]

People are not outcastes by birth and are not brahmins by birth; they are outcastes because of their kamma, and they are brahmins because of their kamma (actions and behavior).[151]

When the four castes—*khattiya, brāhmaṇa, vessa, sudda*—are ordained in the Dhamma-Vinaya set down by the Tathāgata, they leave behind their former name and class and become recluses. We can say that they all become sons of Sakya.[152]

As for all the castes, anyone who becomes a bhikkhu and does away with impurities and unwholesome tendencies, reaches the goal of the Holy Life (*brahmacariya*), successfully completes the tasks that must be done, finishes all burdens, attains the highest benefits a person can reach, does away with everything that binds people in this life, and reaches enlightenment through knowledge—such a person can be deemed higher than any of the castes.[153]

Depend on yourself:

All of you must put forth your own efforts; the Tathāgatas only point the way.[154]

You are your own refuge. Who else can be your refuge? Through proper training you gain a refuge that is difficult to obtain.[155]

Purity and impurity are the result of your own doing. . . . One person cannot purify another.[156]

> Bhikkhus, you have yourself as a refuge. Do not hold anything else as a refuge. Having the Dhamma as a refuge, do not hold to anything else.[157]

Remember the following for the future:

> Women, men, laity, and all those who have been ordained should contemplate the fact that we each have our own kamma and receive the fruits of this kamma. We have the kamma of birth, the kamma of lineage, and the kamma that we depend on. Whatever kamma we perform, be it good or bad, we will reap the fruits of that kamma.[158]

> If you are afraid of dukkha, then do not perform bad kamma, either in secret or openly. If you are planning on performing bad kamma or are doing it right now, even if you could ascend in flight, you would not be able to avoid the consequences (dukkha).[159]

> Grain, wealth, gold, and silver or whatever properties you cling to—including servants, laborers, workers, and those who depend on you—cannot be taken with you; they must all be left behind.
>
> Those who perform any kind of bodily kamma, verbal kamma, or mental kamma, that very kamma is that person's possession and goes with him. Furthermore, that kamma will follow him around like a shadow.
>
> People, therefore, should act out of goodness and accrue things that will be of benefit in the future; goodness is our refuge in the future world.[160]

2. *The Noble Truths* (ariyasacca)

The Noble Truths are important dhammic principles that are more generally known than any others. The Noble Truths are not a part of the principle of dependent origination, rather they constitute the whole of dependent origination. Simply put, the meaning of the Noble Truths envelopes the whole of dependent origination. When someone asks, "What did Lord Buddha attain?", we can respond by saying that he came to know the Four Noble Truths; or we could say that he attained knowledge of dependent origination. But this exact statement is not found in the dhammic principles. I will, however, cite some passages from the canon to illustrate and support this idea.

The Vinaya Piṭaka mentions the circumstances of Lord Buddha's enlightenment.[161] It begins when he had just attained enlightenment, had just tasted the fruits of liberation (*vimutti*), and had been reviewing the forward unfolding of dependent origination (that is, the process of the arising of dukkha) and then the reverse process (the extinguishing of dukkha) for one week. Seven weeks after he had experienced liberation, he decided that he would tell others about this and said the following:

> The Dhamma I have attained is deep, difficult to perceive, difficult to follow. . . . For those who are still caught up in the world, this state of causality (*idappaccayatā*) and dependent origination (*paṭiccasamuppāda*) is difficult to perceive; this state of nibbana is difficult to see.[162]

As for the material found in the Suttas, whenever we find information about Lord Buddha's biography, it is told in the same manner.[163] It begins with the Buddha's contemplation of the four sights [an old man, a sick man, a dead man, and a holy man] that led to his renunciation, his actual embarking on the Holy Life, his studies with the ascetics Alara and Udaka, his practice of austerties and his quitting self-mortification, his return to a normal diet, and his attainment of knowledge, enlightenment, and the Three-fold Knowledge [reminiscence of past lives, the cycle of birth and rebirth according to kamma, and knowledge of the destruction of all mental intoxicants]. Upon his enlightenment the following can be found:

> Having consumed food, energy is regained, sensual urges are quieted, all unwholesome tendencies are quieted, the first *jhāna* [or level of concentration] has been attained. . .the second *jhāna*. . .the third *jhāna*. . .the fourth *jhāna*, there is no dukkha, no sukha. . .and equanimity is the cause of a state of pure mindfulness.
>
> When our mind has reached absorption (*samādhi*), it is pure, clear, without unwholesome tendencies, unclouded, supple, well-suited for work, and free of apprehension. This mental state is conducive to contemplating past lives (*pubbenivāsānussati-ñāṇa*, the First Knowledge). . .it is conducive to contemplating the rounds of births and deaths of all beings (*cutūpapāta-ñāṇa*, the

Second Knowledge) . . . it is conducive for clearly seeing that, "this is dukkha, this is the arising of dukkha, this is the passing away of dukkha, and this is the path to putting an end to all dukkha; these are the intoxicants (*āsava*), this is the arising of intoxicants, this is the passing away of intoxicants, and this is the path leading to the end of all intoxication. The mind is now free from sensual intoxication (*kāmāsava*), the desire to be reborn (*bhavāsava*), and the intoxication of ignorance (*avijjāsava*, completing the Third Knowledge) . . . .[164]

After this, there is a sermon relating the decision to preach the Dhamma, whose content is similar to that of the section from the Vinaya Piṭaka previously cited.

You can see that the Vinaya Piṭaka recounts the time just after Lord Buddha's enlightenment when he had experienced liberation (which the Commentaries say took seven weeks) and was reviewing dependent origination, until he decided he would not preach the Dhamma because of the difficulty of understanding dependent origination and attaining nibbana. As for the Sutta material, it explains the circumstances before enlightenment and proceeds to the attainment of the Three Knowledges, skipping over the section dealing with Lord Buddha's experience of liberation, and then it picks up again when he decided not to preach the Dhamma because of the same difficulties previously mentioned.

Those students who focus on the section in which the Lord Buddha reviews dependent origination in the Vinaya Piṭaka and his decision regarding the preaching of the Dhamma—found both in the Vinaya Piṭaka and the Suttas—claim that Lord Buddha's enlightenment concerns the realization of dependent origination. Those who consider the content of the Suttas, especially the events surrounding the attainment of the Three Knowledges—that is the causal factors leading to true enlightenment (especially the first two Knowledges, which cannot be called true enlightenment and are not necessary for attaining nibbana)—can claim that the meaning of nibbana is the Four Noble Truths, that is, freedom from all mental intoxicants (*āsava*).

At any rate, these conclusions—even if they are both true—have their own unique characteristics and one may be broader or more all encompassing than the other. We should, therefore, try to understand the logic behind each position.

It is easy to see the similarities between the two positions above. To summarize, let us look at the points of the Four Noble Truths together with their definitions and the moral duties expressed in each.

1. **Dukkha** is related to birth (*jāti*), decay-and-death (*jarā-maraṇa*), encountering distasteful things, being separated from the things we love, and not obtaining the things we hope for. To summarize, attachment to the Five Aggregates (*khandha*) is dukkha. In another sense, it is a condition (*bhava*) that has innate repression, pressures, conflict, insufficiencies, and incompleteness—all of which constitute a potential problem that may arise at any time and may reoccur or be reborn in any shape or form. For those still clinging to attachments, their duty towards dukkha is to realize it, come to clearly understand its meaning and magnitude in order to proceed to the next stage of coming to a solution of this problem.
2. **Dukkhasamudaya** (abbreviated as *samudaya*) is the cause of dukkha. It is related to craving (*taṇhā*) that leads to a new existence and is linked with being engrossed and infatuated. It involves seeking increasingly new infatuations, of which there are three types: sensual craving (*kāma-taṇhā*), craving for existence (*bhava-taṇhā*), and craving for non-existence (*vibhava-taṇhā*). To put this another way, it is the desire to create and determine a substantial self, which results in pressures and anxieties, fears, and a constant adherence to fixed notions about yourself; in this state of mind, you are impeded and bound. Your duty is to get rid of these fixations, put them down, and move on to the next stage.
3. **Dukkhanirodha** (abbreviated as *nirodha*) is the extinguishing of dukkha. This stage is related to the complete elimination of craving and involves disentangling yourself from desire, shedding it all, and leaving it completely behind. In another sense, the elimination of dukkha due to the abandoning of craving (*taṇhā*) is not subject to the pressures of any anxieties, fears, or attachments. It is simply a pure state of freedom, peace, unencumbered, clear, and bright. Your duty is to make this state of *nirodha* distinct, manifest, real, and attain the Path.
4. **Dukkhanirodhagāminī paṭipadā** (abbreviated as *magga*) is the Path that leads to the extinction of dukkha. The Noble Eight-fold Path has the following elements: proper understanding (*sammādiṭṭhi*), proper thought (*sammāsaṅkappa*), proper speech (*sammāvācā*), proper action (*sammākammanta*), proper livelihood (*sammā-*

ājīva), proper effort (*sammāvāyāma*), proper mindfulness (*sammāsati*), and proper concentration (*sammāsamādhi*). Your duty is to follow the Path by training yourself and practicing in accordance with it.[165]

Allow me to compare the Eight-fold Path with dependent origination as follows:

1. *Samudayavāra*: ignorance arises → mental formations arise → and so on. . . birth takes place → decay-and-death, along with sorrow and so on. . . and distress follows;
2. *Nirodhavāra*: ignorance is extinguished → mental formations are extinguished → and so on. . . birth ceases to take place → decay-and-death ceases, along with sorrow. . . and distress.

Samudayavāra is the aspect of the cycle of dependent origination referred to earlier as *anuloma*, which explains the arising of dukkha. It amounts to combining the first two parts of the Four Noble Truths, dukkha and *samudaya*, into one. But in the Four Noble Truths these two elements are actually divided into separate points; the final part above (birth, decay-and-death, sorrow, and so on), which are results, are taken as the first portion of the Truths, as a problem that is encountered and must be solved. We then return to the section that describes the whole process of arising, and that is set up as the second Truth. This Truth then leads us to search for the source of our problems.

Nirodhavāra is the aspect of the cycle of dependent origination that explains the process of the extinguishing of dukkha. And it is comparable to the third Noble Truth of extinguishing (*nirodha*). It shows us that when we have correctly solved our problems according to their true sources, then those problems will be cut off at the root of their causal factors. Even though dependent origination, in this sense, is in line with the third Noble Truth, it can be said to extend to the fourth as well, because the process of eliminating problems leads to seeing the way or the method of practice necessary for the solution of problems. That is, it shows us what we must do at every step along the Path.

When we distill the Four Noble Truths, we are left with two things: there is dukkha (Noble Truths 1 and 2), and there is the extinguishing of dukkha (Noble Truths 3 and 4).

In these two senses, in some places dependent origination can be said to define the second and third Noble Truths in order. That is, *samudayavāra* defines the second Noble Truth (*samudaya*), and *nirodhavāra* defines the third Noble Truth (*nirodha*).[166] But according to this definition, craving (*taṇhā*) is singled out and emphasized in the process of *samudaya*, and the extinguishing of craving is emphasized in *nirodha*. This is because craving is the major unwholesome tendency (*kilesa*), it is most obvious and has the most apparent role. At any rate, the process that goes along with craving, which is waiting in the wings, is none other than dependent origination.

The special characteristics of or differences between dependent origination and the Four Noble Truths can be summarized as follows:

1. Both of these dhammic principles are different ways of explaining the truth, each with different aims. Dependent origination explains truth according to a process, according to a natural cycle. The Four Noble Truths are statements of truth related to human intelligence and the search for the fruits of practice. In this sense, the Four Noble Truths are dhammic principles that are linked to the historical search for the truth (*saccadhamma*) embarked upon by Lord Buddha; they begin with encountering dukkha, which becomes problematic, and then continue with a search for the cause. And subsequently, discovering a way to solve problems leads to the attainment of the goal—complete freedom from dukkha. This method or way is then held up as a dhammic principle and is used as a teaching device in order to give students an orderly approach to practice. The method of the Four Noble Truths aims at realizing the final fruits of the teachings and changing the behavior of the student. As for dependent origination, it is the pivotal principle of the Four Noble Truths and contains the intellectual content that must be studied if the Four Noble Truths are to be understood in the clearest and most detailed way possible. Dependent origination is, therefore, the dhammic principle that Lord Buddha reflected upon just after he had attained enlightenment.
2. The most important differences between dependent origination and the Four Noble Truths reside in the dimension of *nirodhavāra* in the cycle dependent origination, which is similar to Noble Truths 3 and 4—extinguishing dukkha (*nirodha*) and the Eight-fold Path (*magga*).

   a. When compared with the third Noble Truth (*nirodha*), you will see that the *paṭiloma* explanation of dependent origination essentially aims at explaining the process of extinguishing dukkha. It does not seek to explain the state of *nirodha* or nibbana itself.[167]

For this reason, in the Buddhist texts, when the Dhamma is revealed it is considered in two parts: At first it refers to dependent origination as explained; then there are statements made by the Buddha to the effect that, "this state is something difficult to see, that is, the quieting of all mental formations, the elimination of all attachments (*upadhi*), the ending of all craving (*taṇhā*), the elimination of lust (*virāga*), the extinguishing of dukkha (*nirodha*), nibbana." This shows that the Dhamma he had attained was divided into two parts: dependent origination (*paṭiccasamuppāda*) and the extinguishing of dukkha (*nirodha*). The third Noble Truth, the extinguishing of dukkha (*nirodha*), puts the condition of extinction as foremost, but it also implies that there is a process leading to the cessation of dukkha, as well.

b. Even though the part of dependent origination referred to as *nirodhavāra* includes the fourth Noble Truth, the Path (*magga*), it still does not clearly specify the fruits of the Path. This is because dependent origination explains a complete natural process and does not clearly specify what a person must do, what the steps of the practice are, and how a person should behave. That is to say, no system of practice is specified that would lead to the successful completion of the Path. We can compare this with a doctor who knows the disease but does not prescribe a medicine or a procedure for the care for the patient. The Four Noble Truths, on the other hand, include the fourth truth, the Path, which is explicitly concerned with specifying a cure; it is stated as a separate Truth, as a point of practice that has already been proven, that is guaranteed to get to the heart of the matter—the elimination of dukkha, that is, nibbana.

The fourth Noble Truth, the Eight-fold Path, explains proper behavior and practice in a detailed and broad manner. It is held to be the practice, or the complete Buddhist system of ethics called *majjhimā paṭipadā*—the Middle Path. When the Four Noble Truths are compared to dependent origination, dependent origination is taken to be an expression of the *majjhena dhammadesanā*—the Middle Way of Expressing the Truth. The Middle Path has its own special characteristics that must be given separate treatment.

Before we proceed to other matters, we should delve into the status of the Four Noble Truths in the system of Buddhist teachings found in the canon, the Tipiṭaka.

Friends, the footprints of all land animals fit within the footprint of the elephant; the elephant's footprint is said to be supreme in terms of size. Similarly, all the merits of the Dhamma can be found within the Four Noble Truths.[168]

Bhikkhus, our knowledge according to the truth has three phases with twelve aspects found in the Four Noble Truths. As long as our understanding is not pure we cannot attain Supreme Wisdom (*anuttara sammā sambodhiñāṇa*). . . .[169]

Bhikkhus, because people are not enlightened and do not understand the Four Noble Truths, they run and wander (throughout all their lives) for a long, long time.[170]

At that time, the Blessed One gave a gradual instruction to the householder Upālī on giving (*dāna*), morality (*sīla*), heaven, finding fault with carelessness, no longer being engrossed with sensual fulfillment (*kāma*), and the merits of renunciation (*nekkhamma*). Upālī's mind was ready, supple, free from hindrances, exuberant, and dedicated, and so he proclaimed the teaching of all the Buddhas (*sāmukkaṁsikā dhammadesanā*), that is, dukkha, *samudaya, nirodha,* and *magga* [or the Four Noble Truths].[171]

Those who lead the Holy Life (*brahmacariya*) stay with the Blessed One for the sake of knowledge, insight, attainment, enlightenment, reaching the things yet unknown, unseen, unattained, that have to be done, and have yet to be achieved (that is,) the existence of dukkha, the arising of dukkha (*dukkhasamudaya*), the extinguishing of dukkha (*dukkhanirodha*), and way leading to the attainment of the extinguishing of dukkha (*dukkhanirodhagāminī paṭipadā*).[172]

Please allow me to emphasize once more that there is one thing that is recognized as part of the nature of the Buddhist teachings: In teaching the truth, only the things that can be put to use in this life are of value; the things that do not lead to beneficial results in this life, even if they may be true, are not taught. The Four Noble Truths, therefore, are considered teachings relevant to the present moment. For this reason, the

Lord Buddha did not waste his time and energy on arguing about various problems pertaining to higher philosophical speculation. There is a very popular passage that expresses this.

> Whoever says that as long as the Enlightened One has not solved the problems concerning whether "this world is eternal or not eternal; whether this self and body are one and the same or the self is one thing and the body another; or whether there is or is not life after death, or whether there is a confirmation of both existence and non-existence or a denial of existence and non-existence after death," I will not live the Holy Life (*brahmacariya*) that the Enlightened One has set down—this person is likely to die before he hears the answers to these questions, because the Tathāgata does not speculate about such matters. We can compare this to a person who is hit with a poison-tipped arrow: This person's relatives and blood kin run out to find an expert surgeon to cut out the arrow. But the unfortunate person who has been struck demands that, "As long as I do not know if the person who shot the arrow is a *khattiya*, a *brāhmaṇa*, a *vessa*, or a *sudda*, I do not know his name and ancestry, I do not know if he is tall, short, or of medium height, I do not know if he has dark, light, or medium complexion, I do not know if he lives in a house, a village, or a city, I will not allow this arrow to be removed. As long as I do not know if the bow that was used was a regular bow or a crossbow, if the bowstring was made of hemp, bamboo bark, gut, fiber, or the membrane of a tree, or if the arrow itself was made from a wild tree or a cultivated tree. . .until I know the kind of arrow that was used, I will not allow it to be removed." In this case, the injured person did not have time to discover any of these things. He most certainly had to die first. Anyway. . .that's it for that person.
>
> Truly, Māluṅkyāputta, when you believe that this world is eternal, you cannot lead the Holy Life; when you believe that this world is not eternal, you cannot lead the Holy Life. Whether you believe this world to be eternal or not eternal, there is still birth (*jāti*), decay (*jarā*), death (*maraṇa*), sorrow, lamentation, suffering, grief and distress. Therefore, we decree that this (whole heap of dukkha) should be eliminated right now!. . .

Therefore, all of you should remember the problems that we will not speculate about, that we have set down as problems not worth speculating about; and you should remember the problems that are worthy of contemplation, that we have set down as worthy of our reflection. We will not speculate about the permanence or impermanence of this world. . . .We do not speculate about this, because it is not beneficial. It is not a part of the fundamental aspects of leading the Holy Life: This kind of speculation does not lead to disenchantment (*nibbidā*), detachment (*virāga*), the cessation of dukkha (*nirodha*), tranquillity, higher knowledge, nor nibbana. The things worth contemplating are: dukkha exists, dukkha arises, dukkha passes away, and there is a way leading to the extinction of dukkha. And why do we contemplate these things? Because they are beneficial; they are the basis for leading the Holy Life; they lead to disenchantment, detachment, the cessation of dukkha, tranquillity, higher knowledge, enlightenment, and nibbana.[173]

The Chief Value of the Noble Truths

The Four Noble Truths, aside from encompassing all of the Buddhist principles—including both the theory and practice previously mentioned—have other important values worthy of our consideration. These can be summarized as follows:

These Truths are a methodology based on wisdom, a rational and systematic procedure to the solution of problems. They are a way of successfully solving problems according to values; and if a goal is to be reached, this procedure must be followed in each case.

These Truths are a way of solving problems and organizing your life intelligently. This is accomplished by applying true and natural principles and putting them to beneficial use. It is not necessary to refer to the supernatural powers of any being or creator, any special powers that transcend nature, or any sacred thing.

These Truths are related to the actual lives of all people. Even if a person were to run amok and become distracted and involved with things that are far afield, if he is to continue to lead a valuable life and relate to external things in a beneficial way, he must become involved with and actually apply the benefits of the Four Noble Truths.

These Truths constitute a central principle linked to our lives; they are really the story of our lives. Even if humans were to create arts or sciences to solve their problems and enhance their lives, and then these arts and sciences were to evolve, degenerate, and become completely lost or new ones might arise in their place, the Four Noble Truths would persevere, remain fresh and new, and continue to be of benefit to future generations.

Notes

26. This is another name for *paṭiccasamuppāda,* which literally means the concurrence of causal factors or a condition based on certain causal factors.

27. S.II.25.

28. M.I.190–191.

29. S.II.79–80, for example.

30. S.II.15, 45–46, 129–130.

31. S.II.92.

32. *Ālaya* = being bound, attached, dependent, leading a life dependent on external factors.

33. Vin.I.3–5; M.I.167–168.

34. S.II.27–28, 64–65, and so on.

35. Vin.I.1–3; S.II.1–2, 64–65.

36. S.II.73–74.

37. S.II.78–79.

38. M.I.55. *Āsava* can refer to influxes and outflowings, and in its psychological sense it tends to refer to thoughts that disturb, engross, or impede the mind. The highest levels of Buddhist practice involve the elimination of these "intoxicating" impulses—trans.

39. See S.II.5–11, 81.

40. For example, S.II.52.

41. For example, M.I.266–267.

42. For example, S.II.77.

43. For example, S.II.11, 101.

44. The Abhidhamma explains these factors in terms of twenty-four different aspects; see *Conditional Relations* (Paṭṭhāna), translated by U Narada Mula Patthana Sayadaw. 2 vols. (London: Pali Text Society. Vol.1, 1969; vol. 2, 1981).

45. For example, S.II.73.

46. S.II.65.

47. S.II.72.

48. S.II.73.

49. *Abhidhamma Vibhaṅga*, Vbh.138–192.

50. Some people translate the term "*avijjā*" as things without knowledge or a state of unknowing, and so they explain matter as the first cause of life; some people explain "*avijjā*" as the unknowable, and therefore they take it to be God. As for "*saṅkhāra*," they take it to cover all conditioned things (*saṅkhata-dhamma*), and so on.

51. See Vism.517–586; VbhA.130–213.

52. And, as we have already noted, in certain English translations—trans.

53. D.III.214–219; S.IV.259; S.V.56.

54. Vism.499; VbhA.93.

55. Dukkha, in terms of *saṅkhāra-dukkha* here, can be summarized as the following: one aspect constitutes conflict, oppression, unrest, and imperfection; a second aspect can be equated with a state of unsatisfactoriness; and a third amounts to a state of being susceptible to suffering.

56. *Kāmupādāna*—clinging to sensuality.

57. *Diṭṭhupādāna*—clinging to erroneous views.

58. *Sīlabbatupādāna*—clinging to rules and rituals.

59. *Attavādupādāna*—clinging to belief in a persistent soul or self.

60. *Kāmasukha* = pleasure derived from the five senses; some basic examples are being enthralled with gambling, drinking alcohol, and various [sensual] entertainments.

61. *Saññutta* = tied up, tied to (and composed of unwholesome tendencies [*kilesa*]—SA.III.77).

62. S.IV.207–210.

63. For the factors of Vibhaṅga, see Vbh.135–192; Vism.517–586; VbhA.130–213; Abhidh-s.36–40; also see Narada Thera, *A Manual of Abhidhamma*. Vols. 1 and 2 (Rangoon: Buddha Sasana Council, 1970), 74–83.

64. For this definition, see, for example, S.II.2–4; Vbh.135–138; and for more information see the references to the *Visuddhimagga* and the VbhA.

65. *Pubbanta—aparanta—pubbantāparanta* (—the past—the future—both the past and the future); see Dhs.183.

66. *Kāya-saṅkhāra* = *kāya-sañcetanā* (physical intentionality) = the 20 intentions of the physical sense-doors (the 8 *kāmāvacara-kusala* and the 12 *kāmāvacara-akusala*); *vacī-saṅkhāra* = *vacī-sañcetanā* (intentionality of speech) = the 20 intentions of the speech sense-door (the 8 *kāmāvacara-kusala* and the 12 *kāmāvacara-akusala*); *citta-saṅkhāra* = *mano-sañcetanā* (mental intentionality) = the 29 intentions of the mental sense-door, which have yet to be explained in terms of gesture (*kāya-viññatti*) and speech (*vacī-viññatti*).

67. *Puññābhisaṅkhāra* (the good things that make up life, the formation of merit) = the 13 good intentions of the sense-sphere and the sphere of form (the 8 wholesome sense-spheres and the 5 wholesome form-spheres); *apuññābhisaṅkhāra* (the bad things that make up life, the formation of demerit) = the 12 unwholesome intentions of the sense-doors; *āneñjābhisaṅkhāra* (the stable things that make up life, formation of the faultless) = the 4 wholesome intentions of the formless-sphere.

68. When expanded, this can be equated with the 32 *lokiya-viññāṇa* (the 5 *viññāṇa* of good consequences + the 5 of bad consequences = 10 + the 22 *mano-viññāṇa*); or it can be equated with the 13 *viññāṇa* (the 5 *viññāṇa* of good consequences + the 5 of bad consequences + the 2 mental elements (*mano-dhātu*) + 1 element of rootless consciousness accompanied by joy), which continue from the initial thought-moment of a life (*paṭisandhi-viññāṇa*) to the final thought-moment (*cuti*), and the remaining 19 types of rebirth consciousness that carry over from the relinking moment to the initial thought-moment of a life.

69. See the explanation in the section on the "Five Aggregates of Existence (*pañca-khandha*)."

70. *Phassa* = the senses coming into contact with external sense-objects and consciousness arising due to this contact.

71. Sensations (*vedanā*) can be divided into three aspects in accordance with their characteristics: pleasurable (sukha), unpleasurable (dukkha) and neutral (*upekkhā*); or feeling can be divided into five types: physical pleasure, physical displeasure, mental pleasure, mental displeasure and equanimity.

72. *Taṇhā* can be divided into 3 types: craving that satisfies the five senses (*kāma-taṇhā*); craving for existence or eternal life (*bhava-taṇhā*), and craving for non-existence or annihilation (*vibhava-taṇhā*). These 3 *taṇhā* multiplied by the 6 *taṇhā* above equals 18; if these 18 are then multiplied by the 2 dimensions of the internal and the external, this yields 36; and this multiplied by the 3 phases of time (past, present, and future) = 108.

73. *Vokāra* refers to constituents of being (*khandha*)—trans.

74. The latter definition under both birth (11.) and decay-and-death (12.) is used in reference to momentary causality (Vbh.145).

75. Once again, the term *arom* is used here to mean mental-objects or ideation rather than its more common usage in Thai meaning "mood"—trans.

76. The choice of terminology is telling here since the Thai believe in maintaining a "cool-heart" (Thai, *chai-yen*), a value influenced by Buddhism. Also, the metaphor of electrical circuitry lends yet another sense to the author's use of the simile of a current or flow to express the interconnected nature of things and the workings of the mind—trans.

77. Vism.576.

78. Vism.576.

79. Vism.529.

80. M.I.54.

81. Thai, *akan*; Pali, *ākāra*—trans.

82. The Commentaries suggest that specifying *avijjā* and *taṇhā* as two different root causes has two different aims: *avijjā* is used for those with improper understanding, and *taṇhā* is used for those with strong craving. The phase with *avijjā* as its root cause was put forth in order to do away with belief in annihilationism (*ucchedadiṭṭhi*); and the phase with *taṇhā* as its root cause was put forth in order to do away with belief in eternalism (*sassatadiṭṭhi*) [two extreme views]; and the phase with *avijjā* as its root cause is intended for womb-born creatures (*gabbhaseyyakasatta*), and the phase with *taṇhā* as its root cause is meant for creatures of spontaneous birth (*opapātika*); see Vism.578.

83. A.V.113; Vism.562.

84. A.V.116; Vism.562.

85. S.II.23.

86. Some Buddhist scholars in Thailand have suggested that this comment is a reference to the teachings of the reformist monk Buddhadasa Bhikkhu. Part of Buddhadasa Bhikkhu's reforms have involved a reification of certain notions of heaven and hell, kamma, and the final goal of Buddhism—nibbana. One aspect of Buddhadasa Bhikkhu's teachings has involved a shift in emphasis from the more traditional explanation of the "three lives" according to Buddhaghosa—that is the force of kamma that is carried over from past lives, to the present, and into future existences—to the importance of realizing the fruits of kamma

from moment to moment. In other words, a person can fall into hell or ascend into heaven in the space of a thought moment, or a person can act unwisely or attain enlightenment in the space of a thought moment (according to Buddhadasa Bhikkhu, like a flash of lightning). This is very different from the long view that is most pervasive in popular Theravada Buddhism, in which a person must accumulate a great deal of merit of the course of several lifetimes before progress down the path (or rather up the ladder) can be made. So, perhaps here, we find the author attempting to be compromising, without mentioning names; he seems to be tempering the teachings of Buddhadasa Bhikkhu, and will demonstrate below that both of these teaching—one pertaining to the "three lives" and the other pertaining to the importance of the present moment—can both be found in the texts. For more on this, see Olson (1989), esp. 336–340; and Buddhadasa Bhikkhu, *Paṭiccasamuppāda: Dependent Origination*, trans. by Steve Schmidt (Bangkok: Sublime Life Mission, 1986), esp. 16–19—trans.

87. *Pubbanta.*

88. *Aparanata.*

89. M.II.31–32.

90. S.IV.327.

91. *Pubbekatahetu.*

92. S.IV.230.

93. S.II.65.

94. In sections to follow this will be dealt with in even more depth.

95. The following example is for the purpose of simplicity; its true meaning will be examined later.

96. S.II.114.

97. The translation of these three types of craving (especially the second and third) continues to cause debate (see Vbh.365; Vism.567–568, for example). Some people compare *bhava-taṇhā* to the "life-instinct" or "life-wish" and *vibhava-taṇhā* to the "death instinct" or "death-wish" according to Freudian psychology (see M. O'C. Walshe, *Buddhism for Today* [London: George, Unwin, and Allen, 1962], 37–40). For a very clear reference to these to terms see It.43–44.

98. For the three *āsava*, see D.II.81; S.IV.256, and so on; for the four *āsava*, see Vibh.373, and so on.

99. Craving for sense-pleasure; craving for self-existence; and craving for non-existence or self-annihilation. See number 7 above under the heading

"Examples Showing Basic Relationships between the Elements of Dependent Origination"—trans.

100. Here, *kāma-taṇhā* translates as wanting, *bhava-taṇhā* as wanting to be, and *vibhava-taṇhā* as wanting to cease to exist.

101. *Sassatadiṭṭhi* = eternalism, constancy.

102. *Ucchedadiṭṭhi* = annihilationism, indeterminacy. Both this concept and the above are improper views related to belief in a self. *Sassatadiṭṭhi* has already been made clear, but *ucchedadiṭṭhi* can be explained brieflyly as follows: because of seeing all things as having a self and as existing as separate entities, a person comes to believe that these things eventually disappear or completely cease to exist. This will be explained in much more detail below in a section entitled, "Dependent Origination Expressed as a Middle Truth (*majjhena dhammadesanā*)."

103. *Kāma* = things that fulfill the needs of the five senses and a desire for things that meet these needs.

104. The most fundamental views (*diṭṭhi*) that satisfy craving (*taṇhā*) are eternalism (*sassatadiṭṭhi*) and annihilationism (*ucchedadiṭṭhi*) and views that are of a similar nature.

105. Phra Ariyananthamuni, *Lak Phraphutthasatsana* (Bangkok: Suwichan, 2499 [1956]), 60.

106. The four *upādāna* can be found in Vbh.375; D.III.231, and so on. This is especially true for attachment to belief in a consistent self or soul (*attavādupādāna*); when we examine this belief, we can see that it relates to attachment to one of the Five Aggregates of Existence. The Pali texts state that, "People. . . tend to understand the body to be the self or think that the self has a body or believe that the body resides in the self or that the self resides in the body. They believe [the same] for sensation (*vedanā*). . . perception (*sañña*). . . mental-formations (*saṅkhāra*). They understand feeling to be the self or believe that the self has feelings or that feeling resides in the self or that the self resides in feelings. . . ."

107. A.II.145.

108. In the case of other doctrines or theories, the term "*vāda*" is an alternative for "*diṭṭhi*." For this reason, the *vāda* listed here might also be referred to as *atthikadiṭṭhi, natthikadiṭṭhi, sassatadiṭṭhi, ucchedadiṭṭhi*, and so on. Also, the term *atthikavāda* can also be called *sabbatthikavāda*.

109. *Sammādiṭṭhi* may be rendered as proper understanding or proper view, and it relates to the proper, correct, or right outlook and perspective for attaining the final goal. As noted above, *diṭṭhi* itself may refer to conclusions, opinions,

and biases that can become an obstacle to clear, unimpeded understanding of the true nature of things. Proper understanding is a fundamental element of the Eight-fold Path and will be discussed in much more detail in part II—trans.

110. S.II.16–17, 76; S.III.134–135.

111. S.II.77.

112. S.II.19–20.

113. S.II.22–23.

114. S.II.39, and so on; for those interested in further references, see D.I.53; S.I.134; D.III.137; Ud.69–70; A.III.336, 440; Vbh.377.

115. Both of these terms have been combined here for the first time. They are the same as *sassataditthi* (eternalism, belief in the continuation of the soul after death) and *ucchedaditthi* (annihilationism, belief in the annihilation of the soul after death).

116. S.II.75.

117. S.II.75.

118. S.II.61–62.

119. S.II.13–14.

120. S.II.64–65.

121. S.II.27.

122. Here, the term "*satta*" refers to the Tathāgata, and this can be found in the Commentaries, MA.II.117; but SA.II.287 says that Tathāgata refers to Lord Buddha, and UdA.340 states that Tathāgata refers to *attā* or Ātman.

123. S.IV.395, and so on. There are many reasons why Lord Buddha decided not to answer the questions related to the so-called higher philosophies, the most important being that they are formed based on a fundamental misunderstandings or assumptions. A question not based on the truth is deemed a false question by Lord Buddha. In other cases, the questions relate to a matter that cannot be ascertained via reasoning. Since the answer cannot be found by applying the senses, speculation about its answer is considered a waste of time. And related to this, when an answer cannot be obtained through reason, sitting around constructing speculative theories does not help anyone in terms of putting an actual teaching into practice in real life. The Lord Buddha encouraged questions that dealt with daily life and practice, questions that would be beneficial. This is the reason why he disregarded certain questions and invited others dealing with the present circumstances—the answers to which would not be a waste of

time. And if certain people were able to arrive at the truth, Lord Buddha encouraged them to get busy and put this into practice; he did not want people to sit around blindly debating ungrounded issues. And finally, we should keep in mind that Lord Buddha lived at a time when many different philosophical questions were being raised and various doctrinal debates were taking place. Therefore, people at that time tended to ask various questions that often took them far afield from the truth and daily life. Getting involved in these ceaseless questions was often a fruitless pastime. Lord Buddha, therefore, simply refused to answer these kinds of questions and get involved in these debates; this became a forceful way to pull people back and focus attention on his teachings. This was one type of psychological method that he employed. For more on this methodology in terms of Buddhist practice, see the section on the "Noble Truths (*ariyasacca*)" below; as for references in the canon, see the following: M.I.426–432, 434–486; S.II.222–223; S.IV.374–403; A.IV.67–68; A.V.193–198, and so on.

124. Relating to acts of the body.

125. Relating to acts of speech.

126. Relating to acts of the mind.

127. S.II.40.

128. See the earlier section on these two terms: Pair 3 under "Dependent Origination Expressed as a Middle Truth (*majjhena dhammadesanā*)."

129. A.I.173; and also see Vbh.367; M.II.214–222.

130. M.II.214.

131. S.IV.230–231.

132. A.I.249.

133. S.IV.319–322.

134. A.III.415.

135. M.III.203.

136. S.I.227.

137. Dh.60.

138. S.I.57.

139. M.I.39.

140. Thīg.240–241.

141. Ud.6.

142. J.I.374.

143. J.I.258.

144. A.I.294.

145. M.III.187, and so on.

146. A.III.47.

147. S.III.153.

148. Kamma translates as action, but in some cases the meaning can be narrower, referring to a person's career or occupation.

149. Sn.612–654.

150. M.II.179.

151. Sn.136.

152. A.IV.202.

153. D.III.97.

154. Dh.276.

155. Dh.160.

156. Dh.165.

157. D.II.101; D.III.77; S.III.42.

158. A.III.72.

159. Ud.51.

160. S.I.93.

161. See Vin.I.1–6.

162. See Vin.I.1–6.

163. See M.I.164–173, 240–249; M.II.93–94, 211–212.

164. See M.I.164–173, 240–249; M.II.93–94, 211–212.

165. There are several definitions of the Four Noble Truths, such as the one in the *Dhammacakkappavattana Sutta*, S.V.420–430; Vin.I.10; S.V.421; Vbh.99–107. The most important thing is knowing and correctly observing each Noble Truth, otherwise misunderstandings and improper practices will result.

Correctly observing each Truth is called tending to the "duty" (*kicca*) of the Noble Truths, which are the following:

1. the duty of dukkha = full comprehension (*pariññā*), understanding and realizing the scope of all problems;
2. the duty of *samudaya* = giving up things (*pahāna*), getting at the root cause of problems;
3. the duty of *nirodha* = realization (*sacchikiriyā*), meaning attaining a state devoid of problems or attaining the goal of clear understanding. Some misunderstandings about Buddhism—such as the view of some critics who say that Buddhism perceives the world as bad or evil—often come from not understanding how to take care of the "duties" of the Four Noble Truths.

166. See S.II.104–105.

167. For an earlier explanation of *paṭiloma-paṭiccasamupāda*, see the section entitled "The Text and Interrelationship of the Principle of Dependent Origination" —trans.

168. M.I.184.

169. See the *Dhammacakkappavattana Sutta*; Vin.I.10; and S.V.420.

170. D.II.90.

171. M.I.379–380; and see A.IV.209-210, for example. *Sāmukkaṁsikā dhammadesanā* is usually translated as the most sublime presentation of the Dhamma and is held in high regard by the Buddhas; or it is teachings that Lord Buddha delivered spontaneously, unlike other sermons or dialogues that are often based on questions posed by other people.

172. A.IV.384–385.

173. M.I.428–432.

PART

II

The Middle Way of Practicing the Truth (*majjhimā paṭipadā*)

The Middle Points of Practice According to Natural Law

How Should We Live Our Lives?
The Middle Path

The Middle Way of Practicing the Truth (*majjhimā paṭipadā*) as a Continuation of the Middle Way of Expressing the Truth (*majjhena dhammadesanā*)

According to the principles of dependent origination, there are two "paths" mentioned in the texts:

- *Micchāpaṭipadā*—Improper practice or the incorrect way; that is, the way leading to dukkha; and
- *Sammāpaṭipadā*—Proper practice or the correct way; that is, the way leading to the end of dukkha.

These can be summarized as follows:

Micchāpaṭipadā: Ignorance (*avijjā*) → mental formations (*saṅkhāra*) → consciousness (*viññāṇa*) and so on → birth (*jāti*) → decay-and-death (*jarā-maraṇa*) leading to sorrow and so on. . .

Sammāpaṭipadā: extinguishing of ignorance → extinguishing of mental formations → extinguishing of consciousness. . . → extinguishing of birth → extinguishing of decay-and-death leading to the end of sorrow and so on. . .[1]

Accordingly, *micchāpaṭipadā* constitutes the *samudayavāra* aspect of dependent origination, or the process of the arising of dukkha; and *sammāpaṭipadā* is the same as the *nirodhavāra* aspect of dependent origination, or the process leading to the cessation of dukkha. As for *micchāpaṭipadā*, we need not speak of it because it deals with the arising of dukkha already explained in some detail. In our consideration of *sammāpaṭipadā* so far, we have shown it to be the aspect of dependent origination called *nirodhavāra*, but we have yet to point out or suggest any of the details of proper practice. We have only suggested that in the course of reaching the final goal, the process of extinguishing must take place. But this principle of *sammāpaṭipadā* does not state what must be done to make the process unfold in a particular way. For this reason, our presentation of *sammāpaṭipadā* has not yet helped to clarify the details of appropriate action.

There are other canonical references that explain dependent origination as a process of eliminating dukkha. These references are different from those referred to so far as the *nirodha* aspect of *sammāpaṭipadā*. They do not mention the extinguishing of dukkha. Rather, they explain a process that takes off from the cycle of the arising of dukkha known as *samudayavāra* as follows:

> ignorance (*avijjā*) → mental formations (*saṅkhāra*) → consciousness (*viññāṇa*) → sense-bases (*saḷāyatana*) → contact (*phassa*) → sensation (*vedanā*) → craving (*taṇhā*) → attachment (*upādāna*) → becoming (*bhava*) → birth (*jāti*) → **dukkha** → confidence (*saddhā*) → delight (*pāmojja*) → joy (*pīti*) → serenity (*passaddhi*) → sukha → concentration (*samādhi*) → knowing things as they are (*yathābhūtañāṇadassana*) → disenchantment (*nibbidā*) → detachment (*virāga*) → liberation (*vimutti*) → final realization (*khayañāṇa*)[2]

Notice that this cycle starts with ignorance and moves on to dukkha, which is actually the *samudayavāra* aspect of dependent origination or the process describing the arising of dukkha (here, dukkha is used in place of the succession of decay and death [*jarā-maraṇa*], sorrow and so on. . .). But when we come to the element of dukkha, instead of the cycle completing itself and beginning again with ignorance, it continues on with confidence (Thai, *sattha*; Pali, *saddhā*) taking its place.[3] From this point, this process continues on in a positive direction until the final goal of realization (*khayañāṇa*) is attained; there is no returning to the ignorance that used to set the previous cycle in motion. It is also worth noting that when dukkha (which appears in bold letters) is taken as the pivotal element, the number of elements in each segment—when counted back to the beginning or forward to the end—is equal.

For the person who already understands ignorance and has studied dependent origination, this process will not seem strange at all, because when one section is eliminated—the process has two sections, from ignorance (*avijjā*) to dukkha and from confidence (*saddhā*) to realization (*khayañāṇa*)—confidence is simply ignorance that has been exploited or worn down. That is to say, this confidence is not blind ignorance: a seed of knowledge and understanding has been planted and its roots are now becoming imbedded in the rich soil of good intentions that will lead to true knowledge and, finally, to the blooming of enlightenment.

Simply put, when the process of the arising of dukkha continues from ignorance to dukkha and dukkha is experienced, we look for a way out. While we are searching, if we happen to receive suggestions or teachings that are correct, or we come to realize the reasons for the existence of dukkha, we begin to establish confidence in these worthy things and begin to feel delight and contentment. This delight and joy lead us to further progress on a course of goodness that is headed towards the final goal.

Actually, the second half of this cycle is the same as the *nirodhavāra* aspect of dependent origination, which shows the extinguishing of ignorance → the extinguishing of mental formations → the extinguishing of consciousness and so on, similar to the initial part; but here the major features of this process are explained in more detail and aim at linking the process of the arising of dukkha with the elimination of dukkha and showing how the two are related.

Lord Buddha explained the extinguishing of dukkha in the following way:[4]

> Ānanda, in this sense, the moral code (*sīla*) of skillful conduct leads to a lack of remorse (being free of worries); it is the essence (of meaning and the fruits of the practice); it is the right result. Having no remorse and experiencing delight are the essence, the right result. Delight that leads to joy is the essence, the right result. Joy that leads to tranquillity is the essence, the right result. Tranquillity that leads to happiness is the essence, the right result. Happiness that leads to concentration is the essence, the right result. Concentration that leads to seeing with the knowledge of things as they really are (*yathābhūtañāṇadassana*) is the essence, the right result. Knowledge of reality that leads to the extinguishing of lust is the essence, the right result. The extinguishing of lust that leads to detachment is the essence, the right result. Detachment that leads to seeing with the knowledge of liberation (*vimuttiñāṇadassana*) is the essence, the right result. The moral

code of skillful conduct completes the other points of the Dhamma and, in this way, leads a person step by step to arahantship.[5]

According to this text, the progression can be simply stated as follows:

skillful moral code (*kusala-sīla*) → absence of remorse (*avippaṭisāra*) → delight → joy → serenity → sukha → concentration → knowing things as they are → disenchantment → detachment → knowledge of liberation

You can see that this progression is similar to the one mentioned earlier. This earlier progression, however, only shows the process of the extinguishing of dukkha. Therefore, let us look at the elements previously mentioned one more time:

ignorance → mental formations → (and so on) → birth → **dukkha** → confidence → delight → joy → serenity → sukha → concentration → knowing things as they are → disenchantment → detachment → liberation → final realization

Both of these progressions, while being the same, do not use the same terminology. In the course of eliminating dukkha, the first progression begins with confidence (*saddhā*) and the other with skillful ethics (*kusala-sīla*) linked with a lack of remorse (*avippaṭisāra*), and from then on they are similar. Actually, their differences are only a matter of terminology and emphasis, and so their meanings remain compatible. The first progression takes confidence as its main feature. And when this confidence has been established, reasoning proceeds with increasing certainty; beliefs are based on goodness and beauty, and there is certainty about the excellence of the Dhamma. At the same time, this mental state is also linked with behavior; that is, good behavior becomes a supporting foundation while confidence continues to maintain this good behavior. With proper behavior as the solid base for this confidence, delight is experienced. As for the other progression that starts with the skillful moral code and a lack of remorse, the same is true; this progression also takes behavior and practice as its major factors. In this case, the mind has also established confidence in reasoning, with goodness as its foundation—a person chooses, therefore, to act properly. And when a person has proper ethics, he experiences delight, has no remorse, is unperturbed, and feels certain about himself and the value of his good deeds—and this is the type of confidence that makes the mind positive and bright. It then follows that confidence becomes a factor in bringing about delight in the second progression, ending with liberation (*vimutti*) and final realization (*khayañāṇa*). The other progression above ends with knowledge of liberation (*vimuttiñāṇadassana*), which can be equated with realization.

The delineation of the preceding steps helps to make the practice clearer. They help us to gain a better understanding of what must be done. However, they do not yet represent a sufficiently detailed system of practice, and the question still remains as to what must be done to set this process in motion.

Before moving on, allow me to present another model of dependent origination in order to expand our understanding of the various dimensions of its elements. This will allow us to see the different aspects of these elements and it will serve as a tool for further understanding as we proceed.

1. The Sustenance (āhāra) *of Ignorance*

Bhikkhus, I declare that ignorance has the following factors:

- Ignorance has sustenance; the sustenance of ignorance is the five hindrances;[6]
- The five hindrances have sustenance. . .three types of improper conduct;[7]
- The three types of improper conduct have sustenance. . .lack of control of the senses;
- Lack of control of the senses has sustenance. . .lack of mindfulness and clear comprehension;
- Lack of mindfulness and clear comprehension have sustenance. . .lack of critical, systematic reflection;[8]
- Lack of proper reflection has sustenance. . .lack of confidence;
- Lack of confidence has sustenance. . .not paying attention to the Dhamma;
- Not paying attention to the Dhamma has sustenance. . .not associating with good people;

  not associating with and having the support of good people means not hearing the true Dhamma and not having it for your support; not hearing the true Dhamma means not having the foundation of confidence. . . .

Having the five hindrances as your support indicates having ignorance as your foundation;
ignorance has sustenance, and it is supported in this way.[9]

2. The Sustenance of Knowledge and Liberation

- Knowledge and liberation have sustenance; the sustenance of ignorance and liberation is the seven constituents of enlightenment;[10]
- The seven constituents of enlightenment have sustenance. . . the four foundations of mindfulness;[11]
- The four foundations of mindfulness have sustenance. . . the three types of proper conduct;[12]
- The three types of proper conduct have sustenance. . . the restraint of the senses;[13]
- The restraint of the senses has sustenance. . . mindfulness and clear comprehension;
- Mindfulness and clear comprehension have sustenance. . . critical, systematic reflection;
- Critical, systematic reflection has sustenance. . . confidence;
- Confidence has sustenance. . . paying attention to the true Dhamma;
- Paying attention to the true Dhamma has sustenance. . . association with good people;

Associating with good, pure people leads to devoting complete attention to the true Dhamma;
devoting complete attention to the true Dhamma leads to perfect confidence. . . and so on. . . .
Having perfected the seven constituents of enlightenment, knowledge of true liberation is attained. Liberation is sustained and completed in this way.[14]

In this progression of teachings, I would like you to take special note of two elements. The following two elements are special in terms of their place in the Buddhist system of practice: one, critical reflection (*yonisomanasikāra*), is the principle used in the Buddhist method of reflection and is considered very important to the internal, psychological process; two, association with good people (= having spiritual friends, *kalyāṇamitta*), shows the importance of having the support of social factors, and it is held to be an important external factor. Both of these elements have confidence as a linking factor, as we will discover in the next section.

Coming to a Basic Understanding of the Middle Path

The Middle Path, or the fourth Noble Truth, constitutes a summary of principles of behavior and practice, or the complete system of Buddhist ethics. It is the section of teachings that will help us to progress to the goal of enlightenment according to the dhammic process that we have come to know. It represents the fruits of practice to be attained in real life. Or, we might say that it is a method that applies the principles of a natural process in order to realize the highest benefits in this life. Please consider the following passage and summary from the Buddhist canon. It will serve as a starting point for understanding the Middle Path.

> Bhikkhus, there are two extremes that bhikkhus should avoid: engaging in self-indulgence of any kind, which is of a lower order and is not noble or beneficial; also, we do not get involved in self-mortification, which constitutes dukkha and is not noble or beneficial.
>
> The Tathāgata reached enlightenment via this Middle Path that avoids these two extremes. The Path gives us eyes (sight), gives us insight (knowledge), and leads to peace, higher knowledge, enlightenment, and nibbana.
>
> What is this Middle Path? It is the Noble Way composed of eight factors: proper understanding (*sammādiṭṭhi*), proper thought (*sammāsaṅkappa*), proper speech (*sammāvācā*), proper action (*sammākammanta*), proper livelihood (*sammā-ājiva*), proper effort (*sammāvāyāma*), proper mindfulness (*sammāsati*), and proper concentration (*sammāsamādhi*).[15]

The First Discourse or the *Dhammacakkapavattana Sutta* summarizes the complete meaning, content, and aim of the Middle Path. We should note that while this Middle Path or Middle Way exists by avoiding the following two extremes, this does not simply mean remaining in the middle of any two extremes or taking a position of compromise in between two incorrect notions: the extreme of sensual indulgence or extreme hedonism (*kāmasukhallikānuyoga*); and the extreme of self-mortification or extreme asceticism (*attakilamathānuyoya*).

> The Noble Path has eight factors. It is the way leading to the end of the accumulation of kamma, that is, [from] proper understanding (*sammādiṭṭhi*) . . . [to] proper concentration (*sammāsamādhi*).[16]

Here, the Middle Path is crucial in putting an end to the build-up of kamma. We should not misunderstand this to mean that this is the end of retribution (Thai, *wen*) and kamma, as many people have very narrowly come to understand it. We should not misunderstand this to mean that we can put an end to kamma by not performing kamma or not doing anything at all, which can begin to look like the doctrine of the Jains. Also, we should not misunderstand the Path to mean that putting an end to kamma involves quitting our usual activities, sitting still, and doing nothing.[17]

First, putting an end to kamma means truly dedicating yourself to the task of its elimination. And this means acting according to the principles of the Middle Path, acting in accordance with a correct methodology, and discontinuing all incorrect activities.

Second, as I have mentioned, extinguishing kamma does not imply sitting still and doing nothing. Rather, it means that we should cease our mundane activities and turn them into noble activities. Simply put, common people are usually driven by craving and attachment; they are attached to notions of good and bad that relate to personal benefits and gain. The actions of common folk are, therefore, referred to in dhammic terms as "kamma" and are divided according to notions of good and bad that are adhered to with craving and attachment. When we stop acting with attachment to what is good and bad, and these notions of good and bad no longer exist, whatever we do can no longer be referred to as kamma, because kamma must be one or the other—either good or bad. The actions of noble people proceed, therefore, according to reason and what needs to be done within a particular context. Their actions have nothing to do with craving or the existence of internal attachments. Noble people do not perform bad deeds, because they no longer have any reason to do so (they lack the greed, ill-will, and delusion that would motivate them to do things merely for personal gain). They only perform good and beneficial acts because their actions are based on wisdom (*paññā*) and compassion (*karuṇā*). However, the "good" of these noble people is not limited to conventional ways of thinking; it is not a good that is related to personal gain. Whenever common folks do something good, they tend to hope for some kind of ultimate reward. And if there is no such obvious hope motivating their actions, there may be a more subtle wish for fame or acknowledgement; or even more subtle than this, they may cling to their good deeds as something that gives them inner warmth or self-satisfaction. As for noble people, when they do something beneficial, they only do this according to a proper purpose, goal, or reason, or because it is necessary in a particular context. Dhammic language, therefore, does not refer to this as kamma. The Path or Middle Way is a method of practice for getting rid of this kamma. All that remains is functional activity. This is the difference between the mundane (*lokiya*) and the supramundane (*lokuttara*). Lord Buddha and all arahants act beneficially and teach people without creating kamma—even though these actions are referred to by common people as "good."

> What is this Holy Life (*brahmacariya*)? Who are those who lead the Holy Life? And what is the goal of the Holy Life?
>
> The Noble Path is composed of eight factors: [from] proper understanding. . . [to] proper concentration. These make up the Holy Life. Anyone who lives according to this Eight-fold Path can be called a Brahma-farer (*brahmacārī*). The dissolution of lust (*rāga*), ill-will (*dosa*), and delusion (*moha*) is the goal of the Holy Life.[18]

The term "Holy Life" is often understood in a narrow way, referring only to monastic chastity and abstaining from sexual intercourse, which is only one sense of the word.[19] Actually, Lord Buddha used the term to refer to a lifestyle in accordance with all of the Buddhist principles, or it was often used as a synonym for Buddhism itself. This first occurred when Lord Buddha sent the disciples out to spread the religion. He told them to go out and proclaim the Holy Life.[20] And Lord Buddha said that the Holy Life will prosper when the four assemblies of Buddhist devotees—monks (*bhikkhu*), nuns (*bhikkhunī*), male laity (*upāsaka*), and female laity (*upāsikā*)—along with the Brahma-farers and householders know and practice the Dhamma well together.[21] Here, *brahmacariya* can be translated as living the Holy Life, as leading an excellent life. According to the Pali texts cited here, the Holy Life is none other than the Middle Path, and the Brahma-farers are those who are walking the Middle Path.

> Ānanda, having a good spiritual friend (*kalyāṇamitta*) amounts to whole of the Holy Life, because those who have found a good friend[22] . . . have the desire to progress along the Noble Eight-fold Path, and they will make great strides down this path.[23]

Bhikkhus, when the sun is rising, its rays break the horizon before it does; these rays are a foreshadowing of things to come. In the same way, having a good spiritual friend is a good sign, a foreshadowing of the Noble Eight-fold Path.[24]

These passages show the importance of having the support of good people in your daily life, people who will provide leadership and set an example of the proper practice of the dhammic principles.

Bhikkhus, I do not support the incorrect way (*micchāpaṭipadā*) for bhikkhus or for laity. Bhikkhus and laity alike who practice incorrectly and are not successful in proceeding along the Noble Path can attribute this to their improper practice. What is the incorrect path? It is improper understanding (*micchādiṭṭhi*)... improper concentration (*micchāsamādhi*).

I uphold the proper way (*sammāpaṭipadā*) for bhikkhus and for laity. Bhikkhus and laity alike who practice correctly meet with success along the Noble Path. They depend on their correct practice for this. What is the proper way? It is proper understanding (*sammādiṭṭhi*)... proper concentration (*sammāsamādhi*)....[25]

Passages that mention the incorrect and correct path have already been cited. These earlier passages explain the process of the arising of dukkha as *micchāpaṭipadā* and the process of the extinguishing of dukkha as *sammāpaṭipadā*. The passages cited here referring to the Path reveal the same factors in the process cited earlier. However, as we now can see, the Path is presented and applied to daily practice as a system of behavior, and *sammāpaṭipadā* is none other than the Middle Path.

In yet another way, these passages emphasize the Middle Path as a set of dhammic principles that lead both monks and laity to aspire to proper practice and the attainment of the final goal.

Bhikkhus, we can compare this to the person who travels a long way and comes upon a large body of water. This shore is dangerous and frightening; but the other shore is safe and tranquil. There is no boat or bridge for crossing over. This person thinks, "This shore is dangerous... if I were to collect grasses, sticks, branches, and leaves and weave them into a raft and then use this raft—paddling with hands and feet—could I safely cross over to the other shore?"

Then, when this person has...constructed a raft...safely crossed over...he thinks, "This raft has been of great benefit; I have depended on this raft...It has allowed me to safely cross over. Should I, therefore, take this raft and carry it on my head or shoulder it around with me at all times?" According to our purpose, bhikkhus, what do you think about this? Has this person acted correctly and performed his duty towards this raft? (The bhikkhus present respond by saying that this is incorrect.)

What can this person do that we would call performing his proper duty towards this raft? Once this person has safely crossed over, he thinks that, "This raft has been of great benefit to me...so now should I drag it up on the shore or leave it moored in the water?" The person who does this can be said to have carried out his duty towards the raft.

The Dhamma can be compared to this raft. I explain it with the aim of using it to cross over, not as something to cling to and parade around. Once all of you come to know the Dhamma, which is comparable to that raft, you should leave the Dhamma alone—not to mention all of the things that are not conducive to the Dhamma (*adhamma*).[26]

Bhikkhus, if we cling to, gloat over, and cherish *diṭṭhi* (theories, principles, and conclusions about the Dhamma) that are pure and bright, calling them ours, consider the parable of the raft just presented. We proclaim the Dhamma so that it can be used for crossing over. We should not tie ourselves to it, right?[27]

Both of these sections from the canon serve as reminders not to cling to the Dhamma (even though it constitutes truth and correctness) and not to attach to the benefits of its meaning, values, and truths. Moreover, these sections point out the importance of viewing the Dhamma as a tool or piece of equipment, as a method for attaining our goals—not as something floating in thin air or as an end in itself. For this reason, whenever we practice in accordance with one dhammic principle or another, we must have a clear realization of the purpose of that principle, along with its relationship to other points of the Dhamma that are a part of the course that leads to the final purpose of Buddhism. Here, the term "purpose" does not mean reaching a final goal and stopping or attaining a wish, as it is often commonly used—it refers especially to the purposes of various points of the Dhamma. In other words, purpose refers to how a dhammic principle is practiced in order to help support or bring about other dhammic principles. And once one principle is mastered, we can know how it leads to other points of the practice. This can be compared to embarking on a long journey that requires many forms of transportation: we might require overland vehicles, ships, and airplanes. It is not enough to simply declare our final destination, we must also know the various types of transportation required for each leg of the trip.[28] Any practice of the Dhamma that lacks a realization of purpose is missing the proper tool, is not linked to the other points of the Dhamma, and will make for practice that is not grounded. This type of practice will be narrow, impeded, and, worse than that, will lead us off the Path, making us miss the point. It will turn the Dhamma into something that is numb, sterile, inert, and ultimately fruitless. Practicing the Dhamma in a way that is not in harmony with the proper aims of Buddhism leads to confusion and loss, and this is especially true when it comes to the important dhammic principles of contentment (*santosa*) and equanimity (*upekkhā*).

The System of the Middle Path

I have already mentioned that the Middle Path amounts to a compilation of the practice of Buddhism. It encompasses the complete Buddhist system of ethics. The Middle Path is both far reaching and detailed. We need not talk about attempting a complete explanation of all of its steps here. This would be impossible. We do not even have the space here to enter into a summary of all of its major factors. Let me, therefore, discuss at least some of the important aspects of the Path with which we should be familiar.

The factors of the Middle Path, or the Noble Eight-fold Path, are as follows:

1. *Sammādiṭṭhi*	Proper understanding
2. *Sammāsaṅkappa*	Proper thought
3. *Sammāvācā*	Proper speech
4. *Sammākammanta*	Proper action
5. *Sammā-ājiva*	Proper livelihood
6. *Sammāvāyāma*	Proper effort
7. *Sammāsati*	Proper mindfulness
8. *Sammāsamādhi*	Proper concentration

These eight components are not eight different paths or eight principles that must be successfully accomplished before proceeding to the next. They are factors of one path. They depend on one another like eight links in a chain, and they must be put into practice at all times. The reason for breaking the Path into factors is to show various prominent phases that occur in different steps of the practice; for example, proper understanding has been set up as the initial step because in the very first stages of practice a person must establish a conducive outlook, correct views, and proper understanding for the course on which he is about to embark. This perspective will then lead to correct contemplation and practice of the Path. The practice of the Dhamma depends on this foundation of understanding as its principal asset; it then moves on to behavior and speech—the external, more blatant aspects of practice—and prepares or conditions them first. From there, attention is focused inward to more refined aspects of mental training that will bear good fruits later. In the course of practicing these aspects of the Path, the knowledge, understanding, and beliefs established along the way as essential assets of the Path will gradually evolve through dependence on this mental training. Finally, wisdom will increase to the point of understanding all things according to their true nature. This will lead to the attainment of enlightenment, nibbana—or, as we have already mentioned, "the Middle Path that gives a person insight (establishes knowledge), gives a person eyes (allows us to see), tranquillity, higher knowledge, nibbana."[29] That is, the final phases of the Path end with wisdom (*paññā*), which is a dhammic factor that plays a major role in attaining the final goal. Beyond the Eight-fold Path are two more factors: Proper insight (*sammāñāṇa*) and proper liberation (*sammāvimutti*).[30]

Accordingly, we can designate a system of practice with the Eight-fold Path divided into broader phases: assuming that the practitioner has already established knowledge, understanding, and belief as primary assets, training starts with proper behavior and speech (ethics, *sīla*); it continues on to mental training (*samādhi*); and then it reaches the final level, developing wisdom (*paññā*) to the point of overcoming ignorance (*avijjā*), craving (*taṇhā*), and attachments (*upādāna*). This system of training is called the Three-fold Training (*tisikkhā*). These trainings are set in the order of *sīla, samādhi,* and *paññā*. They relate to the Eight-fold Path in the following way:

1. Proper understanding 2. Proper thought	*Paññā* (including *sammāñāṇa* in the final phases, as well)

3. Proper speech — *Sīla*
4. Proper action
5. Proper livelihood

6. Proper effort — *Samādhi*
7. Proper mindfulness
8. Proper concentration

As soon as we refer to this more detailed system of practice, we can say that acting in accordance with the Path begins with wisdom and ends with wisdom. That is to say, at the very beginning, the knowledge, views, and beliefs that have been established according to reason constitute proper understanding (*sammādiṭṭhi*). This understanding gradually increases until it becomes knowing and seeing things with complete wisdom, which is called proper insight (*sammāñāṇa*). In this way, proper understanding serves as a bridge linking not-knowing (*avijjā*) with knowing (*vijjā*); as soon as you know, you are enlightened and attain liberation (*sammāvimutti*).

This system of training can be seen in still more broadly defined phases. The following contitutes the sections of practice known as the Three-fold Training (*tisikkhā*) in order:

1. Training in higher morality (*adhisīla-sikkhā*)
2. Training in higher mentality or concentration (*adhicitta-sikkhā*)
3. Training in higher wisdom (*adhipaññā-sikkhā*)

When these three trainings are presented as a model for practice, they become an important part of a principle called the three admonitions (*ovādapāṭimokkha*) or the three major principles of the Buddhist teachings.[31]

1. *Sabbapāpassa akaraṇaṁ*—Do not perform evil deeds (*sīla*)
2. *Kusalassūpasampadā*—Cultivate good, be fully prepared to act properly (*samādhi*)
3. *Sacittapariyodapanaṁ*—Make the mind pure and bright (*paññā*)

The Path, or the Three-fold Training, explains the points of the practice along with the best way to put an end to dukkha, as mentioned earlier; they, therefore, encompass all the various processes in this effort.

The Three-fold Training is called *bahuladhammīkathā*: the dhammic teachings that Lord Buddha often mentioned. There is a passage in the canon that explains the relationship between the parts of the Three-fold Training.

> *Sīla* is like this, *samādhi* is like this, and *paññā* is like this. *Samādhi* infused with *sīla* is very fruitful, very meritorious. *Paññā*

> infused with *samādhi* is very fruitful, very meritorious. The mind infused with *paññā* is completely liberated from all intoxicants (*āsava*)—intoxication of sensuality (*kāmāsava*), intoxication of becoming (*bhavāsava*), and the intoxication of ignorance (*avijjāsava*).[32]

The relationship between these aspects of the Three-fold Training can be seen even in the course of daily life. When a person's behavior is pure and there is confidence in this purity, there is no fear of fault; there is no being startled by the bad intentions of enemies; there is no apprehension towards reprimand or an unwillingness to accept the judgment of society; and there is no mental turmoil due to anxieties, personal shortcomings, or mistakes made. The mind is clear, peaceful, and certain about thought, word, and deed. The more the mind is untroubled, peaceful, and certain, the more contemplation and awareness lead to clarity, competence, and the positive fruits of wisdom. This can be compared to a pond when it is not stirred up—it is still, with the sediment at its bottom undisturbed. The water is clear. And when the water is clear, our view is unimpeded. The higher levels of the practice of Dhamma lead to insight, true knowledge, and the elimination of anything that can taint the mind (*āsava*); and this practice requires a mind that is still, bright, and has firmly established concentration (*samādhi*) to the point of silencing all the various senses. All that remains is the contemplation of mind-objects, which is performed in order to sweep the sediment out of the recesses of the mind so that there is no possibility of them being stirred up again.[33]

There are three factors of the Path that have special importance: proper understanding (*sammādiṭṭhi*), proper effort (*sammāvāyāma*), and proper mindfulness (*sammāsati*). These factors must be related to and practiced with all the other factors. The reason for incorporating these practices can be clearly seen by using a metaphor of travel. Proper understanding gives us a sense of direction or serves as a compass allowing us to see the way and have confidence about our course towards the final goal. Proper effort gives us the strength to take our first steps and provides us the necessary push to get us started. Proper mindfulness works like a governor or a gauge that provides control and can warn us if we go too fast, veer off the Path, or are in imminent danger. Whether the practice is considered from the level of *sīla, samādhi*, or *paññā*, we must still depend on these three essential factors at each step along the way.[34]

The Meaning of Each Factor of the Middle Path

The meaning of each factor of the Middle or Eight-fold Path will be considered here in order to gain a more systematic understanding of the Path.

1. Proper Understanding (sammādiṭṭhi)

The Importance of Proper Understanding

> Bhikkhus, of all the factors of the Path, proper understanding leads the way. How does proper understanding lead the way? Through proper understanding, we come to know improper understanding (*micchādiṭṭhi*) as improper understanding and proper understanding as proper understanding; we come to know improper thought as improper thought and proper thought as proper thought; we come to know improper speech . . . proper speech . . . improper action . . . proper action. . . .[35]
>
> Bhikkhus eliminate ignorance (*avijjā*), cultivate knowledge (*vijjā*), and attain nibbana through proper understanding and proper contemplation of the Path. How is this possible? Because of having established proper understanding.[36]
>
> I see nothing that can make wholesome things that have yet to arise or wholesome things that have already arisen lead to progress and prosperity like proper understanding.[37]

The Definition of Proper Understanding

The most common definition is the following one:

Knowledge of the Four Noble Truths

> Bhikkhus, what constitutes proper understanding? Understanding dukkha, understanding the arising of dukkha, understanding the extinguishing of dukkha, and understanding the way to the extinguishing of dukkha. This is proper understanding.[38]

Aside from this example, there are other definitions:

As Knowing Evil and the Roots of Evil—Knowing Goodness and the Roots of Goodness

As soon as you Noble Disciples come to know evil. . . the roots of evil. . . goodness. . . and the roots of goodness, only then can you be known as having proper understanding; only then is your understanding direct and firmly rooted in the true Dhamma.[39]

As Seeing the Three Characteristics of Existence

Bhikkhus who see body. . . sensation. . . perception. . . consciousness as impermanent have proper understanding. As soon as you have proper understanding, you tire of these things, because you have ceased to be engrossed in them, ceased to be absorbed in them. . . because you have ceased to be engrossed and absorbed in these things, the mind is free—this is called the complete passing beyond.[40]

When bhikkhus perceive the eyes. . . the ears. . . the nose. . . the tongue. . . the body. . . the mind. . . forms. . . sounds. . . smells . . . tastes. . . tangible objects. . . intangible mind-objects as impermanent, this realization is proper understanding.[41]

As Seeing Dependent Origination

(This definition is very prevalent in the canon and will not be referred to any further here, as it has already been cited numerous times.[42])

Dividing Proper Understanding into Tainted (*sāsava*) and Supramundane (*lokuttara*) Levels

Bhikkhus, what is proper understanding? I say that there are two types of proper understanding:

There is proper understanding that remains tainted but is still meritorious and leads to rebirth.[43] And there is proper understanding that is noble, without stain, is supermundane, and is a factor of the Path itself. And what, bhikkhus, is the proper understanding that remains tainted but is still meritorious and leads to rebirth? Believing that, "Giving bears fruit, practicing charity bears fruit, worship bears fruit; the good and the bad kamma that has been done bears fruits and has results; this world exists, the other-world (*paraloka*) exists; there is [merit in serving] mother and father; and there are creatures subject to spontaneous birth (*opapātika*); there are recluses and brahmins who behave correctly, practice correctly, and explain this world and the other-world clearly because they understand the nature of these things." This is proper understanding that is still tainted but is meritorious and can lead to rebirth.

And what is the nature of proper understanding that is most noble, without stain, supramundane, and a factor of the Path? The proper understanding that is a factor of the Path is composed of wisdom, the faculty of wisdom, the power of wisdom, and the factor of enlightenment that investigates phenomena—these are the properties of those with noble and stainless minds, who are endowed with the Path, and who are on the Path. And this is the proper understanding that is without stain, supramundane, and a factor of the Path.[44]

Proper Understanding and the Practice of the Middle Path

From the passages already cited, we can see that proper understanding is the starting point or the guide for anyone beginning the journey along the Middle Path; it is the principal supporting factor that plays a continuous role at each step of the way. At any rate, as a person proceeds along the Path, proper understanding is not simply a refuge or just one factor supporting the other factors. Proper understanding itself receives assistance from the other factors of the Path as well; as a person progresses along the Path, proper understanding continues to mature, be tempered, clarified, and purified. And finally, it becomes an important factor leading to the final goal of the Path. We can say that proper understanding is both the starting point and the end point of the Path.

This gradual process and evolution of proper understanding along the Path shows us that at different stages of practice proper understanding has different levels of quality. It is for this reason that the meaning of proper understanding will be different in its initial phases than in its final phases. Also, these meanings may not coincide with the way the term is more commonly used. In the beginning, "proper understanding" may not be fully realized and may even be undeserving of the term when compared to its fuller potential; and by the time the end of the Path is reached, proper understanding may have developed its own special properties such that could almost go by another name. In fact, separating the two by different names may be beneficial at this point. Because proper understanding is one aspect of wisdom (*paññā*), perhaps the more appropriate term for the latter type of proper understanding is "wisdom," meaning wisdom that has progressed through different phases of the Path and made it to the end point. We should now consider how each phase of the Path might have its own special features, importance, or name.

The System of the Middle Path, Outlining the Progress of Wisdom. Most ordinary people must learn by depending on the suggestions and teachings of other people. The course of training begins with some form of belief, which Buddhism calls faith or confidence (*saddhā*). This confidence may be based on beliefs established due to an initial satisfaction with the teachings, perhaps based on their reasonable nature, or being satisfied that the teacher meets the student's needs. From here on, there is an increased acceptance of the teachings, and so education progresses to the point that a person sees the true logic of the teachings, which is often called proper understanding. When this understanding increases and gradually becomes clearer—through actual practice and by comparing the teachings with actual experience—knowledge and insight become more certain. At this point, we can say that wisdom has reached the level of proper knowledge or insight (*sammāñāṇa*), a level beyond mere faith and beyond mere reason or logic (*diṭṭhi*). This is the end of the road, the attainment of meaning—that is, the freedom of final liberation that is called *sammāvimutti*. For the sake of simplicity, the development of this wisdom can be plotted as follows:

> confidence (*saddhā*) → proper understanding (*sammādiṭṭhi*) → proper knowledge (*sammāñāṇa*) → **proper liberation** (*sammāvimutti*)

Following this progression of the Dhamma, we can say that wisdom is initially hidden or inherent, or that the factors contributing to confidence finally come into their own. When the final point of confidence, *sammañāṇa*, is reached, true wisdom will shine clear and bright, and no trace of confidence will remain because it has been completely replaced by wisdom. When a person has gotten only this far, enlightenment or liberation has yet to be attained. The rest of this process will be discussed in due course.

One thing especially worthy of our attention here is that the confidence referred to in this dhammic progression is confidence for the sake of wisdom, or confidence leading to wisdom. This confidence, therefore, is belief linked with wisdom or belief based on understanding that has reason as its foundation (*ākāravatīsaddhā* or *saddhāñāṇasampayutta*). This does not mean the kind of belief that lets wisdom go as it will without the contemplation of causal factors (*amūlikāsaddhā* or *saddhāñāṇavippayutta*).

The confidence that relates to this dhammic process might be confused with the belief or faith that is found in other religions. Therefore, it is important for us to look into the special nature of this confidence.

A Summary of the Principles of Confidence (*saddhā*)

The following constitutes a summary of the meaning, role, and importance of confidence in the Buddhist belief system.

Confidence is only one stage in the process of the development of wisdom—the very first stage.

The confidence that we aim for is belief rooted in reason. That is to say, it has wisdom backing it up and can, in turn, provide the way to wisdom. It does not amount to simply giving up, letting go, or succumbing to a feeling that everything is all right, without looking into the reasons for things, which tends to follow only the emotions.

Confidence that is based on feelings, or mere emotion, is the kind of blind belief that should be eliminated or at least corrected. The emotional feelings linked with the correct type of confidence can be used in the practice of the Dhamma and be quite beneficial at the initial stages. Eventually, however, these feelings will be completely replaced by wisdom.

Confidence that seeks to develop wisdom can be simply defined as having total confidence in the causes and effects of which you are aware. It is confidence in yourself based on reason, on having determined that the goal you have set is truly attainable and is of value to the seeker. This is confidence that incites a continuous investigation of the true reasons for things. It is a gradual climb to knowledge, to the top of a hill that is opposite another hill, the hill of surrender and emotion, where people are happy to reside without engaging in any further inquiry into cause and effect.

In order to control and check confidence so that it maintains its proper course, various parts of the canon mention that confidence must always be linked with wisdom. Usually, confidence tends to be the initial factor and wisdom the final.[45] But in the instances referring to wisdom, it is not necessary to refer to confidence as well. Wisdom is, therefore, more important than confidence, both in terms of it being a controlling factor and a necessary link.[46] Even when the qualities of people are mentioned in the canon, those who are held in the highest regard are those with the greatest wisdom, such as the chief disciple Sāriputta who did not hold confidence to be of principal importance.

The benefits of confidence are two-fold: in one way, confidence is a factor in bringing about a sense of joy (*pīti*) that leads to cool serenity (*passaddhi*), which in the end brings about concentration (*samādhi*) and wisdom (*paññā*). In another way, confidence leads to striving (*viriya*) and testing the beliefs that have been arrived at through confidence, until the ripening of the final fruits of wisdom are realized. The benefits of both of these can be seen as the result of emotional feelings, but they also depend on a constant and inherent realization of the necessity of wisdom.

Wisdom is the ultimate aim of confidence. For this reason, confidence must support inquiry and critical awareness if progress towards wisdom is to be made. Aside from this, even confidence itself can be firmly established and free of doubt because of having come to certain conclusions about causes and effects. In this respect, the confidence of Buddhism supports inquiry and the search for reason. Imploring people to believe, forcing people to believe established "truths," or threatening people in order to induce belief have no place in Buddhist confidence.

Having faith or confidence in certain people is believed to be insufficient, even confidence in Lord Buddha. Lord Buddha taught that even this should be done away with, because confidence that is strong on emotion can turn into an obstacle, an impediment to enlightenment and final freedom.

Confidence is not a part of the Path because the most important factor for making progress along the Path is wisdom that has been linked with confidence; and, of course, confidence that is of any value must be supported by wisdom. Also, those who have a high level of wisdom, such as Lord Buddha himself or other beings who have attained enlightenment on their own (*paccekabuddha*), take their initial steps along the Path with wisdom already established. They do not have to resort to confidence because the development of wisdom does not always have to begin with confidence. For this reason, the meaning of confidence is incorporated into the factor of proper understanding in the Noble Eight-fold Path.

Even confidence that is devoid of blind beliefs but has never developed to the stages of experimentation cannot be considered correct confidence; nor can practice that does not test the truth be considered correct confidence, because it does not perform its duty according to its true purpose. Both of these are deemed incorrect practice, because they lack an essential ingredient—inquiry.

Even though confidence has a great deal of importance, in the end it must be done away with. If you still have faith or confidence, then you have yet to reach the final goal. As long as you still believe in a goal, you have not truly attained that goal. And as long as you still have confidence, you must depend on other things; wisdom, therefore, must be dependent on other things, and so you have not attained final freedom. For this reason, confidence is not one of the qualities of an arahant. An arahant has no confidence (*assaddha*), which means that the arahant has firmly established knowledge, and so belief is no longer based on the testimony of others or any reported system of logic.

In summary, progress along the Path continues step by step from confidence to proper understanding, or from understanding based on cause and effect (*diṭṭhi*) to the point that perfect knowledge and insight (*ñāṇadassana*) are reached, which is the ultimate burden of confidence.

Whatever the scope and importance of confidence, it is something we must all come to truly understand. We should not inflate its importance nor should we underestimate it, because when confidence is not given due credit, we may easily misunderstand it. For example, self-confidence may easily become a bad tendency (*kilesa*) manifesting itself as egoism or selfishness (*ahaṁkāra-mamaṅkāra*), which can lead to bad results.

In the process of the development of wisdom, certain steps can be established as phases of confidence:

a) Establish a way of looking at the world according to reason; not believing in nor clinging to ideas that have been handed down (similar to the message of the *Kālāma Sutta*).[47]

b) Become a guardian of truth (*saccānurakkha*): that is, being a person who enjoys listening to the principles, theories, teachings, and various views of different people and groups with an open mind, without making hasty judgments about things that have yet to be established as fact, and not simply clinging to the things known to be correct and true.

c) Once you have heard the various theories, teachings, or views of others, consider the merits of their reasons according to your own wisdom; see if the person explaining these theories, teachings, or views is earnest, unbiased, and has sufficient wisdom for you to have confidence in these teachings; and test their truths through the application of your own reasoning.

d) Consider the ideas you have accepted, think about them carefully, and test them with reason until you are certain that they are correct and true, until you can completely accept their rationale and put them into practice in order to test their validity.

e) If doubts still remain, investigate them in an unbiased manner with wisdom, not with the pride of selfishness, and test their reasoning until no doubts remain. This way confidence will be certain and bear the greatest fruits.

Canonical Passages Explaining Confidence

All people—those who hold to certain theories, doctrines, or teachings, or even those who claim no belief system—have a way of forming a worldview based on reason. This is similar to the ideas contained in the *Kālāma Sutta*.[48]

One day the Lord Buddha had come to Kesaputta Village of the Kālāma clan in the kingdom of Kosala. The Kālāma people had heard of the reputation of Lord Buddha and came to pay their respects, but at the same time they showed a certain amount of reluctance toward him. They began their dialogue with the Buddha by posing the following question:

> Oh, Accomplished One, certain groups of recluses and brahmins come to Kesaputta. They explain their own doctrines, but they abuse, look down on, and revile those of others and implore us not to believe them. Moreover, other groups of recluses and brahmins come to Kesputta and do the very same thing. We have doubts and wonder which group is speaking the truth and which one is telling lies?
>
> People of Kālāma, it is good to have doubts, good to wonder. In a doubtful situation, uncertainty arises. Kālāmas, each and every one of you,
>
> —do not let yourself believe reports (*mā anussavena*)
>
> —do not let yourself believe hand-me-down knowledge (*mā paramparāya*)
>
> —do not let yourself believe hearsay (*mā itikirāya*)

—do not let yourself believe the authority of texts (*mā piṭikasampathānena*)

—do not let yourself believe mere logic (*mā takkahetu*)

—do not let yourself believe inferences (*mā nayahetu*)

—do not let yourself believe appearances (*mā ākāraparivitakkena*)

—do not let yourself believe based on agreement with an approved theory (*mā diṭṭhinijjhānakkhantiyā*)

—do not let yourself believe in probability (*mā bhabbarūpatāya*)

—do not let yourself believe based on the notion that "This is our teacher" (*mā samaṇo no gurūti*).[49]

As soon as you come to realize that certain things are unwholesome, flawed, shunned by intelligent people, and when taken up and put into practice they lead to harm and dukkha, you should all abandon them. . . . As soon as you come to realize for yourselves that certain things are wholesome, flawless, praised by intelligent people, and when taken up and put into practice they lead to benefits and sukha, you should live by them.

In the event that the audience did not know, did not understand, and still did not believe, they were not enticed to believe. Teachings were offered for contemplation, and people were invited to decide for themselves based on their own reasoning. For example, concerning the issue of this life and the next, toward the end of the sutta the following can be found:

Kālāmas, Noble Disciples, those with minds free of animosity, those with minds free of malevolence, those with minds free of stains, who are pure will attain four kinds of assurances in the present:

"If there is truly an other-world and there are truly consequences of good and bad kamma, then when this body breaks up I will arise in a happy realm, a heaven; this is a real possibility." This is the first assurance.

"But if there is no other-world and there are no consequences of good and bad kamma, then I will live without dukkha, animosity, and malevolence, happily existing in the present." This is the second assurance.

"And whenever anyone performs evil with evil effects, I do not think of returning this evil. Therefore, how can dukkha come to a person who is free of demerit?" This is the third assurance.

"And whenever anyone performs evil that has no effects, I am clean and clear in two ways." This is the fourth assurance.

For those who had yet to accept any doctrine or religion, Lord Buddha presented the Dhamma in an impartial way—with good intentions for the benefit of these people, as something for them to think about further—without specifying what the teachings are. This method of teaching allowed people to be themselves and did not implore them to believe or put their faith in Lord Buddha himself or a power transcending nature that backed up his teachings. Lord Buddha's method advocates using wisdom to contemplate the reasons and facts that he set down.

Take, for example, the case of the *Apaṇṇaka Sutta*,[50] which explains the reasons for living according to the Dhamma without having to refer to heaven and hell or harboring wishes about the possible rewards of the next life: In the course of his travels, Lord Buddha came to stay in a brahmin village called Sālā. The householders of this village had heard of the reputation of the Buddha, and so they went to visit him. They tended to respond to him as a newcomer, as a visitor whom they did not yet respect. The Lord Buddha asked them the following:

Householders, do you have any teachers with whom you are pleased, in whom, for good reason, you have placed your confidence?

(The Householders respond negatively.)

Since you do not have a teacher with whom you are pleased, you should practice some principles that are correct and certain (*apaṇṇaka-dhamma*). So, from now on, by referring to these teachings and practicing them correctly, you can be of assistance to others and experience long-term sukha. What are these correct principles?

Some recluses and brahmins teach and believe that the gifts that you give are fruitless, that the act of giving is fruitless, that worship is fruitless, and there are no consequences of good and bad kamma; this world does not exist, the other-world (*paraloka*) does not exist, there [is no use in serving] mothers and fathers. . . . Another group of recluses and brahmins teach and hold views completely the opposite of this group. They say that gifts bear fruit, gift-giving bears fruit, worship bears fruit. . . .What do all of you think about this? Do these recluses and brahmins maintain opposing teachings?

(The householders answer affirmatively.)

Of these two groups of recluses and brahmins, the one that teaches and believes that gifts do not bear fruit, gift-giving does not bear fruit. . .aims at doing away with proper behavior, proper speech, and proper thought, which are all three part of the wholesome things (*kusala-dhamma*); and this same group clings to improper conduct, improper speech, and improper thought, which also go against the Dhamma. What is the reason for this? Because these recluses and brahmins do not see the faults, the baseness, and the sorrow associated with these unwholesome things (*akusala-dhamma*). Nor do they understand the merits of renunciation (*nekkhamma*), which leads to the cleanliness and purity of the wholesome Dhamma.

Furthermore, when the other-world exists, they believe that it does not exist—this constitutes improper understanding (*micchādiṭṭhi*). When the other-world exists, they are of the opinion that it does not exist—this constitutes improper thought (*micchā-saṅkappa*). When the other-world exists, they will say that it does not exist—this constitutes improper speech (*micchāvācā*). When the other-world exists, they say that it does not exist and become foes of the arahants who know the other-world. When the other-world exists, they make others come to believe that it does not exist. Making others believe these things goes against the true Dhamma, and making people believe these things and transgress the true Dhamma amount to forcing other people. In this way, from the very beginning, they throw away the excellent ethics (*sīla*); by breaking the precepts, they have improper understanding, improper thought, and improper speech. Being foes of noble people, inviting others to believe in false teachings, raising themselves up and pushing others down, these demerits and bad practices are all a result of improper understanding.

Considering this, the wise man will discover that, "If there is no other-world, when these people die and the aggregates of their existence break up, they are safe. But if the other-world exists, when the aggregates of their existence break up, they may end up in an unhappy state (*apāya*), a world of woe (*duggati*), a realm of suffering (*vinipāta*), or hell (*naraka*). So, even if the other-world does not really exist and we admit the truth of the words of these recluses and brahmins, wise people can still reprimand them now for breaking the precepts and maintaining improper and nihilistic views (*natthikavāda*). And so, if there is an other-world, these brahmins lose out in both scenarios: in the present, they are reprimanded by wise people; and when the aggregates of their existence break up, they end up in an unhappy existence, a world of woe, a realm of suffering or hell. . . .

One group of recluses and brahmins teachs and believes that, "There is no putting an end to becoming (*bhava*)"; and another holds the complete opposite view that, "There is an end to becoming.". . .The wise person will consider this contemplating that I have not really determined that "There is no putting an end to dukkha," and I also do not know if "There is really an end to becoming." Since I have not seen this and do not know for sure, I cannot be absolutely certain that this is the truth and the other a lie—this would not be right. If the teaching of the group of recluses and brahmins who believe that, "There is no putting an end to becoming" happens to be true, there is nothing wrong with the possibility of being born among the gods composed of ideation (*saññāmaya*). If the teaching of the group of recluses and brahmins who believes that, "There is an end to becoming" is true, it is then possible to attain nibbana at the present time. But the views of the recluses and brahmins who teach and believe that, "There is no putting an end to becoming," lead to being engrossed, bound, oblivious, preoccupied, and attached. But the views of the recluses and brahmins who teach and believe that, "There really is an end to becoming" do not lead to being engrossed, bound, oblivious, preoccupied, and attached. Those who correctly contemplate this matter practice to achieve true disenchantment (*nibbidā*), detachment (*virāga*), and the end (*nirodha*) of all becoming.

The following passage from the Buddhist texts explains the limitations of knowledge and thought that have not progressed beyond mere belief and logic. Thought that remains at the level of belief and logic is deemed imperfect, misguided, and cannot be considered to have reached the truth.

Bhāradvāja, there are five things that have two types of consequences (*vipāka*):

1. Confidence/belief (*saddhā*)
2. Being pleased (with something) (*ruci*)
3. Hearing (or learning) (*anussava*)
4. Thinking according to reason (*ākāraparivitakka*)
5. Agreeing with a theory (*diṭṭhinijjhānakkhanti*)

Things that you firmly believe can turn out to be empty or false, or even things that you do not believe can turn out to be true, real, or correct.

Things that you completely agree with can turn out to be empty or false, or even things that you do not agree with can turn out to be true, real, or correct.

Things that you have studied well all along can turn out to be empty or false, or even the things that you have not studied can turn out to be true, real, or correct.

Things that you have thought through can turn out to be empty and false, or even the things you have yet to carefully consider can turn out to be true, real, or correct.

The things on which you have focused your concentration (and claim to be true according to personal views, theories, and principles) can turn out to be empty or false, or even the things on which you have yet to focus your concentration can turn out to be true, real, or correct.[51]

Then the Buddha showed how we should view our own thoughts and beliefs and how we should listen to the thoughts and beliefs of others. This can be called having the perspective of a guardian of truth or truth-lover (*saccānurakkha*).

When the wise person is a guardian of truth, he should not make any absolute statements that, "Only this is true, all the rest are worthless."

Even if people believe [have confidence], as soon as they say, "I believe this!" we can still hold them up as a guardian of truth, but the absolute declaration that, "This is the only truth, all the rest are worthless," cannot be made. By simply observing just this one point of practice, you can be a guardian of truth. But those

I call guardians of truth, those I have declared to be guardians of truth by this practice, have yet to realize the truth.

Even if a person has views that are pleasing. . . is the heir to certain teachings. . . thinks according to reason. . . has ideas based on his own theories, as soon as he says that, "I have views that are pleasing. . . I have studied like this. . . my thoughts are reasonable. . . I have ideas based on my own theories," we can still call him a guardian of truth. But the absolute declaration that, "This is the only truth, all the rest are worthless," cannot be made. By simply observing this one point of practice, you can be a guardian of truth. But those I call guardians of truth, those I have declared to be guardians of truth by this practice, have yet to realize the truth.[52]

The importance of this perspective becomes especially clear when outsiders praise or criticize Buddhism. The disciples of Lord Buddha would often report these public opinions and discuss them with their teacher. On one occasion, Lord Buddha said the following:

Bhikkhus, if other people come and level criticisms against me, criticize the Dhamma, criticize the Sangha, you should not hold any malice towards them, this should not upset you, and you should not feel resentful. Because if you get angry and overly concerned about these criticisms, this will be dangerous for all of you. If other people criticize me, criticize the Dhamma and the Sangha, and if you get angry and upset over these criticisms, how will you know if what they are saying is correct or incorrect?

(The bhikkhus respond by saying that they might not know.)

Bhikkhus, if other people come and level criticisms against me, criticizing the Dhamma and the Sangha, in the event that these are false, you should correct them saying "These points are not true for the following reasons; these points are incorrect, because of such and such." Tell them that these things do not exist in our midst; these things cannot be found among us.

Bhikkhus, if others come to praise me, praise the Dhamma and the Sangha, all of you should not be delighted, happy, or beam with joy. If people come to praise us, praise the Dhamma and the Sangha, if you are delighted and joyful, this will be dangerous for all of you. If people come to praise me, praise the

Dhamma and the Sangha, and if what they say is true, we should accept it as truth saying, "These points are true for the following reasons; these points are correct because of such and such." Tell them that these things exist in our midst; these things can be found among us.[53]

Along with becoming a guardian of truth, Lord Buddha also taught practices leading to realization and the attainment of truth. In the course of these practices, we can gain a clearer picture of the birth of confidence, along with its meaning, importance, and scope.

Through what points of the practice can truth be realized and people can be said to have realized the truth?

As soon as people hear the news that some bhikkhus have come to a village or town and householders and their children have gone to see them, they should look for traces of greed (*lobha*), traces of ill-will (*dosa*), or traces of delusion (*moha*). They should see if these bhikkhus have any traces of greed that have overcome their minds causing them to say, "We know," even though they do not know, or causing them to say, "We see," even though they do not see. Are these bhikkhus inviting other people to head in a direction of long-term dukkha for themselves and others?

Once these people have observed these bhikkhus, they will reach the conclusion that, "These bhikkhus have no traces of any kind of greed that has overcome their minds causing them to say 'We know,' even though they do not know, or causing them to say 'We see,' even though they do not see. These bhikkhus are not inviting other people to head in an unrewarding direction that will lead to long-term dukkha for themselves and others. Furthermore, these bhikkhus have proper behavior and proper speech befitting people who are without greed. The Dhamma that these bhikkhus teach is deep, difficult to perceive, difficult to attain; it is tranquil, subtle, and not easily reached through any detailed logic. Then, wise people will know that this Dhamma is not easily explained by greedy people."

When the people have observed them and seen that they are free of any traces of greed, then they will be interested in making further observations for traces of ill-will . . . traces of delusion . . . .

Once these people have scrutinized these bhikkhus and found them free of any traces of delusion, they will put their confidence (*saddhā*) in them.

Once these people have put their confidence in these bhikkhus, they will seek them out and come sit close by; once seated nearby, they will be intent on listening; once intent on listening, they will pay attention to the Dhamma; once they have paid attention to the Dhamma, they will remember it and contemplate the words they have heard; once they have contemplated these pleasing words, along with various points of the Dhamma that they have tested for themselves and come to agree with, then proper resolve comes about; once proper resolve is established, mental vitality will follow; once there is mental vitality, people will review and compare the teachings to others they have heard; once they have compared the teachings, they will begin to apply them fervently; once they have dedicated their minds to this effort, then higher truth (*paramattha-sacca*) will be realized via wisdom and these practices. This is called realizing the truth. And those who have practiced in this way can be said to have realized the truth—this realization of the truth (*saccānubodha*) can be established by these practices—but this realization is not the same as the attainment of truth.

By what points of the practice can truth be attained and people can be said to have attained the truth?

By observing the Noble Eight-fold Path and making the most of it. . . .[54]

For most people, confidence is a very important, primary step, an ingredient that entices them to make further progress along the path. When put to proper use, it starts people off on the right foot and expedites their pursuit of the ultimate purpose. For this reason, it is often the case that people with a lot of wisdom and a little confidence are slower in attaining the final goal than those with inferior wisdom and strong confidence.[55] If confidence is aligned with correct things, confidence can save people a great deal of time and energy. On the other hand, if confidence is aligned with incorrect things, then this can easily lead people astray and cause them to waste a lot of time. At any rate, Buddhist confidence has reason as its foundation and is based on all-encompassing wisdom. Once confidence is properly established, it is difficult to go wrong, people guided by proper confidence will be able to adjust and correct things. They will not tend to gravitate to things that are incorrect, because they are constantly aware of the process of cause and effect and are steadfastly analyzing and testing their knowledge. Lacking this important factor of confidence can, therefore, become one kind of obstacle that impedes progress. In the words of Lord Buddha:

> Bhikkhus, any bhikkhu who cannot get rid of five stumps in his mind, five stumps that trip up the mind, will not make progress, will not grow, will not prosper in the Dhamma-Vinaya.
>
> The stumps of the mind that have yet to be uprooted are as follows:
>
> 1. Wonder, doubt, reluctance, and not having complete faith in the Teacher. . .
> 2. Wonder, doubt, reluctance, and not having complete faith in the Dhamma. . .
> 3. Wonder, doubt, reluctance, and not having complete faith in the Sangha. . .
> 4. Wonder, doubt, reluctance, and not having complete faith in the Trainings (*sikkhā*). . .
> 5. Being angry, hurt, or shaken to the extent that these feelings arise and become an obstruction, like a stump that trips up those attempting to lead the Holy Life. . . .
>
> The mind of the bhikkhu who still wonders, doubts, is reluctant and does not have complete faith in the Teacher. . .the Dhamma. . .the Sangha. . .the Trainings. . .harbors anger and so on, among those leading the Holy Life, he is not intent on serious effort, is not intent on Training, is not intent on continuous striving nor true involvement. Bhikkhus who are not yet intent on effort. . .can be said to have stumps in their minds that they have yet to uproot.[56]

In this way, lacking confidence, harboring doubts, suspicions, and uncertainties all become great obstacles in the development of wisdom and the pursuit of the Buddhist goal. What must be done is to plant confidence and weed out doubts; but here, the planting of confidence does not mean acceptance or surrender without respect for the value of your own intelligence. Rather, it means thinking and testing with your own intelligence until you clearly see cause and effect, until you are certain and all doubts have been dispelled. Aside from the passage cited in the previous section, there is another that mentions a method of inquiry and testing that takes place before confidence is established.

> Bhikkhus, an inquiring bhikkhu who does not know how to determine the state of mind of another, should observe and examine the Tathāgata to determine if he is the Perfectly Enlightened One or not. . . .
>
> An inquiring bhikkhu who does not know how to determine the state of mind of another, should observe and examine two aspects of a Tathāgata—the things you can know by seeing and the things you can know by hearing:
>
> —As far as you can tell with your eyes and ears, is there anything impure about a Tathāgata? Once you have observed and examined a Tathāgata, you will know based on what you can tell with your eyes and ears that there is nothing impure about a Tathāgata;
>
> —After this, you can observe and examine a Tathāgata further, asking, as far as you can tell with your eyes and ears, is there anything mixed-up (both good and bad) about a Tathāgata? Once you have observed and examined a Tathāgata, you will realize that, as far as your eyes and ears can tell, there is nothing mixed up about a Tathāgata;
>
> —After this, you can observe and examine a Tathāgata further, asking, as far as you can tell with your eyes and ears, is a Tathāgata clean and stainless?. . . You can realize that as far as you can tell with your eyes and ears, a Tathāgata is clean and stainless;
>
> —After this, you can observe and examine a Tathāgata further, asking, is this person competely endowed with true merits that are everlasting or momentary?. . . You will see that the one being investigated is completely endowed with true merits that are everlasting, not momentary;
>
> —After this, you can observe and examine a Tathāgata further, asking, has this bhikkhu who has achieved fame and honor ever been adversely affected by this status? (Because some) bhikkhus do not appear to be adversely affected until they achieve fame and honor. . . . The investigator can know that even though this bhikkhu has achieved fame and honor, he does not appear to have any faults.

—After this, you can observe and examine a Tathāgata further, asking, is he an abstainer (from unwholesome things, *akusala*) because he is fearless or fearful? Does he refuse to get involved in sensual pleasures because he is free of lust, has reached the end of lust?. . . You can know that he is an abstainer because he is fearless, not because he is fearful, and that he does not get involved in sensual pleasures because he is free of lust, because lust has been extinguished. . . .

If someone comes to ask that bhikkhu how he came by his rationale (*ākāra*) and knowledge (*anavayā*), he can answer that he is an abstainer because he is fearless, not fearful; he refuses to get involved in all sensual pleasures because he is free of lust, he has extinguished lust. Bhikkhus, to respond correctly, you should say that it is true that whenever that bhikkhu is in the company of others or is alone, in good company or bad, with leaders, or with people engrossed in objects of pleasure (*amisa*) or not engrossed in objects of pleasure, he does not look down upon anyone for any reason. He can say that he has heard directly from the mouth of the Buddha himself that, "I abstain because I am fearless, not because I am fearful. I do not get involved in any sensual pleasures, because I am free of lust, I have extinguished lust."

Bhikkhus, in that case, press the Tathāgata further, asking, as far as you can determine with your eyes and ears, is there anything impure about the Tathāgata? He will say there is not.

When asked if there is anything mixed up about the Tathāgata . . . he will say there is not.

When asked if he is clean and stainless, the Tathāgata. . .will say yes. I have the clean and stainless teaching as the Path, and for this reason, I am free from craving.

—Disciples should pay attention to a Teacher who responds like this;

—Such a Teacher will continue to explain and compare, in ever-increasing subtlety, "black" dhamma and "white" dhamma in order to show their differences to his disciples;

—However, when the Teacher explains the various teachings to any bhikkhus, they should consider each point until they come to agree with the whole of it. They then have confidence in the Teacher saying, "The Lord is a Perfectly Enlightened One, the

> Dhamma is what he teaches so well, and the Sangha is comprised of those who practice so well."
>
> And if others come to ask that bhikkhu more questions—asking, "How have you arrived at the reasoning and knowledge that make you say the Lord is a Perfectly Enlightened One, the Dhamma is what he teaches so well, and the Sangha consists of those who practice so well?"—in order to respond correctly, he should say, "I sit close to the Lord to hear the Dhamma; he explains the Dhamma to me. . .whatever he explains increases my knowledge until I have come to accept the whole of his Dhamma and have confidence in the Teacher. . . ."
>
> Bhikkhus, a person's confidence in the Tathāgata becomes an impetus and a foundation. According to these qualities, these words, these letters, I call this confidence based on reason (*ākāravati*), which provides a solid lookout (*dassanamūlikā*) for recluses or brahmins, gods or devils (*māra*)—this type of scrutiny does not allow a person to totter.[57] Examining and testing the Tathāgata works this way, and in this way the Tathāgata has been well tested.[58]

Please note from this passage we can clearly see that wondering or having doubts about Lord Buddha are not considered demeritorious (*pāpa*) or bad at all; they are merely things to be corrected until a person sees things clearly and puts an end to doubt by applying wisdom and encouraging continuous inquiry and contemplation. When a person declares his faith in Lord Buddha, before the Buddha acknowledges this, he will first ask if that person's confidence is based on reason.

> On one occasion, Sāriputta approached Lord Buddha and asked, "Lord Buddha, Accomplished One, I have put my confidence in you because there have never been nor are there now any other recluses, brahmins, or any others for that matter who have higher knowledge than you, who have attained Perfect Knowledge (*sambodhiñāṇa*)."
>
> The Lord Buddha responded saying, "This time you have made a very bold statement (*āsabhivācā*)! You have made quite an absolute declaration!. . . Have you applied your mind to the consideration of all Perfectly Enlightened Ones of the past or have you considered that the Enlightened Buddhas of the past estab-

lished certain moral rules (*sīla*) for certain reasons, had certain principles and wisdom as their abode, and had attained enlightenment based on these things?

Venerable Sāriputta: "It's not like that, Lord."

Lord Buddha: "Have you applied your mind to the consideration of all the Perfectly Enlightened Ones to come. . .and thought about how they might come to be?"

Venerable Sāriputta: "It's not like that, Lord."

Lord Buddha: "Have you applied your mind to the consideration of me, the current Perfectly Enlightened One, and wondered why?"

Venerable Sāriputta: "It's not like that, Lord."

Lord Buddha: "So, since you do not have insight into the minds of the past, present, and future Perfectly Enlightened Ones, how can you then make such a grand and absolute declaration [as you stated earlier]?

Venerable Sāriputta: "Lord Buddha, the Accomplished One, it is true that I do not have insight into the minds of the past, present, and future Perfectly Enlightened Ones, but even so, I have realized the way of the Dhamma."[59]

Lord Buddha, the Accomplished One, this can be compared to the border of a king's territory: There is a sturdy fortress, with a thick and well-positioned wall, and there is only one entryway. The one who keeps watch over the gate is a sharp-witted and wise pundit. He turns away strangers and only admits those he knows. He circumambulates the city wall, checking it very carefully for cracks and weak points. If even a cat slips through, he thinks, "All beings, regardless of their size, must enter and exit this city through only one gate." Just as I have realized the way of the Dhamma, so it is that all Perfectly Enlightened Buddhas of the past must break free of the five hindrances (*nīvaraṇa*) that taint the mind and make wisdom feeble, must firmly establish their heart in the four foundations of mindfulness (*satipaṭṭhāna*), and develop the seven factors of enlightenment (*bojjhaṅga*) in accordance with the truth before they can attain final perfect enlightenment. Even all the future Perfectly Enlightened Buddhas [must pass this way]; even the present Perfectly Enlightened Buddha had to break free of the five hindrances, establish his heart in the four foundations of mindfulness, and develop the seven factors of enlightenment in accordance with the truth before he could attain final, perfect enlightenment. . . ."[60]

Faith and confidence, when correctly applied and channeled, are important ingredients for future progress. But at the same time, one of their negative aspects is becoming attached to the object of confidence, which can become an obstacle that blocks your way. The following illustrates the positive aspects of confidence:

> Any Noble Disciple who puts complete confidence in the Tathāgata will not have any suspicions or doubts about the Tathāgata and his true teachings. Truly, the Noble Disciples with devotion are intent on efforts that will put an end to all unwholesome dhammas (*akusala-dhamma*) and work towards carrying out the wholesome dhammas (*kusala-dhamma*) and bringing them to fruition; they are people with vitality, who exert themselves with certainty, and do not neglect all their proper duties.[61]

The negative aspects of confidence are as follows:

> Bhikkhus, the five negative aspects related to putting your faith in someone are as follows:
>
> 1. When the person in whom you have put your confidence must confess to a transgression that causes him to be temporarily suspended from Sangha rites and activities; you suddenly realize that the person you loved and cared about has now been asked to abstain from the activities of the Sangha. . . .
>
> 2. When the person in whom you have put your confidence must confess to something that causes him to have to sit at the tail end of all the other bhikkhus. . . .
>
> 3. . . .the person. . .wanders off to another place. . . .
>
> 4. . . .the person. . .decides to leave the Order. . . .
>
> 5. . . .the person. . .dies. . . .
>
> When these things happen, the faithful person will not seek out other bhikkhus; not seeking out other bhikkhus, he does not

pay attention to the Dhamma; and once he does not heed the Dhamma, appreciation for it declines.[62]

As soon as faith and confidence evolve into love, negative aspects arise in the form of biases that can obstruct the application of wisdom:

Bhikkhus, there are four things that can arise: love that comes from love; ill-will (*dosa*) that comes from love; love that comes from ill-will; and ill-will that comes from ill-will. . . .

How does ill-will come from love? The person you desire, love, and are pleased with is treated in an undesirable, unloving, and dissatisfactory manner by another person. When this happens. . . you can experience ill-will towards this other person [and so on]. . . .[63]

When it comes to personal love, even faith or confidence in the Teacher can be an obstacle to enlightenment or the freedom of the intellect at its highest levels—for this reason, Lord Buddha taught that even this kind of confidence should be eliminated. Sometimes he prescribed quite strong methods for accomplishing this, such as in the case of the Venerable Vakkali, who had very strong faith and confidence in Lord Buddha and wanted to follow him everywhere, stay close to him, and always keep him in sight. Finally, Venerable Vakkali became extremely ill. He wanted to be with Lord Buddha, and so he sent someone to request that the Buddha come to his side. Lord Buddha visited him and said the following in order to set Venerable Vakkali's mind free:

Vakkali: Oh, Accomplished One, I have wanted to come and see you and sit before you for a long time now, but my body has not allowed me to reach the Enlightened One.

Lord Buddha: Never mind, Vakkali. Of what use is this decaying body? Vakkali, whoever sees the Dhamma, sees me; whoever sees me, sees the Dhamma—so when you see the Dhamma, Vakkali, you see me; when you see me, you see the Dhamma.[64]

The Buddha has stated that spiritual progress remaining only at the level of confidence is not stable or safe. This is because a person is still too dependent on external factors that can disintegrate or disappear.

> Bhaddāli, we can compare this to a one-eyed man whose relatives and blood kin do everything they can to protect [his precious] eye, thinking, "Please do not allow him to lose the only eye he has." The same is true for you bhikkhus in the Dhamma-Vinaya if you conduct yourselves and practice only out of confidence or love. In such a case, all bhikkhus must realize that when a bhikkhu conducts himself and practices only out of confidence or love, we have to rouse him on by emphasizing time and again that he get to the heart of the matter. This is done in hopes that the vestiges of his confidence and love will not completely disintegrate and disappear. This Bhaddāli, is the cause, is the reason for our working together to rouse some bhikkhus, causing us to emphasize again and again that they get to the heart of the matter.[65]

So, by confidence alone no further progress is made to the higher stages of wisdom; the fruits of practice are thereby limited only to the heavenly abodes, and a person is not able to attain the final goal of Buddha-dhamma. Lord Buddha stated the following:

> Bhikkhus, our well-established Dhamma is simple, open, clear, and has no strings attached whatsoever:
> —Bhikkhus who are stainless arahants. . .will not be subject to further rounds of rebirth (*vaṭṭa*) and becoming;
> —Bhikkhus who have done away with the first five fetters (*saṁyojana*) will be subject to spontaneous rebirth [without apparent cause] (*opapātika*) and will be enlightened in that state;
> —Bhikkhus who have done away with the three fetters and whose lust (*rāga*), ill-will (*dosa*) and delusions (*moha*) are worn thin will be once-returners (*sakadāgāmi*). . . .
> —Bhikkhus who have done away with the three fetters are stream-enterers (*sotāpanna*);
> —Bhikkhus who are contemplators of the Dhamma (*dhammānussati*) and contemplators of confidence (*saddhānussati*) have the enlightenment of the Buddha as their goal;
> —People who merely have confidence and love have heaven as their goal.[66]

In the course of the development of wisdom, benefits are derived from proper confidence. Wisdom will continue to progress until insight is attained. At higher levels, knowledge and insight have no use for faith or views. Once a person has attained insight, further progress transcends the limits of confidence. Please take note of the following passages from the Tipiṭaka:

> **Question:** Mūsila, is it by not depending on confidence, not depending on thoughts that are pleasing to you, not depending on hand-me-down knowledge, not depending on mere logic, not depending on things that are in agreement with certain theories that, you, Mūsila, have gained knowledge on your own (*paccattañāṇa*), or is it due to the factor of birth (*jāti*) that leads to decay-and-death (*jarā-maraṇa*)?
>
> **Answer:** Saviṭṭha, I know and see what I have said because I understand the factor of birth that leads to decay-and-death without depending on confidence. . . pleasing thoughts. . . hand-me-down knowledge. . . mere logic. . . or things that accord with certain theories.

(From here other questions are posed about the elements of dependent origination—in both its forward and backward unfolding—until the extinguishing of becoming [*bhavanirodha*] leads to nibbana.)[67]

In another place, the following can be found:

> **Question:** Is it true that there are some teachings that suggest a bhikkhu can predict the final stage of his emancipation (*arahatta-phala*) without having to depend on confidence, without having to depend on pleasing thoughts, without having to depend on hand-me-down knowledge, without having to depend on logic, and without having to depend on things that accord with a certain theory, knowing that, "birth has come to an end; the Holy Life (*brahmacariya*) is over; what is necessary to do has been done; and all the things that must be done to reach this state have been taken care of?. . ."
>
> **Answer:** This teaching exists. . . bhikkhus can see form with their own eyes, know their lust, ill-will, and delusion, saying, "we still have lust, ill-will, and delusion," or know that they are free of lust, ill-will, and delusion, saying, "we are free of lust, ill-will, and delusion."

> **Question:** Is it true that...we must know according to confidence, according to pleasing thoughts, according to hand-me-down knowledge, according to logic, or things that accord with a certain theory?
>
> **Answer:** It's not that way.
>
> **Question:** But what you have stated...must be seen with wisdom in order to attain knowledge, right?
>
> **Answer:** That's right, brother.
>
> **Summary:** It is implied that a bhikkhu can predict that final stages of emancipation without depending on confidence [and so on] (and at this point, the text covers each sense-base [*āyatana*] in order).[68]

Once a person has insight—that is, clear knowledge and vision—there is no need for confidence, it is not necessary to have faith in other people. Therefore, the disciples of the Buddha who achieve the highest states of mind know and refer to various ideas without having to make reference to their belief in the Teacher. For example, there is a text dealing with a debate between the Jain Nātaputta and the householder Citta, a lay devotee who was known for his expertise in the Buddhadhamma.

> **Nātaputta:** Householder, do you believe Samaṇa Gotama who teaches that there is a form of concentration (*samādhi*) that has no initialization of thought (*vitakka*) nor sustained thought (*vicāra*), and there is the cessation of the initialization of thought and sustained thought?
>
> **Citta:** First of all, concerning this matter, I do not maintain these views because of my confidence (*saddhā*) in the Fully Enlightened One who says that there is concentration that has no initialization of thought nor sustained thought, and there is the cessation of the initialization of thought and sustained thought.... As soon as I focus my attention...I can enter the first absorption (*paṭhama-jhāna*)...enter the second absorption (*dutiya-jhāna*)...enter the third absorption (*tatiya-jhāna*)...enter the fourth absorption (*catuttha-jhāna*).[69] This is how I know, how I see, and so I do not cling to any recluse or brahmin who maintains that there is a form of concentration that has no initialization of thought nor sustained thought, and there is the cessation of the initialization of thought and sustained thought.[70]

For the reasons cited, an arahant has the highest insight and, therefore, has a quality called "*assaddha*,"[71] meaning a person without *saddhā*; that is, a person who no longer has to rely on belief in other people because he already clearly understands himself. This is evident in another exchange between Lord Buddha and Venerable Sāriputta:

> **Lord Buddha:** Sāriputta, do you believe that the faculty of confidence (*saddhindriya*) that is developed, has done its duty, can lead to the realization of the deathless state (*amata*), have the deathless state as its aim, have the deathless state as its ultimate goal. . . the energy faculty (*viriyindriya*). . . mindfulness faculty (*satindriya*). . . concentration faculty (*samādhindriya*). . . wisdom faculty (*paññindriya*) [in the same manner as above]?
>
> **Venerable Sāriputta:** Lord, the Accomplished One, I do not cling because of faith in the Enlightened One. . . actually, anyone who does not yet understand, see, or know, who remains unclear and does not see with wisdom, that person still clings to their confidence in others. . . . As for those who understand, see, and know, who have clarity and see these things with wisdom, these people have no doubts and are not skeptical about the Teachings. . . . I have come to understand, see, and know; I have gained clarity and see with wisdom. I, therefore, have no doubt that the faculties of confidence. . . energy. . . mindfulness. . . concentration. . . and wisdom, which have already been developed and have done their duties, can lead to the realization of the deathless state, have the deathless state as their aim, and have the deathless state as their ultimate goal.
>
> **Lord Buddha:** Well put, Sāriputta! . . .[72]

In order to summarize the major importance and positive aspects of wisdom, let me quote the following statement by the Buddha:

> Bhikkhus, because you are accomplished, because you have done so much, how many of the sense-faculties (*indriya*) are required for a bhikkhu without stain to predict the final stage of emancipation and clearly know that, "birth (*jāti*) has ceased. . . and there is nothing left to do to attain this state?"
>
> Because you are accomplished, because you have done so much, only one sense faculty is required for the bhikkhu without

> stain to predict the final stage of his emancipation. . .that one sense faculty is the wisdom faculty.
>
> As for those Noble Disciples who have wisdom, they are sustained by confidence. . .effort (*viriya*). . .mindfulness (*sati*). . .and concentration (*samādhi*) based on wisdom—these can sustain you.[73]

If the other sense faculties (that is, confidence, effort, mindfulness, concentration)—whether considered individually or together—lack wisdom, then it is not possible to attain the final fruits of the practice.

Factors Leading to Proper Understanding

Proper understanding is a major factor of the Path. It is the starting point in the practice of the Dhamma; or stated in terms of the Three-fold Training, it constitutes the first level in the system of Buddhist learning. It is an aspect of the Dhamma that must be developed and made pure; it must attain freedom in a progressive manner until final enlightenment is reached. Accordingly, the development of proper understanding is of utmost importance.

The following passage from the Tipiṭaka states the major importance of proper understanding:

> **Question:** Friends, how many factors contribute to the arising of proper understanding?
>
> **Answer:** There are two factors contributing to the arising of proper understanding—learning from others (*paratoghosa*) and systematic, critical reflection (*yonisomanasikāra*).[74]

1. *Paratoghosa*—Listening to others, hearing others spread the word, listening to the suggestions and teachings of others;
2. *Yonisomanasikāra*—Engaging the mind, considering matters thoroughly in an orderly and logical manner through the application of critical or systematic reflection.

Both of these factors support one another. Most people with undeveloped wisdom must still depend on the suggestions and encouragement of others and gradually follow these people until they achieve their own intelligence. But eventually these undeveloped people must practice until they are able to think correctly for themselves and can then proceed to the final goal on their own. Those who have already developed wisdom, who already know how to apply critical reflection to a certain degree, may still have to depend on the proper guidance of others as a compass for plotting their first steps down the Path and as a means of support and encouragement. This initial support will allow them to make increasingly rapid progress in the course of their training.

Establishing proper understanding by listening to the teachings of others (*paratoghosa*) is an initial stage in the establishment of confidence. Confidence then becomes an important impetus. Once the teachings of others are put into practice and applied to a system of learning or training, we must consider if the guidance we have received is good enough to allow us to reach the final goal: Is the teacher well prepared? Does the teacher have the proper abilities? Is the teacher offering a method of training that will bear fruit? Therefore, in the system of Buddhist learning and training, we initially set our sights on observing the teachings of others, supported by a principle of spiritual friendship (*kalyāṇamitta*) or receiving spiritual advice from good friends, along with a second factor, critical reflection (*yonisomanasikāra*), a principle based on wisdom that contemplates how teachings should be correctly applied. When these two factors are brought together, spiritual friends have external importance, while critical reflection has internal significance. And of course the opposite can be true: Any person who is not a spiritual friend may offer poor guidance and misguided thought, which, in turn, can lead to a lack of critical reflection (*ayonisomanasikāra*)[75] or improper understanding (*micchādiṭṭhi*).

Lord Buddha has explained the role and import of these factors in process of practice and training:

1. For bhikkhus, those in the process of learning. . . I see no other external factor more beneficial than having a spiritual friend (*kalyāṇamitta*).[76]
2. For bhikkhus, those in the process of learning. . . I see no other internal factor more beneficial than critical reflection (*yonisomanasikāra*).[77]

A Summary of Two Factors

Having Spiritual Friends (kalyāṇamitta)

Kalyāṇamitta does not mean "good friend" in the usual sense, rather it refers to a person who is well prepared with the proper qualities to teach, suggest, point out, encourage, assist, and give guidance for getting started on the Path of Buddhist training. The *Visuddhimagga* [Path of Purification] mentions that Lord Buddha, his disciples, teachers, and learned wisemen are able to teach and give counsel, even though they may be younger than their students.[78]

In the process of the development of wisdom, having a spiritual friend is an important part of the stage related to confidence. In the Buddhist system of learning and training, the meaning of spiritual friend extends to teachers, advisors, and so on; this also encompasses the qualities of the teacher, his methodology, various strategies, and all of the things a person can do to achieve success in teaching and training. All of these things, which are considered external factors in the process of the development of wisdom, make for a major subject that could easily become a separate volume.

Here, I will only explain the importance and benefits of having a spiritual friend, so that we can see its role in the Buddhadhamma.

> Bhikkhus, when the sun is rising, its rays break the horizon before it does; these rays are a foreshadowing of what is to come. In the same way, having a good spiritual friend is a sign, a foreshadowing of the Noble Eight-fold Path for bhikkhus. Therefore, a bhikkhu who has a spiritual friend can hope for the following: developing the Noble Eight-fold Path and making the most of it.[79]

> Ānanda, having a good spiritual friend. . .encompasses the whole of the Holy Life, because a person with a spiritual friend. . .can hope for the following: developing the Noble Eight-fold Path and making the most of it.

> By depending on us as spiritual friends, beings who are normally subject to birth (*jāti*) can break free of birth; people normally subject to decay (*jarā*) can break free of decay; people who experience death (*maraṇa*) can break free of death; people who are subject to sorrow, lamentation, suffering, grief, and distress can break free. . . [of these].[80]

> Bhikkhus, before the sun breaks the horizon, silver and golden rays can be seen as a sign of its imminent rising. Just so, having

a spiritual friend can serve as a forerunner, a sign of the coming of the seven factors of enlightenment (*bojjhaṅga*) for bhikkhus. Bhikkhus with spiritual friends can hope for the following: developing the seven factors of enlightenment and making the most of them.[81]

I see nothing that can bring about wholesome things that have yet to arise or can make unwholesome things that have arisen fade away like having a good spiritual friend. When a person has a spiritual friend, then anything wholesome that has yet to arise arises, and anything unwholesome that has already arisen fades away.[82]

I see nothing that leads to such great benefit[83] . . .that leads to such certainty, such non-disintegration, and the non-disappearance of the true Dhamma[84] as having a good spiritual friend.

As an external factor, I do not see any other factor that leads to such great benefit as having a good spiritual friend.[85]

For bhikkhus—those who are still learning, have yet to achieve arahantship, and hope for sukha from their supreme efforts—I do not see any other external factor that is of greater importance than having a good spiritual friend. The bhikkhu who has a spiritual friend can put an end to bad things (*akusala*) and nurture what is good (*kusala*).[86]

Bhikkhus who have good spiritual friends can hope for the following:

1. They will be virtuous, well-mannered, and aware of the rules of the Order (*pāṭimokkha*); they will be whole, both in terms of thoughts and deeds;
2. They will (have the opportunity to hear and discuss various ideals with ease) as they see fit. The discussion of these ideals will hewn and polish their character, cleanse their minds, and make them bright. These ideals are contentment. . .effort, moral conduct (*sīla*), concentration

(*samādhi*), wisdom (*paññā*), liberation (*vimutti*), and knowledge of liberation (*vimuttiñāṇadassana*);

3. They will be people whose efforts are well established so that they can put an end to unwholesome things (*akusala-dhamma*) and practice wholesome things (*kusala-dhamma*) until they are perfected; they will be strong and not shirk their duties towards what is wholesome;
4. They will be wise, composed of noble wisdom, fully realizing the arising and passing away of unwholesome tendencies (*kilesa*), which leads to the complete elimination of dukkha.[87]

Applying Critical, Systematic Reflection (yonisomanasikāra)

As mentioned, critical reflection constitutes a method for applying thought correctly. When we examine its role in the process of intellectual development, critical reflection works beyond the level of confidence (*saddhā*) because this is the stage at which people begin to think freely for themselves. As for the role of critical reflection in the system of Buddhist learning and training, it amounts to practicing the application of thought, coming to know the correct method of thinking in a systematic, critical, and deep manner, one that is neither shallow nor superficial. It is an important step in establishing wisdom that is pure and free, which can help everyone to help himself in heading towards the final goal of the true Buddhadhamma.

We can see the importance and benefits of critical reflection in the following statement by Lord Buddha:

> Bhikkhus, when the sun is rising, its rays break the horizon before it does; these rays are a foreshadowing of what is to come. In the same way, preparing yourself through the application of critical reflection is a forerunner, a sign of the coming of the Noble Eight-fold Path for bhikkhus. So, a bhikkhu who has prepared himself by applying critical reflection can hope for the following: developing the Noble Eight-fold Path and making the most of it.[88]

> Bhikkhus, before the sun breaks the horizon, silver and gold rays can be seen as a sign of its imminent rising. Just so, critical reflection is a forerunner, a sign of the coming of the seven factors

of enlightenment (*bojjhaṅga*) for bhikkhus. And so, bhikkhus who have prepared themselves by applying critical reflection can hope for the following: developing the seven factors of enlightenment and making the most of them.[89]

I see nothing that can bring about wholesome things that have yet to arise or can make unwholesome things that have arisen fade away like critical reflection. When a person has critical reflection, then anything wholesome that has yet to arise arises, and anything unwholesome that has arisen fades away.[90]

I see nothing that leads to such great benefit[91]. . . that leads to such certainty, such non-disintegration, and the non-disappearance of the true Dhamma[92] as critical reflection.

As an internal factor, I see nothing that leads to such great benefit as critical reflection.[93]

For bhikkhus—those who are still learning, have yet to achieve arahantship, and hope for sukha from their supreme efforts—I do not see any other internal factor that is of greater importance than critical reflection. The bhikkhu who practices critical reflection can put an end to bad things (*akusala*) and nurture what is good (*kusala*).[94]

I see nothing that brings about proper understanding (*sammādiṭṭhi*) that has yet to arise or makes proper understanding that has arisen continue to prosper like critical reflection. When there is critical reflection, then proper understanding that has yet to arise arises and proper understanding that has already been established continues to prosper.[95]

I see nothing that brings about the factors of enlightenment (*bojjhaṅga*) that have yet to arise or makes the factors of enlightenment that have arisen continue to prosper like critical reflection. When there is critical reflection, then the factors of enlightenment that have yet to arise arise and the factors of enlightenment that already exist continue to prosper.[96]

I see nothing that makes doubts that have yet to arise not arise or eliminates doubts that have already arisen like critical reflection.[97]

Reflecting on disgusting things does not allow lust (*rāga*) to arise and causes the lust that exists to cease. Reflecting on the liberation of mind through the application of loving-kindness (*mettā-cetovimutti*) does not allow ill-will (*dosa*) to arise and causes the ill-will that exists to cease. In general, critical reflection does not allow delusion (*moha*) to arise and causes any delusion that already exists to fade away.[98]

When critical reflection is applied, the five hindrances (*nīvaraṇa*) do not arise and those that have arisen are eliminated. At the same time, it is the cause for the arising and prospering of the seven factors of enlightenment (*bojjhaṅga*).[99]

There are nine dhammic factors that are of great assistance. These nine have critical reflection as their basis: when critical reflection is applied, delight (*pāmojja*) arises; when there is delight, joy (*pīti*) arises; when there is joy, then the body experiences serenity (*passaddhi*); when the body is serene, then happiness (*sukha*) is experienced; those who are happy can have a focused mind (*samādhi*); those who are focused can know the Truth; when things are perceived according to the Truth, disenchantment (*nibbidā*) comes about; when a person experiences disenchantment, detachment (*virāga*) is achieved; and because there is detachment, there is liberation (*vimutti*).[100]

According to the statement made by Lord Buddha, we can illustrate the following simple progression:

Critical reflection → delight (*pāmojja*) → joy (*pīti*) → serenity (*passaddhi*) → happiness (*sukha*) → concentration (*samādhi*) → knowing things as they are (*yathābhūtañāṇadassana*) → disenchantment (*nibbidā*) → detachment (*virāga*) → liberation (*vimutti*).

Let me summarize this for everyone: Those who still lack sufficient wisdom must depend on the guidance of others. The development of wisdom begins with the help of external factors first. That is, first a person must have good spiritual friends, which results in confidence (in other words, confidence according to observation and reason). From here, a person proceeds to the level of internal factors. This progress begins by taking the foundation of understanding well established with confidence and using that understanding to gain freedom of thought through the continued application of critical reflection. This accomplishment, in turn, brings about proper understanding (*sammādiṭṭhi*) and develops wisdom even further until it becomes perfect knowledge (*ñāṇadassana*)—knowing and seeing with certainty.[101] When a person has passed through each of these levels in the course of the development of wisdom, we can see that this process is the same as the sustenance of knowledge and liberation (*vimutti*) that has already been mentioned:[102]

> Association with good people → attending to the study of the Dhamma → confidence → critical reflection, and so on. . . .

When proper understanding has been established, it continues to evolve towards the final goal with the support of various factors:

> Bhikkhus, proper understanding—which is assisted by five factors—brings about liberation of the mind (*cetovimutti*) and the liberation of wisdom (*paññāvimutti*). The five factors are:
> 1. proper conduct (*sīla*);
> 2. knowing how to study, read a text, and make further interpretations (*suta*);
> 3. discussing, debating, and exchanging views; being able to answer other people's questions (*sākacchā*);
> 4. attaining tranquillity and peace of mind, not being deluded (*samatha*);
> 5. using wisdom to consider various phenomena and circumstances in accordance with their conditions, that is, in accordance with reality or their true nature (*vipassanā*).[103]

Finally, therefore, proper understanding relates to seeing in accordance with conditions—seeing according to the true nature of things. In order for proper understanding to develop, a person must consistently depend on critical reflection; this type of reflection prevents superficial inquiry or seeing things only in terms of appearance. Instead, critical reflection allows us to see the make-up of various things—how things have come together, have come to be, and how things proceed along a course of cause and effect. This type of reflection allows us to avoid becoming deluded; it helps us avoid becoming a mechanical dummy easily provoked, incited, and manipulated by phenomena relating to physical sensations, sounds, smells, tastes, tangible objects, and conventions—phenomena that can become a problem for yourself and others. Critical reflection leads to mindfulness and clear comprehension (*sati-sampajañña*), freedom, self-assurance, along with decision making and actions based on wisdom; this is the level at which proper understanding brings its fruits to bear on the other factors of the Eight-fold Path. It is here that the fetters leading to rebirth !*saṁyojana*) are cut—such as, maintaining the delusion of a self (*sakkāyadiṭṭhi*), harboring skepticism (*vicikicchā*), and merely practicing in accordance with rules and rituals (*sīlabbataparāmāsa*).

2. Proper Thought (sammāsaṅkappa)

The second factor of the Eight-fold Path is generally defined in the Buddhist canon as follows:

> Bhikkhus, what is proper thought? It is renouncing thoughts about sensuality (*nekkhammasaṅkappa*), bearing no thoughts of hatred (*abyāpādasaṅkappa*), and giving up thoughts of violence (*avihiṁsāsaṅkappa*)—this is proper thought.[104]

Aside from this, there is another definition that is divided into two perspectives, the mundane (*lokiya*) and the supramundane (*lokuttara*):

> Bhikkhus, what is proper thought? I say that there are two kinds of proper thought: one that is still tainted by intoxication, that is still meritorious and has consequences for the aggregates, and another that is most noble, without stain, supramundane, and is a factor of the Path.
>
> Proper thought that is still tainted . . . renounces thoughts of sensuality (*nekkhammasaṅkappa*) and bears no thought of hatred (*abyāpādasaṅkappa*) or violence (*avihiṁsāsaṅkappa*). . . .
>
> Proper thought that is most noble, without stain, and supramundane (*lokuttara*) and is a factor of the Path involves reasoning, the initial application of thought (*vitakka*), thought (*saṅkappa*),

> the focusing of thought (*appanā*), the determination of thought (*byappanā*), and concentrating on the predispositions of speech (*vacī-saṅkhāra*). Those people who have noble, untainted minds, are endowed with the Noble Path, and are making progress along the Path. . . .[105]

For the sake of conciseness, I am only going to deal with the general definition of proper thought at the mundane level. According to this definition, proper thought constitutes a correct way of thinking, which is opposed to the incorrect or improper way of thinking called *micchāsaṅkappa*. There are three types of improper thought:

1. *Kāmasaṅkappa* or *kāma-vitakka*—Thinking about sensuality; thinking of seeking sensual satisfaction or being preoccupied and caught up in satisfying the desires of the five senses or the various forms of craving (*taṇhā*). Selfish thoughts are thoughts that proceed according to lust (*rāga*) and greed (*lobha*);
2. *Byāpādasaṅkappa* or *byāpāda-vitakka*—Harboring resentment and feelings of revenge, being upset and dissatisfied; the arousal of various thoughts of ill-will (*dosa*); and
3. *Vihiṁsāsaṅkappa* or *vihiṁsā-vitakka*—Thinking with malice and bad intentions; thinking of performing deeds of ill-will.

These ways of thinking are common for most people, because normally when people perceive a certain mind-object, feelings arise in two ways: If a feeling is pleasant and a person likes it, he seeks to prolong it and pursue it. If the feeling is unpleasant and a person does not like it, he resists it and wants it to end. From here, various thoughts proceed according to the strength of a person's likes and dislikes. For this reason, normally people's thoughts are influenced and pulled in certain directions according to biases, and this does not allow them to see the true nature of what they are observing. Thoughts that proceed according to likes and dislikes lead to attachments, entanglements, and biases—becoming *kāma-vitakka*. Thoughts that proceed according to dislike and dissatisfaction lead to anger, distaste, hostility, and a negative attitude—becoming *byāpāda-vitakka*. This extends further to thoughts of using force and doing harm—becoming *vihiṁsā-vitakka*. All of these tendencies lead to an incorrect outlook (or improper intentions).

These kinds of biased thoughts and distorted views come about due to the lack of critical reflection: That is, seeing things superficially, perceiving mind-objects without clear comprehension (*sati-sampajañña*), letting thoughts go according to feeling or likes and dislikes, and not critically examining the make-up of all the factors of a situation in accordance with cause and effect, according to the principle of critical reflection.

In this sense, improper understanding (*micchādiṭṭhi*) means looking at all things without seeing their true nature, which results in improper thought (*micchāsaṅkappa*)—reasoning, thinking, and maintaining views in a distorted or incorrect manner. Improper thought results in improper understanding by causing further misunderstandings and distortions. Both of these factors—improper understanding (*micchādiṭṭhi*) and improper thought (*micchāsaṅkappa*)—complement and support one another.

On the other hand, in order to see all things correctly according to their true nature, critical reflection must be practiced, which implies that thoughts must be clear and free, without preferences, attachments, entanglements, and dislikes tugging at you in an adversarial manner. This means having proper understanding and proper thought and having both of these factors complement and support one another in the same way that their improper counterparts do.

Accordingly, when you have critical reflection, you have proper understanding—that is, seeing and understanding everything according to its true nature. When all things are seen according to their true nature, proper thought is achieved; thoughts and views are correct, unbiased, unattached, and do not turn against you. When thought is free of likes and dislikes and is neutral in this way,[106] this allows you to see things according to their true nature and increases proper understanding. From here, proper understanding and proper thought continue to support each other.

As soon as you are able to practice critical reflection, the mind becomes clear, free, and liberated from biases (including both the positive things that have become attachments and the repulsive things that have been avoided). As with improper thought (*micchāsaṅkappa*) above, proper thought (*sammāsaṅkappa*) also has three types:

1. *Nekkhammasaṅkappa* or *nekkhamma-vitakka*—Renouncing thoughts about sensuality—thinking without greed (*lobha*), without sensuality (*kāma*), not becoming entangled nor mixed up with things that promote desires of any kind; it is thought free of selfishness, that is willing to make sacrifices for others; it is thought that is valuable or meritorious[107] and is free from lust (*rāga*) and greed (*lobha*);
2. *Abyāpādasaṅkappa* or *abyāpāda-vitakka*—Not harboring resentment nor feelings of revenge, not viewing things in a negative way;

this means especially taking dhammic notions such as loving-kindness (*mettā*)—that is, good intentions, friendliness, and wanting others to be happy—and using them as an antidote against thoughts of ill-will (*dosa*);

3. *Avihiṁsāsaṅkappa* or *avihiṁsā-vitakka*—Thinking without malice and bad intentions; this means especially taking dhammic notions, such as compassion (*karuṇā*)—in other words, helping others to overcome dukkha—and using them as an antidote against malevolent intentions (*dosa*).

There is something worth mentioning here, something that the reader may have already noticed. For the good or wholesome dhamma (*kusala*), which are in opposition to the unwholesome dhamma (*akusala*), instead of using an antonym, the Buddhist texts usually employ a negative (using the Pali prefix "*a-*"). This use of the negative often makes some people think that the Buddhist teachings (*Buddhadhamma*) are pessimistic and passive: in other words, they simply advocate not doing evil, sitting still, or being indifferent, and that this is good enough. Such as, here, improper thought (*micchāsaṅkappa*) is equated with *byāpādasaṅkappa*, and proper thought (*sammāsaṅkappa*), instead of being *mettā*, is equated with *abyāpādasaṅkappa*, which opposes the negative (*micchā-*). We will continue to elaborate on the assumption that Buddhism is negative or pessimistic, but here, I would just like to make three short arguments against this misunderstanding.

First, in the case of the factors of the Eight-fold Path, and especially the factor of proper thought (*sammāsaṅkappa*), the Buddhist teachings do not simply express moral values for the sake of proper conduct (usually referred to as *sīla-dhamma*)—the ultimate goal is wisdom (*paññā*). Buddhism does not just teach people not to hate, that is, to have loving-kindness (*mettā*) for one another, and maintain a moral code out of blind faith or a standardized set of religious dogma. There are other aspects of wisdom pertaining to spiritual progress that must be pointed out here. They can be summarized as follows: in terms of proper thought, wisdom is important at all levels and must be constantly maintained, with morality following in its wake. Proper thought requires a bright, clear, and free mind, a mind set on truth—that which we call skilled (Thai, *khlong tua*), unbiased, and unattached, suitable for attaining the unsullied truth according to conditions. In such cases, the use of negative terms is most suitable.

Secondly, as mentioned, one of the linguistic features of the Pali language is the use of "*a-*" as a negative prefix. This does not simply indicate that what is being discussed is not that thing, rather it tends to refer to the opposite of the term under consideration. Or it may, in fact, encompass the opposite as well as anything that is not that thing. Take, for example, the term *akusala* (unwholesome, bad); it does not simply mean not *kusala* (which might be construed as *abyākata*, as an indeterminate or neutral concept, neither good nor evil), instead it means evil, which is just the opposite of *kusala*. The term *amitta*, for example, does not mean neutral people—in other words, people we may not know very well (*mitta*)—instead it refers to enemies. In our discussion of proper thought, the use of "*a-*" carries both a negative meaning and encompasses all opposites: for example, *abyāpādasaṅkappa* refers to *mettā* (loving-kindness), which is just the opposite of *byāpāda*; however, it also expresses the idea that thought must be pure, clear, and free of *byāpāda*, in other words, unbiased. By implication, dhammic concepts—such as *mettā*, for example—are, therefore, aspects of this factor of the Eight-fold Path.

Finally, words that employ the negative "*a-*", aside from having a general meaning, carry a more specific meaning beyond an opposing concept. In such cases, the use of the negative term extends to suggesting that that concept should be completely eliminated, that all belief, traces, or impressions of that thing should be done away with. In this sense, *abyāpādasaṅkappa* means thought that is utterly absent of *byāpāda* or maleviolent intention and is completely taken up with loving-kindness that knows no bounds. This differs from some of the teachings of other religions that ask you to believe in a definition of love or compassion set down by a teacher, that do not consider the actual conditions of certain phenomena, and are therefore limited to a particular scope or group of people who have agreed to such definitions.

There are certain things that we should understand about the relationship between proper understanding (*sammādiṭṭhi*) and proper thought (*sammāsaṅkappa*): one, when they are compared to the unwholesome tendencies (*kilesa*) of the three roots of evil (*akusala-mūla*)—greed (*lobha*), ill-will (*dosa*), and delusion (*moha*)—we can see that proper understanding is the regulator of delusion, the root cause of all unwholesome tendencies; proper thought is the regulator of continuing or subsequent unwholesome tendencies. That is, *nekkhammasaṅkappa* limits lust (*rāga*) and greed (*lobha*); *abyāpādasaṅkappa* and *avihiṁsāsaṅkappa* limit ill-will (*dosa*).

Accordingly, proper understanding and proper thought are linked in all respects.

At any rate, progressing to these two factors of the Eight-fold Path is only the beginning. At this point, wisdom has yet to be completely developed. This all must occur gradually, step by step. For this reason, we should understand some things about the above three types of proper thought: *nekkhammasaṅkappa* does not simply imply its more obvious, symbolic meaning, that is, renouncing the world and being ordained or heading off to lead the homeless life; *abyāpādasaṅkappa* primarily stresses developing loving-kindness (*mettā*); and *avihiṁsāsaṅkappa* puts a great deal of importance on fostering compassion (*karuṇā*). Wisdom that has developed to this point, even if it constitutes proper understanding (*sammādiṭṭhi*) that sees things according to their true nature, is not yet pure and does not yet see clearly enough to reach the level of equanimity (*upekkhā*), which depends on focused concentration (*samādhi*) as its foundation.

Furthermore, even loving-kindness, which is one of the most fundamental stepping stones in the practice of Buddhism, is not the simple step it is often superficially understood to be. Actually, the loving-kindness we often so easily speak of is very difficult to turn into true loving-kindness. For this reason, we should come to an understanding about a few basic things about loving-kindness.

Loving-kindness refers to friendship, love, good intentions, empathy, and establishing a sense of common understanding and happiness among all beings.[108] Loving-kindness is neutral, both in terms of who should have loving-kindness and who should receive it; true loving-kindness is indifferent to seniority, rank, and status—including status measured in terms of wealth, merit, or ordination. It is a fundamental dhammic principle that builds relationships between people, looks at people in a positive and optimistic light, and allows them to listen to one another and exchange ideas freely without feeling disgust or aversion.

Loving-kindness (as well as all the other points of the Sublime States of Mind, the *brahmavihāra*) is a characteristic of great people (Thai, *phuyai*). Traditionally it was said to be "the dhamma of 'big' people" or "brahmins." Brahmins or "big" people here refers to excellent people, those of especially great generosity and goodness. But everyone should nurture the Sublime States of Mind, everyone should practice generosity, not just great people. Today, however, most people understand the Sublime States of Mind to be based on loving-kindness and to be solely a characteristic of so-called great people. We must understand that saying this stresses the responsibility that certain people should have; that is, while everyone should foster the Sublime States of Mind, great people, in their positions of status and leadership, should practice these values first and set a good example for others to follow. If we do come to understand this first and let things go simply believing that loving-kindness or the various aspects of the Sublime States of Mind are the property of great people, we will remain far off the mark.

We must understand something else about the relative success or failure of loving-kindness. According to this principle, the success of loving-kindness relates to stopping vengence, or *byāpāda*; the failure of loving-kindness relates to the arising of lust, or *sineha*.[109] The success of loving-kindness has nothing special worth noting about it, whereas its failure has many things that should be pointed out. The Pali term *sineha* refers to the love that binds certain people together or that relates to self-satisfaction, such as *puttasineha*, love for your children, and *bariyā-sineha*, love for your wife. *Sineha* brings about bias and causes people to help each other for the wrong reasons, which is often called *chandāgati* (misguided love or bias out of love). You have probably heard people say "He has a special love (*mettā*) for me" or "The boss really loves that person"—these are all related to *sineha* and are failures of loving-kindness, not the real thing. True loving-kindness is an important component that helps to maintain the Dhamma. This is because it is a neutral principle that helps people break free of selfishness and biases. True loving-kindness leads to reason and seeks happiness for all people without exception; it is not determined by personal desires and gain. True loving-kindness proceeds as follows:

> The Blessed One cares for people without discrimination—even the archer (who was hired to murder the Buddha), Devadatta [who betrayed Lord Buddha], Aṅgulimāla [the robber who wore a garland of fingers], the elephant Dhanapāla (that Devadatta let loose so that it might trample the Buddha to death), and Rāhula [Lord Buddha's son]—everyone.[110]

The benefits of loving-kindness can be seen in cases of debates, logical arguments, and discussions that make both parties consider the rationale of an argument; these debates help both people to achieve a mutual understanding. For example, when a Jain [named Saccaka] came to confer with the Buddha and used strong language to libel him, Lord Buddha responded in a reasonable manner until finally the Jain responded by saying:

> When it is put this way, I can believe in Gotama, the Accomplished One, as the one who knows the truth. Gotama is well trained in terms of the body and the mind. . . .[111]

> It is amazing! I have never seen this before! Gotama has stood up to my confrontation with him. I prepared my words of cross-examination, and he has accepted them in this way, with a bright complexion, a glowing disposition, like an arahant, an Enlightened One.[112]

In instances that result in proper thought—in which various views are corrected with wisdom—obstinacy, anxiety, and irrationality have no place. Instead, critical reflection (*yonisomanasikāra*) is applied—considering matters according to causes and effects, and contemplating the actual root of the matter. The following text states:

> Bhikkhus, before the attainment of enlightenment, when I was a bodhisatta and had yet to attain Buddhahood, it occurred to me that I should divide thought into two types: 1) *kāma-vitakka* (thoughts of sensual pleasure), *byāpāda-vitakka* (thoughts of hatred or ill-will), and *vihiṁsā-vitakka* (thoughts of violence or cruelty); 2) *nekkhamma-vitakka* (thoughts of renunciation), *abyāpāda-vitakka* (thoughts free of hatred), and *avihiṁsā-vitakka* (thoughts free of violence).
>
> When I was conscientious, tireless, and focused, and *kāma-vitakka* arose, I could clearly know that: *kāma-vitakka* partially worked against me, partially against others, and also worked against both myself and others. It brought an end to wisdom, it became a source of stress and strain, and did not lead to nibbana.
>
> As soon as I realized that it caused conflicts for me, *kāma-vitakka* dissipated. As soon as I realized that it caused conflicts with others, . . . it brought an end to wisdom, it became a source of stress and strain, and did not lead to nibbana . . . *kāma-vitakka* dissipated. I could, therefore, do away with *kāma-vitakka* that used to plague me; I could completely extinguish it.

> When I was conscientious. . .and *byāpāda-vitakka* arose. . . *vihiṁsā-vitakka* arose, I could clearly know that. . .[as stated above]...I could do away with *byāpāda-vitakka*. . .[and the] *vihiṁsā-vitakka* that used to plague me; I could completely extinguish them.
>
> Bhikkhus, the more you think about or dwell on any thought, the more you tend to go in the direction of those thoughts. The more you think about, dwell upon sensuality (*kāma-vitakka*), the farther you are from renunciation (*nekkhamma-vitakka*). The more you dwell on sensuality, the more you are inclined towards sensuality, then your mind is only inclined towards *kāma-vitakka*. . . .The more you think about renunciation, the farther you are from sensuality. If you make the most of renunciation, then your mind is only inclined towards renunciation.[113]

The initial stages of the practice related to the first two factors of the Path can be summarized as follows:

> Bhikkhus, the bhikkhu who is composed of four things can be said to be progressing and practicing correctly; this person can be said to have begun the course eliminating all mental intoxicants (*āsava*). These four things are: *nekkhamma-vitakka, abyāpāda-vitakka, avihiṁsā-vitakka,* and *sammādiṭṭhi*.[114]

3. Proper Speech (sammāvācā)

4. Proper Action (sammākammanta)

5. Proper Livelihood (sammā-ājīva)

All three of these factors of the Path relate to ethics or morality (*sīla*), and this is why they have been put together here. We can see this from the definitions of these terms provided in the texts:

1. Bhikkhus, what is proper speech?	Proper speech is:
a) *musāvādā veramaṇī*	abstention from false speech
b) *pisuṇāya vācāya veramaṇī*	abstention from libel/slander

c) *pharusāya vācāya veramaṇī*	abstention from harsh speech
d) *samphappalāpā veramaṇī*	abstention from vain talk/gossip
2. Bhikkhus, what is proper action?	Proper action is:
a) *pāṇātipātā veramaṇī*	abstention from taking life
b) *adinnādānā veramaṇī*	abstention from taking what is not given
c) *kāmesu micchācārā veramaṇī*	abstention from sexual misconduct

3. Bhikkhus, what is proper livelihood? Proper livelihood is: The Noble Disciples completely stop all improper means of livelihood[115] and sustain themselves according to the ways of proper livelihood.[116]

Aside from this, there is another definition that is divided according to mundane (*lokiya*) and supramundane (*lokuttara*) levels as follows:

1. Proper speech at the supramundane level amounts to "abstaining from, stopping, completely giving up any inclination towards four types of improper speech. The person with a noble mind, free of intoxications (*āsava*), and endowed with the Noble Path is truly progressing along the Noble Path."
2. Proper action at the supramundane level amounts to "abstaining from, stopping, completely giving up any inclination towards three types of bodily misconduct. The person with a noble mind. . . ."
3. Proper livelihood at the supramundane level amounts to "abstaining from, stopping, completely giving up any inclination towards improper livelihood. The person with a noble mind. . . ."[117]

From this description of a central principle of moral training called *sīla-sikkhā*, the Buddhadhamma expands and extends to other practices and aspects of behavior. The details and applications of this training are vast and intricate enough such that the fruits of this practice include helping individuals and society. These details begin with the explanation of the principles of conduct found in the Noble Path, which is called *kammapatha* (course of action), and principles of humane conduct called *pañca-sīla* (five precepts). At any rate, the applied teachings are almost endless in detail and differ according to person, place, and circumstances, which provide the context for each lesson. Unfortunately, there is not enough space to collect and explain all of these teachings here. While the Buddha-dhamma does have its own system of teaching, we will only be able to point out its central principles. As for the various applied teachings, we will let people pursue them according to their own dispositions, lifestyles, and goals.

When the applied teachings are summarized—that is, without reference to a particular person, place, or time—the important underlying principles relate to the quality of life and how life is led. In this sense, there are *sīla,* or the established rules of conduct, which are separated according to rules for laity and rules for ordinands. Those who study the *sīla* must understand the underlying principles and the important essence of each of them; and most important, a person must come to understand the intention of these *sīla*—seeing their differences and common higher purpose as one and the same—which will bring about proper understanding, a sound basis for belief and correct and fruitful practice.

At this point I will explain some examples that expand the meaning of the ethical dimension of the Noble Path. These examples dealing with conduct are direct. They come under the headings of *kāya-kamma* (or *sammākammanta,* proper action), then *vacī-kamma* (or *sammāvācā,* proper speech), and are also often called *kusala-kammapatha* or *sucarita,* being pure in terms of body (*kāya*) and speech (*vācā*) and mind. Some examples are as follows:

At one time, Lord Buddha was staying in the town of Pāvā in the mango grove of a metal worker named Cunda. Cunda came to see him to ask about purification rituals of cleansing (*soceyya-kamma*). Cunda asked him about certain adherents to the rituals and beliefs established by the Pacchābhūmi Brahmins who raise goblets of water, wear seaweed necklaces, worship fire, and observe bathing rites. The practices of these brahmins include touching the earth with their hands as soon as they arise in the early morning; if they do not touch the earth, then they reach for fresh cow dung or green grass; or they tend a fire or put their palms together in respect for the sun, otherwise they are required perform three ablutions at sundown.[118]

The Lord Buddha responded by saying that these Brahmanical notions of cleanliness are one thing and cleanliness according to the Ariya-Vinaya is quite another. They are not the same, and any person who defies the ten proper courses of conduct (*kusala-kammapatha*) is not clean in terms of body, speech, and mind. And when this person gets up in the morning, whether he touches the ground or not, places his hands on cow dung or not, worships fire or not, raises his hands to the sun or not, this will not determine his cleanliness, because any unwholesome course of conduct (*akusala-kammapatha*) is unclean and is the cause of uncleanliness. The Buddha then explained the ten *kusala-kammapatha* as the proper means of cleanliness:

The Three Means to Bodily Cleanliness

1. Abstain from taking life (*pāṇātipāta*); do not harm others with punishment; put down weapons; have shame and loving-kindness towards all beings; assist in the sustenance of all life.
2. Abstain from stealing and taking anything that is not given (*adinnādāna*); do not take anything belonging to others, whether that thing is in a house or in the forest, unless it is offered to you.
3. Abstain from all forms of sexual misconduct (*kāmesu micchācāra*); do not violate women, whether it be those under a family's care, those protected by the law, those with husbands, or those who are already spoken for and engaged to others.

The Four Means to Verbal Cleanliness

1. Abstain from false speech (*musāvāda*); whether you are in good company, in a meeting, among relatives or royalty, if you are asked a question, you should know how to answer properly: when you do not know, say you do not know; when you have not seen something, say you have not seen it; when you know, say you know; when you have seen something, say you have seen it; do not tell a lie; do not declare things for personal reasons; do not declare things because of the influence of others or for gain.
2. Abstain from telling tales (*pisuṇāvācā*); abstain from spreading malicious gossip from place to place; make efforts towards bringing about understanding, unity, and harmony between people.
3. Abstain from harsh speech (*pharusavācā*); abstain from coarse words; use only faultless words that are pleasant, endearing, and polite.
4. Abstain from vain and groundless talk (*samphappalāpa*); speak appropriately, truthfully, with substance; speak meaningfully and

ethically; make reference to things grounded in reality, with purpose and based on proper training.

The Three Means of Cleansing the Mind

1. Abstain from coveting the property of others (*anabhijjhā*)
2. Abstain from harboring ill-will (*abyāpadā*)
3. Maintain proper understanding (*sammādiṭṭhi*)

These last three concepts extend the meaning of the first two factors of the Noble Eight-fold Path, that is, proper understanding (*sammādiṭṭhi*) and proper thought (*sammāsaṅkappa*), and so their details will not be repeated here.

> For those people composed of the ten *kusala-kammapatha*, when you arise from your bed early in the morning and touch the earth, you will be clean, and even if you do not touch the earth, you will be clean.... Because these ten *kusala-kammapatha* are clean and are the cause of cleanliness...![119]

When the meaning of this passage is expanded and applied, it may differ according to various contexts and circumstances. For example, when we refer to a person who has been ordained—a case in which certain points of the moral code change, some new rules are added, and old ones still apply—part of the meaning of ethics changes. Let us take a look at *adinnādāna* and *musāvāda* and compare them to the explanations in the ten *kusala-kammapatha*.

> *Adinnādāna* means abstaining from taking anything that is not given to you; only keeping what has been given; not being a thief; being a clean person.
>
> *Musāvāda* means not telling lies; only telling the truth; being true, upstanding, reliable, and not hypocritical.[120]

There is something worth noting in these passages, and that is that the expanded explanation of the meaning of these points of moral conduct can be divided into two parts. The first part refers to abstaining from evil, and the second part refers to performing proper conduct that is opposed to evil. In short, the first part constitutes a negative statement, and the second part a positive one. These two parts are indicative of a more general trend in Buddhist teachings: They tend to include a negative statement together with a positive one; that is, they follow a principle of "abstaining from evil and then doing what is right." Abstention from evil becomes the starting point, and then the details of proper conduct follow. These details are not simply limited to the factors of the Eight-fold Path. One example of this is *adinnādāna*. We have yet to expand the meaning of the positive aspects of this clearly (we have, however, already mentioned some of the merits of gift-giving [*dāna*], a major principle in Buddhism).

As we have already seen, some Western scholars have criticized Buddhism for being negative, claiming that its teachings only tell people to abstain from various things and do not indicate a positive course of action. Some of these Western critics have also said that the teachings of Buddhism are "subjective" and are merely an "ethic of thought"; they are teachings of renunciation and passivity. These teachings make Buddhists satisfied with merely refraining from bad deeds and trying to avoid demerit (*pāpa*). Accordingly, this has made Buddhists indifferent towards helping the rest of mankind to the extent that loving-kindness (*mettā*) and compassion (*karuṇā*) are not acted upon but rather amount to a wish or hope [hence, an "ethic of thought" or intentions that are not acted upon]. Some of these scholars cite the Tipiṭaka to support their views, maintaining that the Buddhist teachings are only negative; in so doing they refer to only the first part of the definition of the fourth factor of the Eight-fold Path, proper action (*sammākammanta*), such as the following statement by Venerable Sāriputta:

> Friends, what is proper action? Not taking life, not taking what is not offered, and not engaging in sexual misconduct. These, friends, amount to proper action.[121]

Those who study and understand the practice of the factors of the Path as they have been explained will immediately see that these critics, while their intentions may be good, have drawn on only what they have read, or only certain portions of the teachings. They have not noted the larger train of thought of the teachings nor taken a systematic approach to the whole of the Buddhadhamma. By taking a more comprehensive approach to the teachings we can clearly see that the system of ethical conduct related to the Path is not limited to negativity, passivity, nor subjectivity—nor is it merely an ethic of thought. At any rate, when true students of Buddhism study this matter for themselves, they will come to discover what is what.

There are, however, certain reasons why the ethical aspects of the Path must be stated in negative terms. Some of these reasons are as follows:

1. The moral code (*sīla*) is one part of the larger Buddhist teachings (*Buddhadhamma*). This code is not a divine command demanding that followers do this or that in accordance with a divine purpose, a purpose based on ungrounded faith and loyalty that does not require an understanding of interconnected causes and effects. The Buddhist moral code has been determined based on reasons and natural laws, which the practitioner must come to see as as related system. Even if a person does not yet have the wisdom to see this system clearly and is still practicing according to faith or confidence, this confidence must be based on reason (*ākāra-vatīsaddhā*), which, at the very least, must have a basic understanding of cause and effect as its foundation in order for true wisdom to occur.
2. When the process of practice and training is seen as a series of increasingly refined steps, a person must start with abstention, with eliminating bad tendencies first, and then proceed towards better things until purity and the final fruits of the practice are attained. It is like sowing a field: at first, the ground must be cleared and prepared, all obstacles to growth must be eliminated, and then the seeds can be planted and grow until they bear fruit. In the system of Buddhist teachings, the moral precepts (*sīla*) are the very first step; they are the basis for proper behavior, which emphasizes abstention from all evil. After this, a person progresses still higher by doing good, practicing meditation (*samādhi*), and perfecting wisdom (*paññā*), which will gradually assist a person on the Path.
3. According to the Three-fold Training (*tisikkhā*), the moral precepts (*sīla*) alone are not enough to lead a person to the highest level of practice; they only lead to other levels of development, such as the practice of concentration meditation (*samādhi*). *Samādhi,* therefore, is the goal of *sīla*; that is, abstaining from and eliminating all inclinations towards evil makes the mind pure and clear. There is no confusion or worry left to distract or disturb the mind, and the mind is able to become focused easily. When the mind is peaceful and focused, a person becomes accomplished enough

to apply wisdom (*paññā*), investigate cause and effect, and create opportunities for performing beneficial acts as he goes along.

4. Buddhadhamma believes that the mind is of utmost importance. Therefore, its system of ethics must always go hand in hand with an awareness of psychological processes and all aspects of behavior. Buddhadhamma maintains that the mind is the forerunner of all things, and so it takes note of all intentions arising there so that various good deeds are done with true motives, not just to deceive others.[122] This also means, however, that you should not deceive yourself, as well. This type of awareness results in eliminating any conflicts between thoughts and deeds.
5. The ethical dimensions of the Path teach that it is the basic responsibility of everyone not to harbor evil thoughts nor put down or deceive others. When this state of mental purity has been firmly established, it then becomes the responsibility of everyone to expand the scope of their actions and perform more and more good deeds for the benefit of others. Simply put, it is everyone's responsibility to eliminate all their own evil tendencies and then act positively for the good of others.
6. The "negative" aspects of the moral code are a way of expressing the most general aspects of the practice—they keep an eye on evil until all seeds of evil intention are rooted out. But as for the positive aspects of the moral code, they continue on without end. Good deeds can be far reaching, endless, and changeable, depending on particular circumstances and contexts. The determination of improper behavior, however, is more certain. For example, both monks and laity should abstain from telling lies, but their ways of expressing the truth may differ. Therefore, the central principles specify the things to abstain from, the things to be eliminated, but the details of the methodology and the various applications concerning the performance of good deeds remain dependent on time, place, and surrounding conditions.
7. Observing each factor of the Path is essential for anyone who wishes to reach the final goal of Buddhism. For this reason, each factor must be accessible to all; aspects of the Path cannot be limited by status, time, or place. Take *adinnādāna*: refraining from stealing is something everyone can do, but giving gifts depends on other things, such as, having something to give and determining the worthiness of the receiver.

8. When a person is involved in a certain aspect of the practice, attention becomes focused on this aspect. In this case, this person's responsibility towards other dimensions of behavior involve keeping evil at bay. The benefits of ethics (*sīla*) come into play here to help take care of these other dimensions; they make sure that this person's actions remain on target and do not make a turn for the worst at any point. The moral code provides a solid foundation for the performance of good deeds.

Furthermore, there are some points worth noting about the differences between the Buddhist code of ethics and those found in other theistic religions. Some of the differences follow.

According to Buddhadhamma, the moral code constitutes a set of principles of behavior established in accordance with causes and effects that follow natural law. In theistic religions, morality is established according to divine command and a divine principle.

In terms of the negative aspects of the moral code, according to Buddhism, the moral code is composed of rules of training (*sikkhāpada*) that keep evil at bay; but in theistic religions, the moral codes essentially amount to prohibitions or divine commandments.

The motive for the practice of morality in Buddhism is confidence in the law of kamma; that is, a basic understanding of actions and the fruits of actions. The intended outcome of the practice of morality in theistic religions is faith; that is, belief, acceptance, and a willingness to act on divine commandment—a total surrender that does not question cause and effect.

According to Buddhism, proper observance of the moral code constitutes behavioral training beginning with abstaining from evil and then progressing to the performance of various good deeds (which are in opposition to evil); as for the theistic religions, observance of morality involves believing in and strictly adhering to divine commandments.

In Buddhism, the practice of the moral code has a special purpose—it is the foundation of focused attention (*samādhi*). It is a system of training that prepares people and makes them capable of setting their minds on tasks that are of greatest benefit, that proceed towards wisdom and the final goal of liberation. As for any notion such as going to heaven, this would only occur as the result of a person's actions. With theistic religions, however, being moral in accordance with divine commandment results in being looked upon favorably from above; acting according to divine purpose results in being rewarded by God, by being given permission to enter heaven.

For Buddhism, the results of following or not following the moral code are part of a natural process (Thai, *thammachat*); that is, the results of actions have their own natural justice called the law of kamma. These fruits of action have their genesis in the mind and then extend out to a person's character and lifestyle—be it in this life or the next. As for theistic religions, the good and bad fruits of observing or ignoring the moral code (or divine commandment) becomes a matter of retribution—good results, such as ascending to heaven, become rewards, and bad results, such as descending into hell, amount to punishments. And the good and bad rewards depend upon the consideration and judgment from above.

In terms of understanding good and evil, Buddhism teaches that proper ethics have value because they nurture and improve the quality of the mind; ethics make the mind clean, clear, and pure; they raise the mind to higher levels that are called good, moral, or meritorious (*puñña*); they allow the mind and life itself to flourish and blossom; and finally they lead to liberation and freedom of the mind, which allows a person to go forth and act with wisdom in skillful and wholesome (*kusala*) ways. As for evil, it is a condition that causes mental qualities to degenerate, and so it is deemed demeritorious (*pāpa*) and does not result in attaining the final goal of liberation nor the wholesome means mentioned above. In theistic religions, good and evil are a matter of faith based on loyalty to God, the creator. That is, these religions take belief in and acceptance of the divine command as foremost, and moreover, evil refers to transgressing or overlooking the will of God, which amounts to sin.

After citing these differences, we may now note at least two others:

a) The moral code of Buddhism must be understood as a rational, integrated system of ethics so that the Buddhist practitioner can correctly proceed along the Path. In general, the code of ethics for theistic religions amounts to divine commandments or expressions of divine purpose, which are all separate and different. Even when these commandments are brought together they cannot be seen as a system, because the practitioner is only interested in what he must do; it is not necessary to have a systematic understanding of related causes and effects because people believe that everything is in the hands of an all-knowing God. The practitioner need not wonder about these things; he need only have belief, surrender, and carry on in accordance with the will of God.

b) *Sīla*, or the Buddhist system of ethics, is a universal set of objective principles established in accordance with natural truths (referring here to the moral teachings of good and evil rather than the particular points of the Vinaya that are related to specific sanctions), which involves observing mental processes and contemplating the outcome of certain behaviors, habits, and personality traits. And the benefits of this contemplation are not limited to a certain group of people nor is this activity subject to the scrutiny of anyone. For example, no limitations are established saying that only this religion has compassion and so only its adherents can be good—and even if other religions have compassion they will not be as good. Or if you kill adherents of a certain religion it is a sin, but if you kill adherents of other religions it is not a sin. Only people from this religion can make it to heaven; if others do not believe us, they will end up in hell. Some say killing animals (even though they are *not* food) is not demeritorious, because they are food for humans (as if humans are not food for tigers and lions, for example). According to Buddhist ethics, certain limitations and divisions can be made; for example, by observing natural laws, we can determine which people have few demerits and which people have many. We can observe the results and reactions of the workings of the mind, as stated above. As for theistic religions, these principles go according to a divine purpose, as if they are set or decreed by the one who is the legislator and the judge himself.

Because *sīla* are objective principles established in accordance with natural law, the practitioner of Buddhism has to be brave enough to accept the truth, to stare directly into the face of truth. Good and bad, right and wrong, blame and blamelessness all exist; you must be willing to accept these for what they are depending on your actions. You must be brave enough to accept that you are right or wrong according to the facts present, not according to your own inclinations. Natural truths are not measured by personal inclinations. If you do something that can make you fall into hell, it is better to admit that this action is wrong and that you are willing to go to hell for it, than to con yourself into thinking that your deed was not evil.

There are several good things about the commandments of theistic religions that should be noted as well.

First, the determination of what is right and wrong, true and untrue has been clearly designated so that if a person believes and is loyal, the positive results of proper behavior are quick and effective. But a problem subsequently arises: in a rationalistic and positivistic age, what can be done to maintain people's beliefs in these commandments? And in the long run, how will people adhering to different faiths be able to live together? And if belief depends on loyalty to commandments, how will people achieve the freedom necessary to attain true wisdom?

Also, most people find it easiest to accept ethics solely on faith, and this approach guides their behavior quite well. Even a substantial number of Buddhists understand morality in this way. For example, they may view the moral precepts as prohibitions (even though the prohibitor remains vague), and they may view the results of kamma as retribution, reward, or punishment. But essentially the problem stated remains the same: How can belief be sustained?

Finally, it is often necessary to establish certain principles of incorrect behavior to keep people in line, as a means of inducing moral behavior. Buddhism also admits that this method has its benefits, because it is still one more factor that can influence the outcome of people's behavior. For example, saying that it is not a sin to kill animals will take a load off people's minds and not trouble them with guilt; however, this kind of inducement will bring about bad results in other ways and will not lead to wisdom. Buddhism asks you to be aware of the truth at all levels and to make your own decisions; Buddhism often employs a method of inducement, but it asks you to understand all the ramifications of what you are being asked to do. You are invited to apply and test the teachings for yourself. Many inducements that are made in Buddhism will not result in loss or trouble and are only suggested in order to provide the necessary strength to do better things that reap greater results.

6. Proper Effort (sammāvāyāma)

This factor of the Path is the first factor in the section relating to *samādhi* or the higher mental trainings (*adhicittasikkhā*). The following definition of proper effort can be found in the canon:

> Bhikkhus, what is proper effort? Proper effort means that you bhikkhus in the Dhamma-Vinaya should,
>
> 1. Develop proper resolve (*chanda*), apply yourselves, be tireless, arouse your minds, and become focused in order to (guard against) the arising of any unwholesome things (*akusala-dhamma*) that have yet to arise;

2. . . . in order to get rid of any demeritorious unwholesome things that have already arisen;
3. . . . in order (to cultivate) wholesome things (*kusala-dhamma*) that have yet to arise and cause them to arise;
4. . . . in order to bring about the continued prosperity and maximum development of wholesome things that have already arisen.[123]

In the Abhidhamma texts this is expanded even further:

> What is proper effort? It is a concentration of mental effort (*virayārambha*), progress, perseverance, persistence, exertion, hard work, a pressing forward, a firmness and certainty, not backing off, not losing proper resolve (*chanda*), not putting down your task until it is finished, applying effort (*viriya*), the faculty of energy (*viriyindriya*), and the power of energy (*viriyabala*). Proper effort is one of the seven factors leading to enlightenment (*bojjhaṅga*), and it is linked to the Path.[124]

Also, according to another passage in the Suttas, there are four kinds of proper effort—the four correct efforts (*sammappadhāna*[125] or four *padhāna*[126]). They are designated as follows:

1. *Saṁvarappadhāna*—The effort to prevent or avoid (unwholesome things from arising);
2. *Pahānappadhāna*—The effort to do away with or limit (unwholesome things that have arisen);
3. *Bhāvanappadhāna*—The effort to develop or establish (wholesome things that have yet to arise); and
4. *Anurakkhanappadhāna*—The effort to conserve, nurture, and sustain (wholesome things that have already arisen).

In certain places in the canon, the four kinds of effort are explained by example:[127]

Saṁvarappadhāna means that having seen a form with your eyes you do not cling to its afterimage and its attending details; practice composure of the faculties because when they are out of control this can cause demerits and unwholesome dhammas (*akusala-dhamma*) to arise, such as covetousness (*abhijjhā*), and then grief may overcome you. Keep a watch over the faculty of sight until you attain composure; listen with your ears, smell with your nose, taste with your tongue, feel things with your sense of touch, and know mind-objects [with the same composure].

Pahānappadhāna means not allowing thoughts of sensual pleasure (*kāma-vitakka*), thoughts of ill-will (*byāpāda-vitakka*), thoughts of violence (*vihiṁsā-vitakka*), or any demerits (*pāpa*) or unwholesome dhamma (*akusala-dhamma*) that have arisen to remain. You must be willing to let go, release, and completely eliminate all of these things.

Bhāvanappadhāna means developing the seven factors of enlightenment (*bojjhaṅga*), which are inclined towards solitude (*viveka*), detachment (*virāga*), and the extinguishing of dukkha (*nirodha*), in order to reach the final goal.

Anurakkhanappadhāna means nurturing the positive signs observed while meditating (*samādhi-nimitta*), that is, the arising of the six senses.

Effort is a quality of utmost importance in Buddhism. Proper effort is one of three central factors (proper understanding, proper effort, and proper mindfulness) around which all others revolve.[128] And in other parts of the teachings that discuss practice, you will find effort incorporated in one way or another, as well. We can see the emphasis put on effort in the following passages:

> This Dhamma is for those who are industrious, not for those who are lazy.[129]

> Bhikkhus, I clearly understand two valuable things about the Dhamma:
>
> 1. I am not merely content with the good things I have already done;
> 2. I do not allow any backsliding in the course of ceaseless efforts.
>
> Therefore, all of you should know that we will establish effort that does not cease, until only skin, sinew, and bones remain. Our tissue and blood may dry up, but we will continue to seek the fruit that can be attained via human energy, hard work, and struggle. There is no slack in our efforts—all of you should know this and carry on in this way.[130]

Aside from the points already mentioned, the reason for stressing effort relates to one of the fundamental tenets of Buddhism: The Truth (*sacca-dhamma*) is comprised of natural laws or true principles to be found naturally.

Lord Buddha and other great teachers discover these laws and reveal them to others. The fruits of practice are attained in accordance with a natural process of causes and effects—the teacher is not a creator who metes rewards. For this reason, all people must exert their own efforts in order to attain any goal. There should be no time spent sitting around hoping or imploring other sources for benefits without lifting a finger. We have already cited the following maxim: *tumhehi kiccaṁ ātappaṁ akkhātāro Tathāgatā*—all of you must put forth your own efforts; the Tathāgatas only point the way.[131]

At any rate, expending effort is just like any other point of practice. You must prepare your mind in the correct manner first, and then gradually extend your efforts to the external world in a way that maintains harmony. You should not simply think, "Oh, I should put forth effort," over exerting yourself and going all out, which could easily become torturous, until you are burnt out. For this reason, effort must be linked with other parts of the Dhamma; this means applying mindfulness and awareness, knowledge, understanding, and wisdom to make your efforts appropriate, not too tense nor too relaxed.

At the time of Gotama Buddha, a monk named Soṇa was staying in the Sītavana forest near the city of Rājagaha. He was practicing with unrelenting effort and was performing walking meditation until both of his feet were cracked and bleeding, but he had yet to attain enlightenment. Once, even though he was in a tranquil setting, the following thought occurred to him: "Among the disciples of the Blessed One who have put forth great effort, I am one, who in spite of effort, has yet to attain freedom from mental intoxicants and attachments. My family is well off; we can use our wealth to do good things. So perhaps I should just quit these robes and do good deeds that way."

Lord Buddha heard about the ruminations of Soṇa and met him to discuss the matter:

> **Lord Buddha:** So, Soṇa, you've been doing some thinking lately?
>
> **Venerable Soṇa:** Yes, I have, Lord.
>
> **Lord Buddha:** And what have you been thinking? In the past, as a layman, you were quite accomplished at playing the harp, right?
>
> **Venerable Soṇa:** That's right, Lord.

Lord Buddha: So what do you think? When your harp's strings are too taut, could your harp make beautiful music?

Venerable Soṇa: It couldn't, Lord.

Lord Buddha: What do you think? When the strings of your harp were too loose, could your harp make beautiful music?

Venerable Soṇa: It couldn't, Lord.

Lord Buddha: And when the strings of your harp were neither too taut nor too loose but were just right, then did your harp make beautiful music?

Venerable Soṇa: Yes it did, Lord.

Lord Buddha: Just so, Soṇa, expending too much effort causes disruption, and being too relaxed causes laziness. For this reason, you should train yourself to be balanced and just right. You should understand what is sufficient and appropriate for all the sense-faculties,[132] and you should hold to this overall picture of what is balanced and just right.[133]

7. Proper Mindfulness (sammāsati)

Sammāsati is the second factor in the *samādhi* section of the Eightfold Path; it is a part of the higher mental training.[134] The usual definition of *sammāsati* given in the Suttas is as follows:

> Bhikkhus, what is *sammāsati*? This is called *sammāsati*, namely, that a bhikkhu in this Dhamma-Vinaya:
>
> 1. Contemplates the body in the body with effort, clear comprehension (*sampajañña*), and mindfulness (*sati*), eliminating greed and grief related to the world;
> 2. Contemplates sensations in sensations with effort, clear comprehension, and mindfulness, eliminating greed and grief related to the world;
> 3. Contemplates the mind in the mind with effort, clear comprehension, and mindfulness, eliminating greed and grief related to the world;
> 4. Contemplates dhammas in dhammas with effort, clear comprehension, and mindfulness, eliminating greed and grief related to the world.[135]

Another definition, which appears in the Abhidhamma texts, is as follows:

> What is *sammāsati*? *Sati* means to reflect upon or bring to mind. *Sati* is the state of recollecting, the state of remembering, the state of non-dissipation, and the state of non-forgetting. *Sati* means the *sati* that is a sense-faculty, *sati* that has power, *sammāsati*, the *sati* that is a factor of enlightenment (*bojjhaṅga*), *sati* that is a factor of the Path and is linked with the Path—this is what is called *sammāsati*.[136]

Sammāsati, as defined in the Suttas, is a principle of the Dhamma known as the four foundations of mindfulness (*satipaṭṭhāna*). The four elements of this group have the abbreviated names of:

Kāyānupassanā (contemplation or mindfulness of the body);
Vedanānupassanā (contemplation or mindfulness of sensations);
Cittānupassanā (contemplation or mindfulness of mind);
Dhammānupassanā (contemplation or mindfulness of dhammas).

Before investigating the meaning of *sammāsati* in terms of the four foundations of mindfulness, we should clarify a few general points on the subject of *sati* to serve as a basic foundation for our study.

Sati as *Appamāda*[137]

Sati is most simply rendered as "recollection," but such a translation may convey the idea that it is merely an aspect of memory. While memory is certainly a valid aspect of *sati*'s function, it does not do justice to the full meaning of the term. To put this in a negative sense, apart from meaning "non-forgetting" (the direct counterpart of the positive term "recollection"), *sati* also refers to "non-carelessness," "non-distraction," and "non-fuzziness." These negatively expressed meanings of *sati* point to the positive qualities of carefulness, circumspection, and clarity about one's duties and the condition of being constantly prepared to deal with situations and respond appropriately. Especially when speaking of ethical conduct, the functioning of *sati* is often compared to that of a gatekeeper whose job is to keep his eyes on the people passing in and out, restricting entry and exit to only the proper people. Thus, *sati* is of major importance to ethics. It oversees the performance of our duties, and it guards and restrains us; this is accomplished by preventing us from taking foolish pleasure in the bad and preventing evil from sneaking into the mind. Simply put, *sati* reminds us to open the door to the good and close it to the bad.

Buddhadhamma emphasizes the importance of *sati* at every level of ethical conduct. Mindfully conducting your life and your practice of the

Dhamma is called *appamāda*, or conscientiousness. *Appamāda* is of central importance to progress in the Buddhist system of ethics, and this concept is usually defined as non-separation from *sati*. *Appamāda* also implies constant carefulness and circumspection, not allowing yourself to stumble into harmful ways, not allowing yourself to miss any opportunity for improvement, and maintaining a clear awareness of what needs to be done and what has been left undone. *Appamāda* involves continual attention to and appreciation of your duties, non-negligence, and the performance of daily tasks with sincerity and unflagging efforts aimed at improvement. In other words, *appamāda* constitutes Buddhist responsibility.

In terms of importance, *appamāda* is classified as an internal factor, as, you will recall, is *yonisomanasikāra* (critical reflection), which is linked with its external counterpart, *kalyāṇamittatā* (association with good and noble friends). The Buddha's description of the significance of *appamāda* occasionally overlaps with descriptions of *yonisomanasikāra*—and these two supporting factors are of equal importance, although they differ in application. *Yonisomanasikāra* is a member of the *paññā* section of the Path; it is a tool to be used. *Appamāda*, on the other hand, is a member of the *samādhi* section; it governs the use of the tool of *yonisomanasikāra* and serves as a motivating force to further progress.

The importance and scope of the application of *appamāda* at various levels of moral practice can be gleaned from the words of the Buddha:

> Bhikkhus, the footprints of all land animals fit within the footprint of the elephant; the elephant's footprint is said to be supreme in terms of size. Similarly, all wholesome dhammas having conscientiousness (*appamāda*) as their base fall within the bounds of conscientiousness. Conscientiousness may be said to be supreme amongst those dhammas.[138]

> I see nothing that can bring about wholesome things that have yet to arise or can make unwholesome things that have arisen fade away like conscientiousness. When a person is conscientious, then anything wholesome that has yet to arise arises, and anything unwholesome that has already arisen fades away.[139]

> I see nothing that leads to such great benefit[140] . . . . I see nothing that leads to such certainty, such non-disintegration, and the non-disappearance of the true Dhamma as conscientiousness.[141]

> As an internal factor, I see nothing that leads to such great benefit as conscientiousness.[142]

Even the final instructions given by the Buddha before he passed away and entered Parinibbana are concerned with *appamāda*.

> All conditioned things are subject to decay. Strive on conscientiously![143]

> When the sun is rising, its rays break the horizon before it does; these rays are a foreshadowing of things to come. In the same way, conscientiousness is a forerunner, a good sign foreshadowing the coming of the Noble Eight-fold Path. . . . The single dhamma that leads to the Noble Eight-fold Path is the perfection of conscientiousness. . . . I see no other dhamma that has such power to bring about the Noble Eight-fold Path that has yet to arise and make the Noble Eight-fold Path that has already arisen come to maturity and fruition. A bhikkhu who is conscientious can hope for the following: developing the Noble Eight-fold Path and making the most of it.[144]

> Bhikkhus, you should apply *appamāda* in four areas:
> 1. Abandon bad behavior. Cultivate good behavior. Neglect neither.
> 2. Abandon bad speech. Cultivate good speech. Neglect neither.
> 3. Abandon bad thought. Cultivate good thought. Neglect neither.
> 4. Abandon improper understanding. Cultivate proper understanding. Neglect neither.
>
> When a bhikkhu has abandoned bad actions, has cultivated good actions. . .abandoned improper understanding and cultivated proper understanding, he does not fear his inevitable death.[145]

> Bhikkhus, a bhikkhu should establish *appamāda*, maintain mindfulness, and be attentive of these four states:
> 1. . . .My mind will not attach to anything that invites attachment;

2. . . . My mind will not be averse to anything that invites aversion;
3. . . . My mind will not be deluded by anything that invites delusion;
4. . . . My mind will not be intoxicated by anything that invites intoxication.

When a bhikkhu's mind, because of the absence of lust, does not attach to anything that encourages attachment, is not averse. . . is not deluded. . . is not intoxicated, he will be without fear or disturbance, will not be scared or startled, and does not have to believe in anything, even the words of a sage.[146]

Question: Is there any single thing that provides both sorts of benefits, both present and immediate benefits and future or higher benefits?

Answer: Yes, there is.

Question: What is it?

Answer: It is conscientiousness.[147]

Your Majesty, the Dhamma that I have put forth is for those with good and noble friends, good and noble companions, good and noble people as associates. It is not for those with foolish immoral friends, foolish immoral companions, foolish immoral people as associates. . . . Having good and noble friends can be equated with the whole of the Holy Life.

Therefore, Your Majesty, you should dedicate yourself to having good and noble friends, good and noble companions, and good and noble people as associates. The king who has good and noble friends should lead his life in accordance with one essential principle—being conscientious about wholesome things.

When the King is conscientious and leads a life of conscientiousness, then his inner circle, the nobles of the court. . . the royal guard. . . right down to the townsfolk and villagers will all think, "His Majesty the King is a conscientious person; he conducts his life conscientiously. We should also be conscientious; we should conduct our lives conscientiously."

Your Majesty, if you are a conscientious person and live your own life conscientiously, you will be cared for and protected. The inner circle will receive care and protection. . .everything right down to the houses and barns of your subjects will receive care and protection.[148]

Sati as a Social Value

The following quotation from the *Sedaka Sutta* reveals the value of *sati* very well. It links the meaning, in practical terms, of the nature and value of *sati* to that of conscientiousness (*appamāda*). The passage helps to further clarify our understanding of both of these concepts and, at the same time, to demonstrate the Buddhist attitude towards the social dimensions of life. It is evidence that the Buddhadhamma sees the internal life of the individual as intimately related to the external life of society and holds that values in the two realms are inseparably connected, compatible, and are, in fact, one and the same thing.

Bhikkhus, once there was an acrobat who set up his bamboo pole and called to his student, saying, "Come here and climb the pole and stand on my shoulders," and the pupil did as he was told.

Then the bamboo acrobat said to his pupil, "Now, you take good care of me and I'll take good care of you. By watching over and protecting each other like this, we will show off our skills, get a good fee, and safely descend from the bamboo pole."

At these words, the pupil said to his teacher, "Teacher, I don't think I can do that. You look after yourself and I will look after myself. If we both watch and protect ourselves then we will be able to show our art, get a good fee, and safely descend the bamboo pole."

The Blessed One said, "That was the correct thing to do in that case: Just as that pupil spoke to his master, when thinking, 'I will protect myself,' you must be mindful, and when thinking, 'I will protect others,' you must also be mindful.

Bhikkhus, protecting yourself, you protect others; protecting others, you protect yourself.

And how is it that while protecting yourself you protect others? By earnest practice, development, training, and making the most of it. In this way, when you protect yourself, you protect others.

And how do you protect others by protecting yourself? By proper resolve (*chanda*), by non-violence, by possessing a heart

> of loving-kindness and compassion. In this way, protecting others, you protect yourself.
>
> Bhikkhus, when thinking, 'I will protect myself,' you must be mindful. When thinking, 'I will protect others,' you must also be mindful. In this way, protecting yourself can be called protecting others, and protecting others can be called protecting yourself.[149]

The Role of *Sati* in the Process of Developing Wisdom, or Eradicating Mental Intoxicants and Unwholesome Tendencies

Appamāda, or conscientiousness, refers to the uninterrupted presence of *sati* in our life and its constant application in daily activities. *Appamāda* makes us careful; it keeps us from evil and degenerative ways. It provides restraint, and it reminds us not to become caught up in mindless indulgence. It motivates us not to become complacent and stimulates us to make continual effort. It makes us ever aware of our duties by providing a clear perception of what should and should not be done, what has already been done, and what remains to be done. It helps us do our work in a meticulous and cautious way. As stated above, *appamāda* is, therefore, a very important ethical concept.

At any rate, the ethical importance of *appamāda* has a wide-ranging impact on people's lives. Its significance starts at the level of keeping the precepts and continues right on up to the practice of *samādhi*. At these levels, mindfulness (*sati*) has a key responsiblity in linking and holding together other dhammic principles, particularly that of effort (*vāyāma*), with which it is constantly linked. If we only look at it in terms of the mind during the process of the development of wisdom—or in terms of using wisdom to cleanse the mind internally—*appamāda* becomes something that offers external inspiration and encouragement. At this level, attention is confined to the workings of the mind, discriminating between the various phenomena present on a moment-by-moment basis. It is at this point that mindfulness has fulfilled its duties completely and most clearly—and it is at this point that "mind-full-ness" plays the major role that its name implies.

We can understand the essential meaning of mindfulness by noting the practical duties of mindfulness on occasions when its role is most clearly distinguishable from that of other points of the Dhamma, such as in the practice known as four foundations of mindfulness (*satipaṭṭhāna*). In the case of these four foundations, mindfulness may be summarized as follows:

The basic function of mindfulness is to prevent the mind from becoming unfocused; it does not allow daydreaming nor aimlessly drifting along with the flow of mind-objects. It focuses the mind's eye of attention on each passing impression that comes into consciousness, and it turns our gaze on the flow of thought. When we wish to concentrate on a particular object, it fixes our attention on it, not allowing the object to drift away or disappear.[150] There is a simile that compares mindfulness to the major pillar of a building's foundation (Thai, *sao lak/sao ek*), because it is firmly embedded in its object; or it can be compared to a gatekeeper, because it guards over the various sense-doors through which impressions pass, checking everything that happens. The proximate causes for the arising of mindfulness are awareness of perceptions (*saññā*—a stable and clear perception of mind-objects) or any of the different foundations of mindfulness that will be described.

When examined from the point of view of ethics, the negative and positive aspects of the role mindfulness become evident. When put in negative terms, mindfulness is a safeguard. It keeps the mind from becoming unfocused, misguided, and holds it to the "straight and narrow." It allows no opportunity for bad thoughts to enter the mind and turn thoughts for the worst.

On the positive side, mindfulness is the overseer and inspector of the stream of consciousness and all thought and action, ensuring that they remain within determined bounds and stay with the designated mind-objects. Mindfulness can be used as a tool for grasping or embracing any thoughts and bringing them before the mind for consideration and further action.

In Buddhist practice, great emphasis is placed on the importance of mindfulness. Lord Buddha stated that mindfulness is necessary (should be applied) in every situation. Mindfulness is also compared to salt, which must be used in every curry, and to a country's leader, who must take an interest in all aspects of government. Mindfulness may either restrain the mind or support and sustain it, depending on the needs of the situation.[151]

When we note all the duties of mindfulness mentioned, we can see the following aims and practical benefits. Mindfulness can:

- Help to maintain a determined state of mind by monitoring the cognitive process and the flow of thought—accepting only that which is conducive and barring all that is not. Channeling and stabilizing the flow of thought, facilitating concentration (*samādhi*);

• Allow the body and mind to dwell in a state that may be called its "true nature" (Thai, *pen tua khong tua eng*), because they are unburdened, relaxed, and happy in accordance with their own nature—in a state of preparation ready to face any circumstances in this world and put things right;

• Focus concentration in order to guide the cognitive process and the flow of thought and alter or expand its own dimensions;

• Enable a person to "grasp" an object of meditation and lay it before the mind, so that subsequent investigation by the wisdom-faculty may proceed with optimum clarity, as a basis for the development and perfection of wisdom (*paññā*);

• Purify all volitional actions (of body, speech, and mind), making them clean, liberated, and purposeful, no longer under the influence of craving and attachments, and, together with clear comprehension (*sampajañña*), mindfulness can make a person's actions wise, based on impartial reasoning.

The last two benefits listed here are goals at a more advanced level of development and may be obtained only through a specially prescribed method of practice that, according to our definition of *sammasāti*, is called the four *satipaṭṭhāna*.

Satipaṭṭhāna as *Sammāsati*

Satipaṭṭhāna is sometimes translated as the "foundation of mindfulness" or the "emergence of mindfulness." Simply put, it is the application of mindfulness or a method of practice that reaps the maximum benefits of mindfulness, which the Buddha put forth in the *Mahāsatipaṭṭhāna Sutta*:

> Bhikkhus, this is the main path that leads to the purification of all beings, to going beyond sorrow and lamentation, to the elimination of dukkha and grief, to the attainment of the supramundane path, to the attainment of nibbana, namely, the four *satipaṭṭhāna*.[152]

The development of *satipaṭṭhāna* is a very popular method of practice that is highly regarded and revered. It incorporates both the cultivation of *samatha* (concentration meditation) and *vipassanā* (insight meditation). The practitioner may develop concentration in order to attain certain states of absorption (*jhāna*)—which will be discussed in the following section on *sammāsamādhi*, the final factor of the Eight-fold Path—and then move on to developing *vipassanā* based on the four *satipaṭṭhāna* as a way of reaching the final goal; or a person may develop the basic levels of *samādhi* as deemed necessary and then develop *vipassanā* in accordance with the *satipaṭṭhāna* we have mentioned, until the final goal is attained.

According to the Buddhist tradition that we have come to know, *vipassanā* is a most important principle of practice. While it is widely known, it is often misunderstood; it is, therefore, a matter that deserves some clarification. The following basic outline of *satipaṭṭhāna* will help to improve our understanding of the meaning of *vipassanā*: We will examine its essential nature and the breadth of its scope, the extent to which it can be applied in daily life, as well as the benefits that can be derived from the practice of insight. However, we will not be able to make a thorough study of *vipassanā* here; our aim is only to understand it in the context of the essential aspects of *satipaṭṭhāna*.

In brief, *satipaṭṭhāna* can be defined as follows:

1. *Kāyānupassanā*, contemplation of the body;
   a) *Ānāpānasati*, going to a secluded place, sitting cross-legged, and being mindful of breathing, inhaling and exhaling, and other states of the body;
   b) *Iriyāpatha*, focusing on the state of the body in the various postures of standing, walking, sitting, or lying down;
   c) *Sampajañña*, maintaining clear comprehension in every kind of action and movement, such as moving forward, looking around, opening the hand, dressing, eating, drinking, chewing, excreting, urinating, waking up, going to sleep, speaking, and keeping silent;
   d) *Paṭikūlamanasikāra*, contemplating the body, from the top of the head to the bottom of the feet, as a composite of numerous unclean elements;
   e) *Dhātumanasikāra*, contemplating the body as four constituent elements;
   f) *Navasīvathikā*, looking at corpses in nine different stages of decay, from one newly dead to one reduced to crumbling bones, and, in each case, reflecting on our own condition, accepting that our body will one day meet a similar fate.

2. *Vedanānupassanā*, contemplating sensations (*vedanā*). In other words, when feelings of sukha, dukkha, or equanimity (*upekkhā*) arise, whether they are associated with sensual desires or unassociated with them, see them for what they are.
3. *Cittānupassanā*, contemplation of mind. Understanding our state of mind at any given moment—be it consumed with lust (*rāga*) or non-lust, ill will (*dosa*) or non-ill-will, delusion (*moha*) or non-delusion, be it unfocused or concentrated, liberated or unliberated, see it for what it is.
4. *Dhammānupassanā*, mindfulness of dhammas.
   a) *Nīvaraṇa*[153] (hindrances)—Realizing at any given moment if the five hindrances are present in the mind or not; knowing how the unarisen hindrances arise, how hindrances already arisen may be eliminated, and how hindrances already eliminated may be prevented from arising again;
   b) *Khandha* (aggregates)—contemplating the nature of each of the Five Aggregates and knowing how they arise and how they pass away;
   c) *Āyatana* (sense-bases)—understanding each of the internal and external sense-bases, understanding the fetters that arise dependent on them, how those already arisen may be eliminated and how those already eliminated may be prevented from arising again;
   d) *Bojjhaṅga* (factors of enlightenment)[154]—Clear comprehension of whether or not any of the seven factors of enlightenment are present in the mind, knowing how those yet to arise may arise and how those already arisen may be developed to perfection;
   e) *Ariyasacca*—Clear comprehension of each of the Four Noble Truths.

At the end of every one of the above points, there is a refrain that is identical to a passage in the *Mahāsatipaṭṭhāna Sutta:*

> The bhikkhu contemplates the body in the body internally (= your own body), contemplates the body in the body externally (= other's bodies), and contemplates the body in the body both

internally and externally. He contemplates phenomena, the dissolution of the body; he contemplates phenomena, both the arising and dissolution of the body. He possesses clear mindfulness that "the body exists" as a source of information and as a reference. In this way, he lives independently, not clinging to anything in this world.[155]

The Important Essence of *Satipaṭṭhāna*

From this summary, we can see that the practice of *satipaṭṭhāna* (along with *vipassanā*) does not require withdrawal from society nor a fixed time schedule. For this reason, many wise teachers have encouraged its integration into general daily life.

According to the preceding outline, we can know that when we practice we do not merely apply mindfulness; its application is carried out in conjunction with other points of the Dhamma. One such point not specifically mentioned above is *samādhi*, which must be present, at least in an undeveloped form, to assist these efforts.[156] Three concepts singled out by name in the definition of *sammāsati* are:

1. *Ātāpī* = effort exists (this refers to *sammāvāyāma*, or proper effort, the sixth factor of the Noble Eight-fold Path, which entails guarding against and abandoning what is evil and creating and maintaining what is good);
2. *Sampajāno* = clear comprehension exists (this refers to the wisdom-faculty);
3. *Satimā* = mindfulness exists.

The second concept, *sampajāno*, which can be rendered as clear comprehension (*sampajañña*), is noteworthy. *Sampajañña* is a concept that usually appears coupled with *sati*. *Sampajañña* is the wisdom-faculty (*paññā*). For this reason, training in mindfulness is part of the process of wisdom development. *Sampajañña*, or *paññā*, is the clear and penetrating understanding of the object of mindfulness; or it is establishing the purpose of a mind-object, its nature, and knowing how to deal with it in a way that is free of delusion and misunderstanding.

The earlier statement, ". . .eliminating greed and grief related to the world. . .," demonstrates the attitude that results from the possession of mindfulness and clear comprehension (*sati-sampajañña*): one of neutrality, objectivity, and freedom, a state unfettered by unwholesome tendencies that can be linked to desire or disappointment.

The common refrain mentioning the arising and passing away of phenomena points to an understanding of the Three Characteristics of Existence. This "seeing" results in an outlook, a perception of other things according to their nature. For example, saying that "the body exists," means to be aware of the body as it actually is, without clothing it in conceptualizations, interpretations, or attachments, not labelling it as a person or as self, as "him," "her," "me," or "mine." This attitude is free, independent; it is not contingent on external conditions, and it is not bound by attachment to or craving for the things of this world.

Some scholars in the West have compared *satipaṭṭhāna* with contemporary methods of psychotherapy. In their assessment of the relative merits of the two systems, they have concluded that *satipaṭṭhāna* provides better results, because each person can apply it himself; it can be practiced at any time for achieving good mental health.[157] However, these views will not be criticized here; instead, I would like to summarize the important aspects of *satipaṭṭhāna* in a new way.

Practice as Process

The constituent factors in this process of practice are two-fold: the active (that which focuses attention, observes, concentrates, and contemplates) and the passive (that which is focused on, observed, concentrated on, and contemplated).

The passive constituents are ordinary, mundane things common to all of us: the body and its movements, thoughts and feelings, and so on, which are observed as they occur, that is, in the present moment.

The active constituents of focusing, concentrating, observing, and contemplating form the basic agents of *satipaṭṭhāna* and are functions of mindfulness (*sati*) and clear comprehension (*sampajañña*). Mindfulness grasps the object of contemplation; clear comprehension is the wisdom-faculty that realizes the nature and conditions of the thing being contemplated, determining what it is and what its purpose is. For example, when contemplating physical movement, such as walking, know why you are walking and where you are going. Understand things and actions for what they are, without coating them with personal feelings and impressions.[158]

The conditions that are being observed should be noted according to their true nature at that moment; that is, merely watch, see, and understand what is what, what is happening, and what is the outcome. This does not involve reacting, criticizing, or judging what is happening as good or bad, right or wrong; you do not involve your own feelings, biases, and attachments concluding that the object of contemplation is agreeable or disagreeable, pleasant or unpleasant. You see things for what they are without embellishing them with notions such as "mine," "his/her," "me," "him/her," "Mr. A.," "Ms. B.," and so on. For example, when contemplating the feelings in your mind, at a given moment you may experience dukkha; there is anxiety; and you know that dukkha has arisen. You can also know the way in which this dukkha has come about and the way in which it is passing away. This kind of contemplation can be fun—studying and examining your own dukkha can actually be enjoyable! When it is purely dukkha that is presently arising and passing away, it is no longer "my dukkha" or "I am experiencing dukkha," and so that dukkha loses its power over the person who is able to contemplate it. Whatever form of good or bad appears, it is met face to face, without avoidance. It is viewed as it is, from the moment of its occurrence until it meets its own end, and then attention shifts to something else. It can be compared to a doctor performing an autopsy or that of a scientist observing the subject of his experiment. It is not like a judge listening to the evidence of the prosecutor and the defendant in a trial. It is objective rather than subjective observation.

The Fruits of Practice

Purity: When mindfulness is fixed exclusively on a determined object and clear comprehension sees that thing as it is, then the stream of consciousness and thought will be naturally maintained in its purity. There is no opening for unwholesome tendencies to pass through. When examining and analyzing phenomena simply as they are, without involving emotions and conceptualizations based on subjective prejudices and preferences, there will be no clinging. This is the method for eradicating existing intoxicants (*āsava*) and protecting the mind from the interference of those that have yet to arise.

Freedom: When this pure state of mind has been attained, freedom comes with it. This freedom is attained by being unperturbed by the various sense-impressions that impinge upon it, by utilizing impressions as material for objective study. When sense-data are not interpreted according to the dictates of mental intoxicants, then impressions exert no subjective influence over the person who experiences them. That person's behavior is liberated from the unwholesome tendencies that act as unconscious drives or motivations. This is what is meant by living "independently, not clinging to anything in this world."

Wisdom: When a person enters the flow of the mental process in this way, the wisdom-faculty will function with maximum effectiveness. The absence of distortion or diversion by emotions, biases, and prejudices ensures the perception of things as they actually exist, the awareness of the true nature of things.

Liberation from dukkha: When the mind is in an awakened state, it understands things as they are and is able to maintain this focus. Positive and negative notions based on impure reasoning do not occur. Feelings of greed (*abhijjhā*), grief (*domanassa*), and anxiety do not arise. This is a state of mind that has gone beyond dukkha. The mind is unburdened and relaxed, existing in accordance with its true nature (Thai, *pen tua khong tua eng*).

In fact, all of the fruits of practice mentioned are different, related aspects of a comprehensive whole. When summarized according to dependent origination and the Three Characteristics of Existence, we can note that at first, human beings are ignorant of the fact that the self to which they cling does not really exist. Human life consists of a current of numerous intricate corporeal and mental phenomena that exist in accordance with interdependent causes and conditions. When people are unaware of this truth, they cling to the feelings, thoughts, desires, habits, views, beliefs, opinions, and impressions that arise at each moment and take this to be the self, even though this so-called self is continually changing. These people feel that, "I was that, now I am this; I felt that way, and now I feel this way," and so on. People delude themselves by thinking that "I am this way or that," in perceiving an "I" as a subject who is aware of certain things or is subject to certain conditions. This deluded condition of the mind is the beginning of misguided thought. It follows that a person's thoughts, feelings, and actions are subject to the powers of this self-clinging. In the practice of *satipaṭṭhāna*, every kind of material and mental phenomenon within the flow of the mental current is seen to be arising and passing away in accordance with its nature. When a person is able to perceive the various interconnected elements of this process, understand their make-up and their temporal sequence, and perceive the continuity of change—the processual nature of our existence—then phenomena lose their power to entice and there is no interest in clinging to a notion of self.

If this insight is deep and clear, then liberation is attained. This freedom allows the mind a whole new way of being. It is an unburdened course, free and unimpeded by prejudices and the internal knots of attachment.

Attainment of this freedom constitutes the birth of a new personality. To put it another way, it is a state of perfect mental health, comparable to a body in perfect health when, in the absence of any disturbing illness, all of its organs function smoothly, to full capacity with complete efficiency. In this sense, the practice of *satipaṭṭhāna* is viewed as a method of cleansing the mind of all mental illnesses, eliminating all knots and impediments to its smooth functioning. *Satipaṭṭhāna* creates an expansive mind, one ready to move forward in life, to face up to and deal with everything in the world with determination and joy.

This matter may be summarized with the following words of the Buddha:

> Bhikkhus, there are two kinds of diseases: Physical diseases and psychological disorders. Some people in this world can claim that they have been without physical disease for a whole year. And you can find some people who can claim that they have been without physical disease for two years. . .three years. . .four years. . .five years. . .ten years. . .twenty years. . .thirty years. . .forty years. . .fifty years. . .a hundred years. But it is hard to find anyone who can claim that he has been free of mental disturbances, even for a single moment, except for those who have destroyed all mental intoxicants (*āsava*).[159]

> **Vernerable Sāriputta:** Householder, you look very fit, your countenance is radiant. Surely you have been listening to a Dhamma talk by the Blessed One.
>
> **Householder Nakulapitā:** Venerable One, how could it be otherwise? I have just been sprinkled with the ambrosia of the words of the Blessed One who blessed me with the words of the Dhamma.
>
> **Venerable Sāriputta:** What kind of ambrosia did the Blessed One sprinkle upon you?
>
> **Householder Nakulapitā:** Accomplished One, I came before the Blessed One, paid my respects to him, and having sat down in an appropriate place I spoke to the Blessed One saying, "Lord, I am at the end of my life, I am a broken-down old man, I am far gone in years, my body is plagued by illnesses and is in constant pain. Moreover, I have seldom had the opportunity to behold the joyous sight of the Lord and the Sangha. May the Lord, out of compassion, give me a teaching that will lead to long-lasting

benefits and happiness." Then the Lord Buddha said the following: "That is correct, Householder, it is so. This body is constantly surrounded by illness, just as an egg is covered by a shell. Anyone who has a body and attests to being without illness, even for a moment, is a fool. Therefore, householder, you should train yourself thinking, 'Even though my body is plagued with illness, my mind will remain healthy. . . .' " Venerable One, this was the nature of the ambrosia that the Lord Buddha sprinkled upon me.[160]

8. Proper Concentration (sammāsamādhi)

Proper concentration is the final factor of the Path. Because it involves deep psychological and mental training, the factor of concentration has a substantial amount of material associated with it for study; it is detailed and involved—both in terms of the peculiarities and refinements of the mind but also in terms of practice—and it is a point of convergence for many points of the Dhamma. In giving an account of proper concentration, please note that if I were to explain it in the same orderly manner that I did with the other factors of the Path, this matter would be difficult to understand. I will, therefore, summarize the important points first and then elaborate these later.

The Meaning of Proper Concentration

"*Samādhi*" means stilling the mind or establishing one-pointedness of the mind (*cittassekaggatā* or *ekaggatā*). Or it can mean focusing the mind on a single mind-object—that is, not being scattered or disturbed.

Samādhi can be divided into three levels:[161]

1. Momentary concentration (*khaṇika-samādhi*)—which most people put to good use at work or in everyday life;
2. "In the neighborhood" concentration (*upacāra-samādhi*)—concentration that is collecting itself, is "almost there"; and
3. Attainment concentration (*appanā-samādhi*)—which is the highest level of concentration. Concentration is fixed and absorbed, undistracted in the various levels of absorption. This is held as the final goal in the development of *samādhi*.

According to the definition of "proper concentration" in various passages found in the Buddhist canon, it constitutes the four absorptions (*jhāna*).[162] At any rate, this definition should be viewed as a model or example, because most practitioners are only able to develop insight via the very first levels of concentration, which is called *vipassanā-samādhi*, or *samādhi* between the levels of momentary concentration and "neighborhood" concentration.[163]

Attaining Positive Results by Developing Concentration

The development of concentration involves a gradual progression through various levels culminating with attainment concentration. These various levels are known as absorptions (*jhāna*), and the higher a person goes, the more mental states and functions are progressively stilled.[164] Generally speaking, the absorptions are divided into two major sections that are then further divided into four, totaling the eight that follow:

The Four Absorptions of the Material Sphere (*rūpa-jhāna*)

1. First absorption (*paṭhama-jhāna*)—Consisting of the following five elements: initial application of thought (*vitakka*), sustained application of thought (*vicāra*), joy (*pīti*), happiness (sukha), and one-pointedness (*ekaggatā*);
2. Second absorption (*dutiya-jhāna*)—Consisting of the following three elements: joy, happiness, and one-pointedness;
3. Third absorption (*tatiya-jhāna*)—Consisting of the following two elements: happiness and one-pointedness;
4. Fourth absorption (*catuttha-jhāna*)—Consisting of the following two elements: equanimity (*upekkhā*) and one-pointedness.

The Four Absorptions of the Formless Sphere (arūpa-jhāna)

1. Sphere of infinite space (*ākāsānañcāyatana*);
2. Sphere of infinite consciousness (*viññāṇañcāyatana*);
3. Sphere of nothingness (*ākiñcaññāyatana*);
4. Sphere of neither-perception-nor-non-perception (*nevasaññānāsaññāyatana*).

The efforts that are put forth to attain these levels of *samādhi* are called *samatha*. Whatever effort human beings put into the practice of concentration meditation, they can only attain to these levels. In other words, all of *samatha* can only lead to a mental state, the highest level of absorption, which is called the sphere of neither-perception-nor-non-perception.

Those who have reached all possible levels in the practice of both *samatha* and *vipassanā* are never-returners (*anāgāmi*) or arahants and are able to attain to an even higher, more refined state. We can call this the ninth level, and that is the cessation of perception and sensation (*saññāvedayitanirodha* or *nirodha-samāpatti*), the highest level of sukha.

Methods for Developing Concentration

There are many methods and strategies for reaching the various levels of concentration indicated above. The commentator to the canon—that is, Buddhaghosa—compiled a list of forty meditative devices for contemplation.

1. Ten *kasiṇa*—These are external devices used to compose the mind or focus concentration.
   - earth (*paṭhavī*)
   - water (*āpo*)
   - fire (*tejo*)
   - air (*vāyo*)
   - the color blue (*nīla*)
   - the color yellow (*pīta*)
   - the color red (*lohita*)
   - the color white (*odāta*)
   - light (*āloka*)
   - space or emptiness (*ākāsa*);
2. Ten kinds of foulness, corpses at different stages of decay (*asubha*);
3. Ten recollections or bases for mindfulness (*anussati*), such as the Buddha, the Dhamma, the Sangha, *sīla*, and so on;
4. Four unbounded states of mind (*appamaññā*)—Developing the Sublime States of Mind or *brahmavihāra*: loving-kindness (*mettā*), compassion (*karuṇā*), joy in the success of others (*muditā*), and equanimity (*upekkhā*);
5. Perceiving the loathsomeness of food;
6. Meditation on the four elements (*dhātu-kammaṭṭhāna*—Earth, water, fire, and air);
7. Four absorptions of the formless sphere (*arūpa*)—Contemplating the four formless spheres mentioned.

These practices are called the forty subjects of meditation (*kammaṭṭhāna*);[165] and each meditation practice will reap different results. Therefore, when engaging in different practices it is best to examine the character and tendencies of the meditator first, which we can refer to as temperaments (*cariyā*).[166] For example, contemplation of corpses may be good for a person with strong lust (*rāga*); and the practice of loving-kindness (*mettā*) is suitable for a person with a lot of hatred (*dosa*). There are six types of temperaments:

1. *Rāga-cariyā*—A person who is full of lust, who is infatuated with beauty;
2. *Dosa-cariyā*—A person who harbors hatred and is impatient and hotheaded;
3. *Moha-cariyā*—A person who is deluded, forgetful, and "foggy";
4. *Saddhā-cariyā*—A person who is full of confidence in others and is too gullible and impressionable;
5. *Buddhi-cariyā*—A person who has a good deal of wisdom, is accomplished, and likes to examine causes and effects;
6. *Vitakka-cariyā*—A person who likes to think, who tends to speculate and worry.

Anyone who has any of these tendencies will be identified according to a particular temperament. We do not have the space, however, to go into the details of each of these character traits.

The Sphere of Importance of Concentration

It is true that concentration is an important aspect of Buddhist practice, but at the same time its sphere of importance in the pursuit of the final goal of liberation (*vimutti*) has its own dimensions.

The benefits of concentration that lead to the final goal of Buddhism are applied in order to attain wisdom and seek the highest good. The concentration that is used in this pursuit does not have to be of the highest order. If a person merely attains to the highest level of concentration but has no wisdom, there is no way he will be able to reach the final goal.

The various eight levels of absorption (*jhāna*), while being profound, are still only the result of the practice of *samatha* and therefore remain at a mundane level (*lokiya*) that is not associated with the final goal.

In the states of absorption attributed to concentration, various types of unwholesome states of mind (*kilesa*) are eliminated to the extent that we can call this achievement "liberation." This liberation, however, tends to be momentary and is only maintained while in a state of absorption. As soon as the meditator returns to his usual state of mind, this liberation is lost. Therefore, these kinds of liberation are referred to as *lokiya-vimokkha* (mundane liberation), *kuppa-vimokkha* (liberation that can disintegrate);[167] and *vikkhambhana-vimutti* (liberation based on repression; a type of liberation that occurs because concentration still holds sway over unwholesome tendencies; it is like taking a flat stone and covering some grass with it—as soon as you remove the stone, the grass starts to flourish again).

From the points mentioned, we can see that in the practice that leads to the essence of Buddhadhamma, the final, most important element or causal factor is wisdom (*paññā*), and wisdom at this level of practice is called *vipassanā*. For this reason, the practice must always lead to *vipassanā*. As for the application of *samādhi*, while being necessary, we can be selective in choosing which level to engage in. For example, we might start at the first level called *vipassanā-samādhi*, which is at the level of momentary concentration (*khaṇika-samādhi*) and "neighborhood" concentration (*upacāra-samādhi*), and then go from there. This method of approaching the essence of Buddhadhamma, while still requiring the integration of all the factors of the Noble Eight-fold Path, seems to be distinguished by the two ways in which *samādhi* is put to use.

One is the method already suggested in the previous section on proper mindfulness (*sammāsati*). In this method, mindfulness plays an important role and applies *samādhi* only at the most elemental level, or uses it merely for assistance. According to this method, mindfulness is crucial to focusing and holding attention. This perception then allows wisdom to contemplate or investigate various objects of attention. This method is called *vipassanā*.

The second method emphasizes *samādhi* and gives it a role of utmost importance. It involves using *samādhi* to make the mind tranquil and fixed, to the point that it reaches a state of attainment (*samāpatti*) or absorption (*jhāna*). This practice makes the mind firmly linked with its object of attention until it is ready for action; when this has been achieved, the mind is open, flexible, and yielding, ready for engaging in activities that can lead to the highest good. In this mental state, various types of unwholesome tendencies and intoxicants (*kilesa-āsava*), which normally disrupt thought and cause pressures and stress to build, are quieted, stilled, and minimized. This can be compared to throwing fine sand in a still pool and being able to watch it settle all the way to the bottom because the water is still and clear. This mental state is most suitable for making further progress and starting to use wisdom to eliminate all sediment in the mind. At this level, we can refer to this practice as *samatha*. If the practitioner does not simply stop here, he can continue on and apply wisdom to the complete elimination of unwholesome tendencies and mental intoxications (*kilesa-āsava*), that is, to the level of *vipassanā*. But we can say that after practicing *samatha*, it may be easier to apply wisdom because the mind has been prepared. This method involves practicing both *samatha* and *vipassanā*.

The results of the first type of practice are called *paññāvimutti*—liberation (emancipation and the elimination of mental intoxicants, *āsava*) by means of wisdom. As soon as *paññāvimutti* exists, the initial *samādhi* that was established as a foundation of practice becomes stable, pure, and complete as it becomes linked with wisdom and progresses to liberation of the mind (*cetovimutti*). In this case, however, the deliverance of mind is not fully accomplished and remains only in its initial stages until it achieves completion via *paññāvimutti*.

The results of the second method of practice can be divided into two parts. The first is the result of *samatha* called *cetovimutti*—meaning liberation of the mind (freedom from the power of unwholesome tendencies [*kilesa*] due to the power of *samādhi*). The second, being the last level, is called *paññāvimutti* (similar to the first method)[168]—as soon as *paññāvimutti* is attained, the previously achieved *cetovimutti*, which was subject to deterioration or loss, does not regress.

When the results of practice are divided, a person who has followed the first method and clearly has *paññāvimutti* is known as a *paññāvimutta*—one who has been liberated through wisdom and understanding; and a person who has followed the second method is called an *ubhatobhāgavimutta*—one who has been liberated in both ways (through mental attainments and the Noble Eight-fold Path).

Those who have followed the second method, using *samatha* and *vipassanā* to become an *ubhatobhāgavimutta*, can attain certain abilities in the process of practicing the absorptions (*jhāna*). These are often referred to as the six "superknowledges" (*abhiññā*):[169]

1. mental powers (*iddhividhi*)
2. clairvoyance or divine ear (*dibbasota*)
3. telepathy or mind-reading (*cetopariyañāṇa*)
4. clairvoyance or divine eye or the ability to know of the decease and rebirth of beings according to their kamma (*dibbacakkhu*)
5. recollection of former existences (*pubbenivāsānussatiñāṇa*)
6. knowledge of the extinction of all mental intoxicants (*āsavakkhayañāṇa*)

The person who follows the first method of practice will only realize the extinction of mental intoxicants (*āsava*) but will not gain these special types of knowledge or insight.

Those who follow the second method must practice both of its aspects. No matter what level of absorption (*jhāna*) is attained, if only *samatha* is used and *vipassanā* is not linked with the practice, there is no way to reach the final goal of Buddhadhamma.

Putting Concentration to Good Use

The training and development of concentration aims at achieving various benefits. Please note the following passage, which cites some of these benefits:

> Bhikkhus, the development of concentration (*samādhi-bhāvanā*) has four aspects:
> 1. concentration that is already developed and accomplished leads to a life of fulfillment in the present (*diṭṭhadhammasukhavihāra*);
> 2. . . . leads to knowledge and insight (*ñāṇadassana*);
> 3. . . . leads to mindfulness (*sati*) and clear comprehension (*sampajañña*);
> 4. . . . leads to the complete elimination of mental intoxicants (*āsava*).[170]

The concentration leading to fulfillment in the present, referred to in number 1 relates to the development of the four absorptions of the material sphere (*rūpa-jhāna*). This is one method of experiencing sukha, and this sukha can, in turn, be divided into ten increasingly refined levels:
- sukha related to sensuality (*kāmasukha*);
- sukha of the four levels of absorption in the material sphere (*rūpa-jhāna*);
- sukha of the four levels of absorption in the formless sphere (*arūpa-jhāna*);
- sukha attributed to the cessation of perception and sensation (*nirodha-samāpatti*).

Lord Buddha and most other arahants advocated practicing the four absorptions of the material sphere whenever they were at leisure in order to relax and experience peace. This is called experiencing sukha in the present moment (*diṭṭhadhammasukhavihāra*).

As for number 2, the Commentaries state that this refers to obtaining divine eyes (*dibbacakkhu*), which is an example of using concentration to achieve special powers or "miracles" (*pāṭihāriya*).

Number 3 has already been made clear.

Number 4 relates to using concentration to achieve wisdom or as a basis for *vipassanā* that leads to the final and highest goal of Buddhism—liberation and the complete elimination of mental intoxicants (*āsava*).

Understanding the benefits and goals of the practice of concentration (*samādhi*) will help to eliminate some misconceptions about this method of training. Many such misconceptions have been formed based on certain monk's lifestyles and the practice of Buddhism in various cultural contexts today, such as taking the practice of concentration to mean isolating yourself from society or seeking complete solitude and not bearing any social responsibilities. The following points might help to prevent and eliminate the perpetuation of some of these misconceptions:

- The practice of concentration meditation (*samādhi*) is a means to an end, not an end in itself. The person who initially engages in the practice of *samādhi* may, for a time, have to sever certain social contacts to focus attention on this practice and training. This temporary isolation may be maintained until this person is ready to resume his proper role in society. Furthermore, generally speaking practicing *samādhi* does not mean that you have to sit still all day and into the evening; there are many methods of practice to chose from that are suitable for various lifestyles.
- The path a person chooses to take also depends upon his expertise, character, and personal preferences. Some people may feel compelled to go to the forest, and others, while they may want to live in the forest, are not able to do so; there is even one example in which Lord Buddha did not give permission to certain monks to reside in the forest.[171] And even for those who do live in the forest, the Vinaya does not permit them to sever their social responsibilities, similar to the recluses and holy men in some other religions.[172]
- Through the practice of concentration and the attainment of the absorptions (*jhāna*), Buddhadhamma aims at achieving a state of mind that is malleable and ready for work; once this is achieved, the mind is then put to the task of applying wisdom, as stated above. Using concentration and the absorptions for purposes other than these is viewed as something exceptional and, in some cases, is not really warranted nor recommended by Lord Buddha: such as, using concentration to achieve psychic powers (*iddhipāṭihāriya*). Any person who actively seeks these powers is working with false

motives. These powers can lead to tragic results, not allowing a person to achieve the final goal of Buddhadhamma at all. However, anyone who attains psychic powers after having applied himself towards achieving the goal via the path of wisdom and having passed through the stages of concentration is deemed exceptional indeed. But for the person whose practice is progressing correctly, but has yet to achieve the final goal, these psychic powers are almost always dangerous. Such powers can easily become the cause of distraction and preoccupation for the practitioner and those around him; and they can cause unwholesome tendencies (*kilesa*) to mount up to the point that no further progress is possible. One is stuck with a fascination for psychic powers. Lord Buddha, while having an abundance of such powers, did not advocate using them, because they do not lead to wisdom and final liberation. From what we know of the life of Lord Buddha, he used psychic powers to curb psychic powers or to restrain the desire to use psychic powers.

• Those who have made significant strides along the Path, or have even achieved the final goal, tend to favor practicing concentration and attaining the absorptions as a way of relaxing and experiencing sukha when they are at their leisure. For instance, even though Lord Buddha wandered about teaching to large gatherings of people without discriminating between class or caste, and he had the additional responsibility of guiding a large community of monks, he still maintained his practice of the absorptions (*jhāna-sīlī*) and found peace of mind (sukha) this way (as did the other Noble Disciples). This is called *diṭṭhadhammasukhavihāra*, living happily in the present moment. And there were occasions when Lord Buddha led a solitary existence for up to three months in order to develop concentration and find sukha in the absorptions.[173] Anyone who engages in these practices will discover a certain amount of personal freedom; but if a person becomes too attached to that freedom, this may result in that person exhibiting a certain lack of social responsibility. It is crucial to keep in mind that if a person attains the higher, more refined levels of the Holy Life, social responsibility continues to be an important Buddhist principle. Whether the Buddhist community experiences prosperity or loss, stability or imbalance, all depends on the amount of importance placed on social concerns.

❦ ❦ ❦ ❦

The two larger parts of this volume have attempted a systematic explanation of the major principles of the Buddhist teachings or Buddhadhamma. There has only been enough space to consider the major principles related to attaining the final goal of Buddhism. Much more could be said about the practice and application of these principles, but we will let that be our future task.

Notes

1. S.II.4.

2. S.II.31. Here, *khayañāṇa* refers to realizing the extinguishing of all unwholesome tendencies and mental intoxications (*kilesa-āsava*), or attaining the final fruits of arahantship.

3. The Pali term *saddhā* is often translated as faith, confidence, or even devotion. The author will soon distinguish it from the kind of faith often found in theistic religions. In order to avoid confusion with the broader sense of faith, I have translated *saddhā* as having confidence or confidence in someone or something. The author makes it clear that this confidence must constitute belief based on reason, experience, and experimentation—trans.

4. Compare with Nanamoli, *The Guide* (London: Pali Text Society, 1977), 192–193.

5. A.V.312–313. In A.V.1–2 there is a similar passage, but it puts disenchantment (*nibbidā*) and the absence of lust (*virāga*) together as the same element. Aside from this, see A.III.19, for example.

6. *Nīvaraṇa:* sensual desire (*kāmachanda*), ill-will (*byāpāda*), sloth (*thīna-middha*), distraction and anxiety (*uddhacca-kukkucca*), and uncertainty (*vicikicchā*)—trans.

7. *Duccarita:* misconduct of act (*kāya-*), word (*vacī-*), and thought (*mano-*)—trans.

8. *Yonisomanasikāra*. The author deals with this pivotal concept in detail below—trans.

9. A.V.113–114.

10. *Bojjhaṅga:* mindfulness (*sati*), truth-investigation (*dhammavicaya*), effort (*viriya*), joy (*pīti*), tranquillity (*passaddhi*), concentration (*samādhi*), and equanimity (*upekkhā*)—trans.

11. *Satipaṭṭāna*. See section below on "Proper Mindfulness"—trans.

12. *Sucarita:* just the opposite of *duccarita*—trans.

13. *Indriyasaṁvara,* composure of the sense faculties, does not mean covering your ears and eyes, not hearing nor seeing. At a basic level it means

controlling the mind and controlling the senses. Whenever anything is perceived, you will not be distracted and overtaken by unwholesome tendencies (*kilesa*). At a higher level, once the sense faculties have become more developed, *indriyasaṁvara* can come to mean having the ability to take feelings and direct them in certain ways you see fit. See the *Indriyabhāvanā Sutta,* M.III.298.

14. A.V.114–116.

15. Vin.I.10; S.V.421.

16. A.III.414.

17. See section in part I on "Kamma" for another reference to the Jains—trans.

18. S.V.7, 16–17, 26–27.

19. The Commentaries (MA.II.41) explain the Holy Life in twelve different ways. Some of the most important are: the whole of the Religion, following and practicing the Eight-fold Path, the four Sublime States of Mind (*brahmavihāra*), gift-giving (*dāna*), being steadfast to your mate, abstaining from sexual intercourse (*methunadhamma*), and so on.

20. Vin.I.20–21.

21. M.I.490–494.

22. The term *kalyāṇamitta* does not simply mean friend. Rather it refers to someone—be it a monk, guru, teacher, friend, or helper—who makes valuable suggestions and provides direction and spiritual support.

23. S.V.2.

24. S.V.29–30.

25. S.V.18–19; *ñāyadhamma* = *lokuttaramagga, saccadhamma,* and *nibbāna.*

26. M.I.135.

27. M.I.260.

28. The *Rathavinīta Sutta* (M.I.145–151) emphasizes this point. It contains general material as well as specific points of the Dhamma, such as the seven stages of purity (*visuddhi*).

29. See the *Dhammacakkappavattana Sutta* previously cited.

30. When these two concepts (*sammāñāṇa* and *sammāvimutti*) are added to the Path it is referred to as the ten proper states (*sammatta*) or the ten qualities of the adept (*asekhadhamma*); see D.III.271, 292.

31. D.II.49; Dh.183; this expression of the Three-fold Trainings can be found in Vism.4.

32. D.II.123.

33. Here, again, mind-objects = *ārammaṇa* (Thai, *arom*), that is, objects of consciousness. This term will gain increasing importance in sections below dealing with the final steps of the Eight-fold Path related to the practice of concentration meditation—trans.

34. Concerning the arising of these three elements of the Middle Path and other elements, see the *Mahācattārīsaka Sutta*, M.III.71.

35. M.III.71, 76.

36. See S.V.10, 43–49.

37. A.I.30.

38. D.II.312; M.I.62; S.V.8; M.I.48; Vbh.104, 235, and so on.

39. M.I.46–47; three root causes of bad actions (*akusala-mūla*) = greed (*lobha*), ill-will (*dosa*), and delusion (*moha*); three causes of good actions (*kusala-mūla*) = generosity (*alobha*), love (*adosa*); wisdom (*amoha*).

40. S.III.51.

41. S.IV.142.

42. See, for example, S.II.17; M.I.47–56.

43. "Leads to rebirth" could be translated more literally as "having consequences for the Aggregates," ultimately an undesirable result because the Buddhist goal is to go beyond any kamma that would lead to rebirth—trans.

44. M.III.72.

45. There are many examples of concepts and progressions related to this, such as: *samparāyikattha-saṁvattanika-dhamma* (virtues leading to spiritual welfare), *vuddhi-dhamma* (virtues conducive to growth), *bala* (power) and *indriya* (controlling faculty), *vesārajjakaraṇa-dhamma* (qualities that give courage), and *ariyadhana* (Noble treasures).

46. Such as with *adhiṭṭhāna-dhamma* (bases for tranquillity), *bojjhaṅga* (enlightenment factors), and *nāthakaraṇa-dhamma* (virtues that serve as a refuge).

47. See the next section below for a detailed presentation of this sutta—trans.

48. This is called the *Kesaputtiya Sutta*, A.I.188.

49. In previous editions, "do not let yourself believe (Thai, *ya plongchai chüa*)" was rendered as "do not cling to (Thai, *ya yütthü*)." This was changed for purposes of clarity and differentiation. In other words, do not arrive at decisions or come to any definitive conclusions based on these premises.

50. M.I.400–413.

51. M.II.170; compare with M.II.218.

52. M.II.170–171.

53. D.I.2–3.

54. M.II.172–173; this passage can be compared to the *Kiṭāgiri Sutta*, M.I.480, which explains the enlightenment process as a gradual, orderly progression.

55. Such as in the case of Sāriputta who attained enlightenment much later than others, even though he was renown for his wisdom.

56. D.III.237–238; M.I.101 (there are four separate things that can overcome the mind, but they have not been specified here because they do not directly apply).

57. The Commentaries correct this saying that the path of stream-entrance (*sotapattimagga*) is the basis.

58. *Vīmaṁsaka Sutta*, M.I.317–320.

59. Pali, *dhammanvaya* (the way of the Dhamma); Thai, *naeotham*.

60. D.II.83; D.III.101. For more details see D.III.99–116.

61. S.V.225.

62. A.III.270.

63. A.II.213.

64. S.III.120.

65. M.I.444.

66. M.I.141.

67. S.II.115–118.

68. S.IV.139–140.

69. From the level of *dutiya-jhāna* and higher, this is *samādhi* that has no initial application of thought (*vitakka*) nor sustained application of thought (*vicāra*).

70. S.IV.298.

71. Dh.97.

72. S.V.220–221.

73. S.V.222.

74. M.I.294.

75. The prefix *a-* is used to form negatives in Pali. Below, under the section dealing with proper thought, the author explains the significance of the use of negatives in light of the portrayal of Buddhism by some scholars as a pessimistic religion—trans.

76. It.10; compare this with S.V.102.

77. It. 9–10; compare this with S.V.101.

78. See Vism.99–100.

79. S.V.29–30, and so on.

80. S.V.2–4, and so on.

81. S.V.78.

82. A.I.14.

83. A.I.16.

84. A.I.17.

85. A.I.17.

86. It.10.

87. A.IV.352–353, 357–358; Ud.36–37.

88. S.V.31, and so on.

89. S.V.78.

90. A.I.13.

91. A.I.16.

92. A.I.17–18.

93. A.I.17.

94. It.9.

95. A.I.31.

96. A.I.14.

97. A.I.5.

98. A.I.200–201.

99. S.V.85.

100. D.III.288.

101. Note that there are two levels knowledge in Buddhism. Buddhism maintains that both of these levels comprise the truth but have different intellectual meaning and value:
1) Knowledge according to the five senses—eyes, ears, nose, tongue, and touch—are considered conventional or relative truth (*sammuti-sacca*);
2) Knowledge of conditions obtained via wisdom—gaining insight into impermanence, suffering, and no-self, for example—are considered higher or absolute truth (*paramattha-sacca*). This knowledge is used to keep pace with all changing conditions, to live a life of freedom, and to put all things to their proper use depending on the circumstances at the present moment.
It must also be noted that within both of these spheres of knowledge, Buddhism only accepts empirical knowledge.

102. See pages 185–186.

103. The essence of this is taken from A.III.20.

104. D.II.311–312; M.III.251; Vbh.104, 235.

105. M.III.73; Vbh.106, 237.

106. When this attitude or state of mind develops further, it becomes the state of equanimity (*upekkhā*), an important aspect of applying thought to bring about good results—it does not mean passivity or indifference. This will be discussed in greater detail.

107. *Nekkhamma* = *alobha* (VbhA.74), *nekkhammadhātu* = *kusala-dhamma* (PsA.I.68).

108. In Nd[1].488, we find the following definition: *mettāti yā sattesu metati mettāyanā mettāyittataṁ anudā anudāyanā andāyittataṁ hitesitā anukampā abyāpādo abyāpajjho adoso kusalamūlaṁ* [*mettā* means that which in beings is loving, the act of loving, the state of loving-kindness, care, forebearance, consideration, concern for others, compassion, the absence of malice, kindness, the lack of anger, the root of good action]. In SnA.I.128, we find the following: *hitasukhūpanayanakāmatā mettā* (since it has the nature of a desire to lead on to welfare and happiness it is called *mettā*). [I especially thank Charles Hallisey for his help with these passages—trans.]

109. Vism.97–98.

110. DhA.I.146, and so on. [For more information on these people, see, for example, Marie Beuzeville Byles, *Footprints of the Buddha* (Wheaton, IL: The Theosophical Publishing House, 1957)—trans.]

111. M.I.239.

112. M.I.250.

113. M.I.114–115.

114. A.II.76.

115. *Micchā-ājīva* means "scheming (or deceiving), currying favor, conniving, intimidating people, and seeking gain with gain"; M.III.75.

116. D.II.311–312; M.I.62; M.III.251; Vbh.105, 235.

117. M.III.74–75, compare with Vbh.106–107, 237.

118. Please note that such strict adherence to mere rule and ritual (*sīlabbataparāmāsa*) was present in ancient India and is still an aspect of life there today. The elimination of these kinds of beliefs and practices was clearly the aim of Lord Buddha and continued to be a major aspect of Buddhist practices and teachings; elimination of caste was another aim of Buddhism, as well as diverting attention away from metaphysics and unanswerable questions concerning the problems of daily life. Adherence to mere rule and ritual increased with the decline of Buddhism in India, but such adherence can also contributed to this decline. We can say that it is this strong adherence to ritual that has made India what it is today; and, furthermore, it can be said that wherever this adherence prospers, Buddhism degenerates. Also, strong adherence to rules and rituals is often the major cause of abrupt, radical social changes and revolutions; and it is these changes that have often brought about the end of such rules and rituals in various stages of human history.

119. A.V.263; several other references refer to the expanded explanation above, such as A.V.283, 288, 292, 297, 301.

120. D.I.4, 63, 100, and so on; M.I.268; M.I.345; A.V.205.

121. This is the same definition as M.III.251, which is referred to in Albert Schweitzer, *Indian Thought and its Development* (New York: Henry Holt and Co., 1936), 112, and is also picked up and referred to in Joseph L. Sutton, *Problems of Politics and Administration in Thailand* (Bloomington: Institute of Training for Public Service, Dept. of Govt., Indiana University, 1962), 3. In the latter book (pages 2–8), Professor Sutton refers to many other points of the Buddhist teachings to support his positions, such as kamma, rebirth, seeking isolation from or escaping from the world or the problems of life. As for misunder-

standings about kamma, please refer to the previous statements that attempt to correct these misperceptions. Sutton states the following: The possibility of rebirth makes people easygoing and disinterested in performing good acts (Christianity believes in one life); Buddhism believes that it is very difficult to be born as a human being, it is more difficult than a turtle trying to stick his head through a single ring floating in the ocean; and there is no opportunity to have your sins forgiven or to have your responsibility lifted through confession. And as for isolating yourself from worldly matters, Professor Sutton refers to the Buddha's statement that, "Those who love nothing in this world are rich in joy and free from pain," which comes from a Pali passage "*tasmā hi te sukhino vītasokā yesaṁ piyaṁ natthi kuhiñci loke*" (Ud.92). Here, the term "love" is equivalent to the Pali "*piya*," meaning love related to lust that causes personal attachment. This passage describes the feelings of a person who has already experienced liberation, who has no remaining traces of lust, only loving-kindness (*mettā*), which has taken its place. For this reason, this passage relates to a person who has a freed mind, who performs various acts out of loving-kindness without attachment, bias, or selfishness that would cause others to be upset. Various interpretations of dhammic passages can yield different values depending on the standards used. Whether his intentions and interpretations are correct or not, the criticisms of Professor Sutton are beneficial, because they serve as reminders to Buddhists to study harder and help each other clarify the true meaning of the various points of the teachings. And we must also accept the fact that the widespread beliefs about Buddhist principles that have been passed on to most people in Thai society allow the above criticisms to be made; Professor Sutton is not alone, there are many other Westerners who have reached similar conclusions.

122. For one of the most explicit statements on the primacy of mind, see the very first line of the *Dhammapada*—trans.

123. D.II.311–312; M.I.62; M.III.251; Vbh.105, 235.

124. Vbh.106–107, 237.

125. A.II.15. (This can be translated as proper or complete effort.)

126. A.II.74.

127. A.II.16.

128. See M.III.72–76.

129. A.IV.229.

130. A.I.50.

131. Dh.276.

132. The five faculties are confidence (*saddhā*), effort (*viriya*), mindfulness (*sati*), concentration (*samādhi*), and wisdom (*paññā*).

133. Vin.I.181; A.III.374.

134. See section on "The System of the Middle Path"—trans.

135. D.II.313; M.I.62; M.III.251; Vbh.105, 236.

136. Vbh.107, 238.

137. Here, note the way these terms are used in English: *sati* is translated as mindfulness, attentiveness, or detached watching; *appamāda* is often rendered as heedfulness, watchfulness, earnestness, diligence, zeal, carefulness, or, stated negatively, non-neglect of mindfulness. [To convey this wider range of meaning, I have generally translated *appamāda* as conscientiousness—trans.]

138. S.V.43; A.V.21.

139. A.I.11.

140. A.I.16.

141. A.I.17.

142. A.I.16–17.

143. D.II.156.

144. S.V.31, 32, 33, 35, 36, 37, 41–45.

145. A.II.119–120.

146. A.II.120.

147. S.I.86; A.III.364.

148. S.I.87–89.

149. S.V.168–169.

150. You can see that "*sati*" does not have the same meaning as "memory," but rather reflection or recollection, which are an aspect of memory and are one dimension of *sati*. This dimension of *sati* can be found in many parts of the teachings, such as when the term *buddhānussati* appears. But here, the true meaning is best expressed by the English term "mindfulness."

151. Vism.130, 162, 464.

152. D.II.290; M.I.55.

153. *Nīvaraṇa* (hindrances that prevent the mind from making progress) are as follows: sensual desire (*kāmachanda*), ill-will (*byāpāda*), sloth and torpor (*thīna-middha*), distraction and remorse (*uddhacca-kukkucca*), and uncertainty (*vicikicchā*).

154. *Bojjhaṅga* (factors that contribute to enlightenment) are as follows: mindfulness (*sati*), truth-investigation (*dhammavicaya*), effort (*viriya*), joy (*pīti*), tranquillity (*passaddhi*), concentration (*samādhi*), and equanimity (*upekkhā*).

155. The term "*kāya*" can become *vedanā* (sensation), mind (*citta*), or dhamma in different contexts.

156. This is called *vipassanā-samādhi* and is between the level of momentary concentration (*khaṇika-samādhi*) and "neighorhood" concentration (*upacāra-samādhi*). [For further details, see the section below on proper concentration (*sammāsamādhi*)—trans.].

157. See, for example, N. P. Jacobson, *Buddhism: The Religion of Analysis* (Carbondale: Southern Illinois University Press, 1970), 93–123.

158. Addition from a later edition of *Buddhadhamma* (Bangkok: Mahachulalongkorn Buddhist University, 2529 [1986), 816–817: There is a point to be wary of which should be stressed here, concerning a misunderstanding that may lead to misguided and fruitless practice. Some people misconstrue the meaning of the common translation of *sati* as "recollection" and of *sampajañña* as "self-awareness." They establish *sati* on the sense of self and then feel aware of themselves as the agents of the various actions, "I am doing this; I am doing that," their practice thus becoming a creation or strengthening of the concept of a self. . . . *Sati* should pay attention to the action being performed or to the state that is presently occurring to the extent that there is no room to think of oneself or an "actor."

159. A.II.142–143.

160. S.III.1–2.

161. See DhsA.207, for example.

162. See, for example, D.II.312–313; M.I.112; M.III.252.

163. See PsA.150.

164. Most of the time when the term *jhāna* is used, it tends to mean the four meditative absorptions of the material sphere.

165. See Vism.118–228 and 229–406.

166. See Vism.101–102.

167. PsV.40.

168. Liberation through concentration (*cetovimutti*) frees the mind from the powers of lust (*rāga*) and related feelings of ill-will (*dosa*), but it does not eliminate delusion (*moha*), which is the last unwholesome tendency (*kilesa*). It is, therefore,

necessary to experience liberation through wisdom (*paññāvimutti*). Liberation through wisdom frees the mind from delusion—the root of passion (or greed, *lobha*) and ill-will—and leads to complete attainment of the final goal.

169. See Vism.373–435.

170. A.II.44; D.III.222.

171. A.V.201–202; M.I.104–105; M.III.58.

172. See, for example, the disciplinary regulations related to the relationship between ordinands and laity regarding the proper way to seek sustenance; and see the regulations describing how ordinands should participate in and govern their own community or Sangha.

173. See S.V.325–326.

Index